VERHANDLUNGEN

DES

VII. INTERNATIONALEN

ORIENTALISTEN-CONGRESSES.

ARISCHE SECTION.

Druck von Adolf Holzhausen,
k. k. Hof- und Universitäts-Buchdrucker in Wien.

Actes du 7e congrès international des orientalistes, Vienne, 1886.

Section arienne.

VERHANDLUNGEN

DES

VII. INTERNATIONALEN

ORIENTALISTEN-CONGRESSES

GEHALTEN IN WIEN IM JAHRE 1886.

ARISCHE SECTION.

MIT ZEHN TAFELN.

WIEN, 1888.

ALFRED HÖLDER

K. K. HOF- UND UNIVERSITÄTS-BUCHHÄNDLER.

I., ROTHENTHURMSTRASSE 15.

Ueber gewisse Kürzungen des Wortendes im Veda.

Von

R. v. Roth.

Unsere Vedenerklärung, die von Friedrich Rosen an gerechnet noch nicht fünfzig Jahre alt ist, wird mit Schwierigkeiten lexikalischer Art noch lange kämpfen. Und wenn hundert Hindernisse geräumt sind, wird gleichwohl stets ein unlösbarer Rest bleiben. Das liegt in der Art einer so alten Litteratur, zum Theil auch in den Mängeln einer jeden Ueberlieferung.

Leichter fand und findet man sich in den grammatischen Besonderheiten des Veda zurecht. Auf diesem Gebiet dürften die Hauptsachen erledigt sein, und eine sorgfältige Beobachtung wird weiter ans Licht ziehen, was noch dunkel scheint. So habe ich im XXVI. Band der Zeitschrift für vergleichende Sprachforschung, S. 50 ff., auf einen nicht genug benützten Schlüssel hingewiesen, der das Geheimniss mancher unerklärten Form erschliesst, auf ein richtiges Verständniss des Sandhi und seiner Behandlung im Padapâṭha.

Ich erlaube mir heute ein weiteres kleines Hilfsmittel für den Erklärer aufzuzeigen, das in manchen Fällen die Lösung bringt, eine Wohllautsregel nicht grammatischer Art, sondern eher rhetorisch zu nennen. Ihre Wirkung ist in einzelnen Fällen längst bemerkt, aber grammatisch gedeutet worden. Unsern indischen Lehrmeistern ist etwas der Art ganz geläufig gewesen, nur manchmal am falschen Ort angewandt worden und so bei uns in übeln Ruf gekommen. Es ist das bekannte *supo luk*, im

Anschluss an Pâṇini 7, 1, 39, der Commentatoren, womit sie uns in der Regel etwas verblüffen.

Die Thatsache des Abfalls einer Casusendung ist richtig, aber erstens kann dieser Abfall nicht willkürlich eintreten, sondern er muss einen Anlass haben und zweitens ist nicht jeder Fall, in welchem eine Endung fehlt oder zu fehlen scheint, ein Abfall in diesem Sinne z. B. nicht bei Locativen, wie *sadman çarman,* Formen, welche nach Lanman's Zählung in den Texten sogar erheblich zahlreicher sind, als die vollen: *sadmani çarmaṇi.* Fälle dieser Art gehören in einen anderen Zusammenhang. Dagegen versuche ich an etlichen Beispielen jenen wirklichen, grammatisch unberechtigten, Abfall zu zeigen und näher zu bestimmen.

1. Im Rigveda 1, 67, 9 (5) lesen wir:

वि यो वीरुत्सु रोधन्महित्वोत प्रजा उत प्रसूष्वन्तः

Man wird den Vers nicht anders verstehen können als: Agni, der mächtig wächst in den Kräutern und in den Kindern im Leibe ihrer Mütter. Wie soll aber *prajâ,* oder wie der Padapâṭha will *prajâḥ,* ein Locativ sein? Zugleich ist darauf zu achten, dass das in fünfsilbigen Gliedern sich bewegende Versmass verlangt: *uta prajâ u* | *prasûshu antaḥ,* wie schon Grassmann im Wörterbuch s. v. *uta* richtig gesagt hat, nur dass er mit Unrecht dem Pada folgend *prajâs* annimmt. Durch die uns vom Metrum aufgedrängte Verbesserung, die Ersetzung des zweiten *uta* durch *u* wird der Sinn erst tadellos: die treibende Kraft des Feuers lässt sowohl die Kräuter wachsen als die Leibesfrucht in den Müttern, nicht aber: Kräuter, Frucht und Mütter, wie man verstehen müsste, wenn jenes *uta* berechtigt wäre.

Halten wir also *uta prajâ u* (*uta u* wie *uta vâ u* 10, 142, 3) als ursprünglichen Wortlaut fest, so drängt sich die Vermuthung auf, dass der Dichter den Gleichklang *prajâsu prasûshu,* obwohl das metrisch gepasst hätte, vermeiden wollte und dem Hörer überliess an *prajâ* das *su* aus dem folgenden *prasûshu* zu ergänzen. Den Verfasser des Pada aber treffen wir, wie weiterhin in ähnlichen Fällen, auf falscher Fährte, wenn er aus dem Hiatus *prajâ u* auf ein *prajâḥ* schliesst.

Stünde dieser Fall ganz vereinzelt, so könnte ein solches rhetorisches Auskunftsmittel, so nahe es liegt, immerhin Bedenken machen, sehen wir uns also nach ähnlichen Vorkommnissen um.

Rr. 8, 11, 1 lautet:

त्वम॑ग्ने व्र॒तपा अ॑सि दे॒व आ मर्त्ये॒ष्वा । त्वं य॒ज्ञेष्वीड्यः॑ ॥

Ich übersetze: Du, o Agni, bist Wächter der Ordnung unter den Göttern, unter Sterblichen. Zu übersetzen: als Gott bei den Sterblichen (Ludwig) verbietet das doppelt stehende *â*. Ich nehme also an, dass hier, wie oben, der Pada falsch auflöse in *devaḥ*, dass vielmehr *deve* zu verstehen, vermutlich auch zu sprechen sei.

Der Commentar zu der Stelle, so wie er in der Ausgabe lautet, sieht etwas confus aus, enthält aber eine Bestätigung unserer Ansicht, wenn er umschreibt: *he agne devo dyotamânas tvam martyeshv â manushyeshu ca deveshu ca madhye vratapâ asi.* Der Herausgeber gibt keine Variante. Ich möchte glauben, dass die Worte *ca deveshu ca* von einem klügeren Leser an den Rand gesetzt wurden, der so erklärte wie wir. Die Ausleger desselben Verses in Vs. 4, 16, Ts. I, 1, 14, 4 bleiben bei dem Nominativ.

Im Vorübergehen nur will ich erwähnen, dass auch 6, 3, 7

वृषा॑ रु॒क्ष ओष॑धीषु नूनोत्

wahrscheinlich *rukshe*, d. h. *ruksheshu* = *vṛksheshu* zu verstehen ist: das Feuer braust in Stämmen und Stauden. Der Padapâṭha hat auch hier *rukshaḥ*.

Auffälliger nach unserem Gefühl ist dieselbe Erscheinung in umgekehrter Folge, die volle Form voranstehend, die gekurzte folgend, wie z. B. 1, 105, 5. 8, 58, 3

त्रि॒ष्वा रो॑च॒ने दि॒वः

rocane für *rocaneshu,* in den drei Lichträumen des Himmels, oder 1, 81, 1

तमिन्महत्स्वाजिषूतेमर्भे हवामहे स वाजेषु प्र नोऽविषत्

ihn rufen wir in grossen und in kleinen Streiten. Hier ist also eines von vier *su* — wenn man metrisch liest — abgeworfen. Den Singular gelten zu lassen ist ja nicht unmöglich, aber nachdem wir die Vorgänge haben, nicht wahrscheinlich.

2. In einem Agni-Liede, 1, 31, 7, lesen wir:

यस्तातृषाण उभयाय जन्मने मयः कृणोषि प्रय आ च सूरये

Dass Agni selbst dürstend anderen den Durst lösche, was der Wortlaut besagen würde, wenn man mit Padapâṭha *tâtṛshâṇaḥ* voraussetzt, das wäre eine wunderliche Vorstellung. Machen wir aber Gebrauch von unserer bisherigen Erfahrung und verstehen *tâtṛshâṇâya ubhayâya,* so ergibt sich der gute Sinn: der du beiden lechzenden Geschlechtern (Menschen und Thieren) Erquickung schaffest, Labung unserem Gebieter.

3. Die Worte einer Anrede an Agni in 6, 3, 1

यं त्वं मित्रेण वरुण सजोषा देव पासि त्यजसा मर्तमंहः

so einfach sie aussehen, machen den Erklärern Schwierigkeit. Ludwig sagt: den du als Varuna eines Beliebens mit Mitra, o Gott, schützest den Sterblichen durch Vernichtung der Bedrängniss. Er mutet uns dabei zu, den Agni, der aus der Bedrängniss rettet, als einen Varuna zu betrachten und zwar nicht als eine einfache, sondern als eine im Einklang mit einer zweiten handelnde Person. Das ist eine mystische Unklarheit, und man sieht nicht ein, weshalb Agni das Geschäft nicht in eigener Person sollte besorgen. Grassmann's Uebersetzung: wenn du, o Gott, und Varuna mit Mitra vereint beschirmt durch kräftige That vor Unglück, ist im ersten Pâda der Sache nach richtig, aber aus dem Wortlaut, der vorliegt, nicht zu gewinnen. Er hat das unschuldige ‚und' hineingedacht und sich darüber weggesetzt, dass statt *pâsi* doch wohl *pâtha* stehen müsste.

In diesem Fall hat nicht, wie in dem obigen, der Pada allein geirrt, sondern der Fehler ist in den Text selbst hineingekommen, dessen Aufzeichner mit einem *váruṇa* in dieser Verbindung nichts machen konnte und dafür *váruṇaḥ* schrieb. In der That also steht ein als ursprünglich vorauszusetzendes *mitréṇa váruṇa sajóshâḥ* für *mitréṇa váruṇena sajóshâḥ* (vgl. 4, 39, 6): welchen Sterblichen du, o Gott, im Vereine mit Mitra, mit Varuna schützest. Die Schlussworte werden weiter unten berührt werden.

4. Längst bemerkt ist die Zusammenstellung *návyasâ vácas* mit ganz neuem Spruch, 2, 31, 5. 6, 48, 1. 8, 39, 2, sowie *divítmatâ vácas,* 1, 26, 2. Sâyaṇa beruft sich richtig auf seinen Pâṇini und fasst *vacas* als *vacasâ*. Die sämmtlichen anderen Fälle eines ähnlichen Instrumentals von *as*-Stämmen, welche Lanman, Noun-Inflection, p. 562, mehr oder weniger zweifelnd anführt, und welchen kein zweiter Instrumental, auf *â* auslautend, unmittelbar vorhergeht oder folgt, gehören, wie ich glaube, nicht hieher und ich getraue mir dieselben auf andere Weise zu erklären. Sie bilden für mich also vorläufig noch keine Instanz gegen die Erklärung des Abfalls der Casusendung aus Gründen des Wohllautes.

Dagegen rechne ich in unseren Kreis die unter 3. angeführten Worte: *yám pâsi tyájasâ mártam áṅhaḥ,* 6, 3, 1, welchen Sterblichen du behütest in Verlassenheit, in Noth; also *aṅhas* für *aṅhasâ*, Instrumental bei Zeit und Ort.

5. Eine weitere Lösung liefert unsere Regel für 6, 4, 5:

तुर्याम यस्त आदिशामरातीरत्यो न ह्रुतः पततः परिह्रुत्

Ludwig: wir wollen überwinden deiner Anweisungen Anfeinder, wie ein Renner, der die Sturz bewirkenden auf der Flucht fällt. Mit *hrut* soll ‚der Feind in religiös-moralischem Sinn‘ bezeichnet sein. Den verfolgt man aber wohl nicht mit Ross und Wagen, und in der Metapher fehlt die Hauptsache, nämlich das was übersprungen werden soll. Grassmann: lass schlagen uns die deinen Plänen feind sind, dem Renner gleich die fliehenden Feinde stürzend.

Statt *arâtîs* verlangt das vorangehende *yas* die Form *arâtis*. Das mag ein Versehen sein, begünstigt durch das häufige Vorkommen von *arâtîs* am Padaschlusse. Lanman, 376. Im Veda haben ja die Reminiscenzen häufig Einfluss, wenn auch keinen so verderblichen wie in der Ueberlieferung des Avesta. Ich nehme an, dass in unserer Stelle das dritte *as* abgeworfen, also für *parihrut* ein *parihrutas* im Sinne des Dichters zu denken sei, und erhalte dadurch den abgerundeten Satz: wir möchten hinwegsetzen über den, der eurer Befehle sich weigert, wie ein Renner (Ross) über die Fallen (Hemmnisse), die den Eilenden fällen. Zu *hrut* vergleiche man 9, 61, 27.

6. Nicht unmittelbar zwingend, aber wie mir scheint durch den richtigen Geschmack geboten, ist die Anwendung unserer Regel in 8, 64, 6:

तस्मै नूनमभिद्यवे वाचा विरूप नित्यया ।
वृष्णे चोदस्व सुष्टुतिम् ॥

Was darauf führt, ist der Gegensatz zwischen *virûpa* und *nitya*, von welchen jenes die veränderte, wechselnde, dieses die bleibende, bisherige Modulation *(vâc)* oder alte und neue Melodie bezeichnet. Das natürliche Sprechen pflegt als Beigabe zu Cultushandlungen nicht zu genügen. Es vergeht zu rasch und macht nicht den Eindruck des Ungewöhnlichen, Feierlichen. An seine Stelle tritt, wo nicht wirklicher Gesang, doch ein Singsang, der aus pathetischer Declamation sich entwickelt, ähnlich dem sogenannten Recitativ. Davon werden gewisse Formen sich ausgebildet haben, zu deren Handhabung einige Fertigkeit nöthig war. Und dass die vedischen Dichter und Sänger ihre Leistungen für schön hielten, ja überzeugt waren, die Götter hören ihrem Concerte mit Genuss zu, das zeigen viele lobende, fast prahlerische Bezeichnungen.

Ich nehme also an *vâcâ virûpa nityayâ* vertrete ein *vâcâ virûpayâ nityayâ:* lass erschallen schönen Preisgesang in verändertem und üblichem Ton, d. h. in alten und neuen Weisen. Der Sammler des Veda musste *virûpa* als Vocativ behandeln, also unbetont lassen. Und dieser Umstand hat dem Rishi Virûpa zur Ehre der Autorschaft unseres Liedes verholfen, und daraus, dass im vorangehenden Vers der fungirende Priester als Angiras angeredet wird, ist der Virûpa ein Âṅgirasa geworden.

7. Eine willkommene Hilfe leistet unsere Regel in der auf anderem Weg nicht aufzuklärenden Stelle 5, 52, 9, wo von den Marut gesagt wird:

उत स्म ते परुष्ण्यामूर्णा वसत शुन्ध्यवः ।
उत पव्या रथानामद्रिं भिन्दन्त्योजसा ॥

Bei einem Versuch die Worte zu deuten wird man sich bald überzeugen, dass nicht von dem Flusse Parushṇî die Rede sein kann, welchen Sâyaṇa und Nachfolger hier finden. Mir scheinen die sichtbar verwandten Worte in 4, 22, 2:

श्रिये परुष्णीमुषमाण ऊर्णां यस्याः पर्वाणि सख्याय विव्ये

ein helles Licht aufzustecken, indem *parushṇîm ûrṇâm* unserem *parushṇyâm* (zu sprechen *parushṇiyâm*) *ûrṇâ* entspricht, wie *ushamâṇas* dem *vasata* und *çriye* ähnliches aussagt wie *çundhyavas.* Also wird wohl *ûrṇâ* für *ûrṇâyâm* stehen, eine abgekürzte Form, und wir hätten zu übersetzen: und sich herausputzend hüllen sie sich in das bunte (oder krause) Vliess (d. h. in die flockige Wolke, vgl. 5, 63, 6) und mit den Felgen ihrer Wagen spalten sie wuchtig die Felsen. Dass 1 *vas* nicht wie sonst mit dem Accusativ des Gewandes, sondern mit dem Locativ verbunden wird, kann schwerlich einen Einwand gegen die Erklärung begründen, da dieser Casus sachlich so nahe liegt.

Die parallelen Worte aus 4, 22, 2 übersetze ich: Indra, welcher sich zum Putze das bunte Vliess anzieht, dessen Büschel (Zotten) er seinem Gefolge überbreitet. Zugleich ein Bild von Indra's Grösse, wenn die Flocken seines Vliesses, d. i. einzelne Ballen der Wolke (*parvan* passt mehr für die Wolke als für das Vliess) zureichen, um auch seine Gefolgschaft, die Marut, einzuhüllen.

8. Als letztes Beispiel führe ich die gewaltsamste dieser Kürzungen auf. In diesem Fall bin ich aber keineswegs der

Erfinder, sondern gehe in den Fussstapfen des Commentators, der schon den Abfall der Endung behauptet, freilich den Sinn der Worte verfehlt hat. Sie lauten 1, 187, 7:

यददो पितो अजगन्विवस्व पर्वतानाम् ।
अत्रा चिन्नो मधो पितो ऽरं भक्षाय गम्याः ॥

Ich suche zunächst einige Nebenfragen zu erledigen. Das *ado pito,* nach Padapâṭha *adaḥ,* also gegen die Lautregel, ist am ungezwungensten als Sandhi für *adas u* zu fassen, wie z. B. 10, 93, 10 *râyótá* für *râyas uta* steht. Indessen vereinfacht der Atharvan der Paippalâda, wo das ganze Lied vorkommt, die Sache und liest *yad adash pito.* Der Genitiv *parvatânâm* kann nicht von *ajagan* abhängen, sondern gehört zu *adas,* entsprechend etwa dem Gebrauch desselben Casus im Latein bei Ortsadverbien, wie ubi terrarum, eodem loci. Aehnlich bei dem nächstverwandten adverbialen *idam* in Av. 4, 16, 4 *diváḥ spáçaḥ prá carantîdám asya* (nämlich *divaḥ*).

Nehmen wir also mit Sâyaṇa an, dass *vivásva* apocopiert stehe für *vivásvatâm,* so sagen die Worte: bist du fort in das leuchtende Gebirge gegangen, o Saft, so stelle dich doch zum Trunk uns hier bereit, o süsser Saft. Die Berge sind aber nicht die Wolken, wie Sâyaṇa und Genossen glauben, und der Trank ist nicht der Regen, sondern die Berge sind Berge, die mit ihren Schneegipfeln zu dem Sprecher herüberstrahlen, und der Trank ist der Soma, der von den Höhen ins Thal herabgebracht wird.

Das ist zugleich ein anschauliches Beispiel dafür, dass wir im Veda nicht immer zwischen Metaphern und gezwungenen Allegorien wandeln und uns mit Mühe durchwinden müssen, sondern dass bei jenen alten Poeten, guten und schlechten, auch eine natürliche Anschauung und gemeinverständliche Redeweise zu Hause ist. Je sicherer wir im genauen Verständniss ihrer Sprache, d. h. ihres Sanskrit, werden, desto menschlicher und vernünftiger werden sie uns erscheinen. Aber für manches Auge liegt der Nebel indischer Schulweisheit noch immer auf jenem

Altertum. Wie viel Ungereimtes würde z. B. vermieden, wenn unsere Uebersetzer sich entschliessen könnten, das eine Wort *vṛshan* nicht immer mit ‚Stier, stierartig, stierkräftig' oder, wo das schlechterdings unmöglich ist, wenigstens mit ‚regnend' oder ‚tauend' zu übersetzen, wie die Commentare ihnen vorsagen — es kommt sogar ein ‚stierkräftiger Rauch' vor — sondern zuzugeben, dass das Wort gar nicht von derjenigen Wurzel *varsh* hergeleitet werden darf, die nur ‚regnen' und lediglich nichts anderes bedeutet. Werden jene Hirten ihre Stiere die Regner genannt haben? Hat denn ihre natürliche Function irgend eine augenfällige Achnlichkeit mit Regen? Ist es dagegen nicht ganz natürlich, dass der Stier, dessen gewaltige Gestalt über Kühe und Kälber sich emporhebt, auch der Hervorragende, Hohe, Grosse genannt werde? Eine Hekatombe ihrer Stiere könnten unsere Uebersetzer opfern, ohne dadurch zu verarmen.

9. Was ich oben zusammengestellt habe, das sind nur Proben, gelegentlich aufgelesen, seit ich auf die Erscheinung zu achten angefangen habe. Es lässt sich erwarten, dass weitere Beispiele derselben und wohl auch anderer Arten gefunden werden. Nach den vorliegenden Fällen kann man etwa folgende Sätze formulieren:

Die Endkürzung findet sich an einem von zwei — oder auch mehreren — benachbarten Wörtern, welche gleiche Schlusssilben haben. Das gekürzte Wort geht dem vollen voran oder folgt ihm. Ersteres mag das häufigere und der Ursprung der Erscheinung sein. Beide Wörter folgen entweder unmittelbar aufeinander oder sind nur durch eine Partikel oder Präposition, selten durch ein bedeutenderes Wort, wie unter 4. in dem Beispiele aus 6, 3, 1, getrennt.

In vereinzelten Fällen wird gekürzt, wo die Endungen sich nicht vollkommen decken, sondern nur ähnlich sind, wie unter 8., wo vor der Endung *tânâm* die vorangehende *tâm* abgeworfen ist. Unter einen ähnlichen Gesichtspunkt fiele, bei 3., das *mitreṇa varuṇa*. Das genau entsprechende *varuṇe* war unzulässig, weil dadurch der Sinn geändert wurde. Indessen liegt in diesem Fall die Möglichkeit vor, dass die Ueberlieferung ungenau sei und ursprünglich ein alter Instrumental *várunâ* gestanden habe.

10. Der nächste Anlass zu dieser Kürzung, die eine wirkliche Verstümmelung ist, liegt in dem Streben nach Vermeidung des Gleichklangs, das ja auch sonst in die Sprache gewaltsam eingreift. Und als mitwirkend ist das jeweilige metrische Bedürfniss zu betrachten.

Suchen wir nach Aehnlichem, so wüsste ich aus den classischen Sprachen nichts beizubringen. Dagegen bietet uns das Deutsche selbst Stoff genug, wenn schon die geschultere Neuzeit diese Licenz ablehnt, und bald nur noch einige bequeme und eingewurzelte Kanzleiformen, wie die ‚kaiserlich deutsche Reichspost‘ und dergleichen, überleben werden.

Unsere Sprache duldet die Kürzung nur bei unmittelbarer Aufeinanderfolge von Adjectiven oder bei ihrer Verbindung durch ‚und‘. Die Dichter sind bis in unsere Zeit sehr freigebig damit:

In still und feuchten Buchten.
Herden klein und grosser Thiere.
Ein stolz verdriesslich schwerer Mann.
Ein unerwartet ungeheures Schicksal.
Das ungeheuer unerwartete.

Also Kürzung der Endungen e, en, er, es. Die ältere Zeit kannte aber nicht blos den Abfall von Casusendungen, sondern ein güt und väterliches Zureden, und Göthe sagt, freilich mehr scherzhaft: gegen inn und äussern Feind setzt er sich zur Wehre; und ein bekannter Arzt in Halle, Michael Alberti, hat eine seiner zahllosen Dissertationen betitelt: de crimine rugarum oder von lasterhafter Verursach und Verstellung der Runzeln. Halle 1747. Was uns geschmacklos erscheint, war damals elegante Kürze, und dem Dichter dienten die gekürzten Endungen, eben weil sie in der Sprache des täglichen Lebens nicht üblich waren, bei gehobenem und feierlichem Ausdruck. Die vedischen Poeten aber haben für ihre Kürzungen diesen Anspruch gewiss nicht gemacht.

Der Ursprung des Rumänischen.

Von

P. Hunfalvy.

Wenn ich mir die Freiheit nehme, geehrteste Versammlung, über die Frage: Wo kann die rumänische Sprache entstanden sein? Einiges vorzutragen, so glaube ich damit dem orientalischen Charakter des Congresses keinen Abbruch zu thun. Oesterreich-Ungarn bildet ja nach der allgemeinen Meinung den Uebergang vom Occident zum Orient; und Siebenbürgen, die grösste geographische Unterlage dieser Frage, ist vielleicht den meisten gegenwärtigen Herren ein überaus orientalischer Landstrich.

Noch etwas Anderes muss ich im vorhinein hervorheben. Ich bin nämlich der Meinung, dass es viel leichter sei, im Allgemeinen über den Ursprung der Sprache Behauptungen aufzustellen, gegen welche man kaum etwas Triftiges vorbringen könnte, als den Ursprung nicht nur einer gewissen Sprachenclasse, sondern selbst einer einzelnen Sprache der gewissen Classe zu erklären. Man könnte, denke ich, alle physiologischen und psychologischen Vorbedingungen, welche die Möglichkeit des Sprechens darthun, genau kennen, ohne doch zu wissen, warum z. B. das bekannte *açva,* im Griechischen ἵππο, im Lateinischen *equo,* in den ugrischen Sprachen aber *lov, ló, lu, lav,* und in den türkischen *at* heisst? Warum das sanskritische *apa,* das im Lateinischen *aqua* lautet, im Rumänischen ebenfalls *apa* heisst? sowie das lateinische *equa* im Rumänischen *épa (eapa)* lautet. Ich sehe nicht die Entstehungsursache der angeführten

Wörter; ich weiss auch nicht, warum der Lautwechsel in *açva, equo* und ἵππο, in *aqua* und *apa,* in *equa* und *épa (eapa)* entstanden ist. Man sagt: der Gutturallaut kann in einer verwandten Sprache zum Labiallaut werden, was viele Beispiele bestätigen; oder genauer gesagt, die Sprachenfacta sind der Grund jenes abstracten Ausdruckes geworden. Aber ich fühle weder physiologisch noch psychologisch die Nöthigung zu diesem Lautwechsel; und ich wage zu behaupten, dass auch Andere diese Nöthigung nicht fühlen, weil bekanntlich dieselben Sprachen beide, sowohl Guttural- als Labiallaute in grosser Menge anwenden. Ebenso wenig weiss ich einen physiologischen oder psychologischen Grund anzugeben, warum die türkischen Sprachen, denen der *r*-Laut nicht fremd ist, denselben doch im Anlaut vermeiden, so dass sie z. B. das *‚rus‘ ‚urus‘* sprechen; weshalb auch im Ungarischen der Russe *‚orosz‘* heisst, ein in uralten Zeiten dem Türkischen entnommener Ausdruck, denn im Ungarischen ist das *r* auch im Anlaut sehr gebräuchlich.

Diese Vorbemerkung wollte ich deswegen machen, damit ja Niemand wähne, ich werde mit der Frage: Wo kann die rumänische Sprache entstanden sein? auch das Wie und Warum diese Sprache so entstanden ist, wie sie eben ist, erklären; obgleich ich das Warum doch auch ein oder das andere Mal aufzufinden versuchen werde.

Die rumänische Sprache hat zwei Hauptdialecte, den südlichen, transdanubianischen, den man makedo-rumänisch, und den nördlichen, cisdanubianischen, den man dako-rumänisch nennt. Wo kann nun diese Sprache entstanden sein? Auf diese Frage sind dreierlei Antworten möglich und auch ausgesprochen worden. Nämlich:

1. Die rumänische Sprache ist im Norden der Donau, und zwar in Siebenbürgen entstanden, von woher sie sich dann nach dem Süden in die transdanubianischen Provinzen verbreitet hat.

2. Die rumänische Sprache ist sowohl im Norden, d. h. in Siebenbürgen, wie auch im Süden, auf der Balkanhalbinsel entstanden.

3. Die rumänische Sprache ist im Süden, auf der Balkanhalbinsel entsprungen, und hat sich von daher nach dem Norden in die cisdanubianischen Provinzen, folglich auch nach Siebenbürgen, verbreitet.

Um die dreierlei Antworten richtig beurtheilen zu können, ist eine Kenntniss des Rumänischen beider Dialecte, den Hauptzügen nach, erforderlich, welche ich möglichst kurz andeuten will.

Das Rumänische ist eine romanische Sprache, denn ihr Grundstock ist lateinisch, wie der aller anderen romanischen Sprachen. Es steht am nächsten dem Italienischen, und könnte für einen Dialect desselben angesehen werden, wenn es nicht solche Eigenthümlichkeiten hätte, die es von allen anderen romanischen Sprachen unterscheiden. Es zeigt auch überhaupt einen grösseren Lautschwund, als das Italienische, wobei ich sogleich bemerke, dass ich nur die italienische Schriftsprache mit der rumänischen Schriftsprache vergleichen kann, demnach die mannigfachen Ortsdialecte beider Sprachen ausser Acht lassen muss. Es behaupten aber Sprachgelehrte, wie Emil Picot (Documents pour servir à l'étude des dialectes roumains, recueillis et publiés par Emil Picot. I. Paris. Extrait de la Revue de Linguistique et de Philologie comparée. T. V., fasc. 3), dass das Rumänische, verglichen mit dem Italienischen, sehr wenig Dialectverschiedenes aufzeigt. Nach Picot wäre das Makedo-Rumänische bei weitem nicht so abweichend von dem Dako-Rumänischen, wie das Neapolitanische von dem Toskanischen oder von dem Venetianischen. Wenn man dennoch die verschiedenen italienischen Dialecte nur für Mundarten einer und derselben Sprache hält, so dürfen umsomehr die beiden rumänischen Hauptdialecte nur für Mundarten einer Sprache gelten. Ich kann mich auch auf meine eigene Erfahrung berufen. Ich verstehe das im Makedo-Rumänischen Gedruckte nicht mit mehr Schwierigkeit, als die Fritz Reuter'schen Schriften; ich finde demnach zwischen dem Makedo-Rumänischen und dem Dako-Rumänischen keinen grösseren Unterschied, als zwischen dem Fritz Reuter'schen Plattdeutschen und der deutschen Litteratursprache.

Der Wortschatz beider rumänischen Dialecte enthält zuerst eine grosse Menge solcher Ausdrücke, welche der Form und Bedeutung nach, so zu sagen, identisch sind mit den lateinischen Wörtern. Die Beispiele werden immer in der dako-rumänischen Form vorangestellt, worauf die makedo-rumänische folgt.

Dako-Rumänisch	Makedo-Rumänisch	Lateinisch	Deutsch
acu	*acu*	*acus*	Nadel
albu	*albu*	*albus*	weiss
altu	*altu*	*altus*	hoch
amu	*amu*	*habeo*	ich habe
arbore	*arbore*	*arbor*	der Baum
ardu	*ardu*	*ardeo*	ich brenne
ascundu	*ascundu*	*abscondeo*	ich verberge
audu	*avdu*	*audio*	ich höre
barba	*barba*	*barba*	der Bart
bou	*bou*	*bos*	der Ochs

u. s. w.

Ein kleiner Unterschied zeigt sich in dieser Kategorie der Wörter, dass der Lautschwund im Dako-Rumänischen noch grösser ist als im Makedo-Rumänischen, z. B.

chiemu	*clemu*	*clamo*	ich schreie
chiaie	*cliae*	*clavis*	der Schlüssel
muiare	*muliare*	*mulier*	das Weib
ochiu	*ocliu*	*oculus*	das Auge

u. s. w.

Dann lautet *c* vor *e*, *i* im Dako-Rumänischen *tsch*, im Makedo-Rumänischen *tz*, als:

čine	*cine*	*quis*	wer
če	*ce*	*quid*	was
četate	*citate*	*civitas*	die Stadt
čina	*cina*	*coena*	das Abendmahl
čingu	*cingu*	*cingo*	ich umgürte

u. s. w.

Wegen dieser Aussprache nennen die Dako-Rumänen ihre südlichen Sprachbrüder Tsintsaren, weil sie *tz* und nicht *tsch* sprechen.

Weiter entspricht dem *f*- und *v*-Laut im Makedo-Rumänischen *h* und *j*, als:

ferbu	*herbu*	*ferveo*	ich siede
fia	*hilia*	*filia*	die Tochter
fiu	*hiliu*	*filius*	der Sohn
ficatu	*hicatu*	*ficatus*	mit Feigen gestopft
verme	*jermu*	*vermis*	der Wurm
vinu	*jinu*	*vinum*	der Wein

u. s. w.

Doch finden wir auch:

ventu	*vintu*	*ventus*	der Wind
vina	*vina*	*vena*	die Ader
focu	*focu*	*focus*	das Feuer

u. s. w.

Die lateinischen Gatturallaute werden in beiden Dialecten häufig zu Labiallauten, was in der italienischen Schriftsprache nicht vorkömmt, als:

apa	*apa*	*aqua*	das Wasser
lapte	*lapte*	*lac (lactis)*	die Milch
lemnu	*lemnu*	*lignum*	das Holz
limba	*limba*	*lingua*	die Zunge, Sprache
opto	*opto*	*octo*	acht
patru	*patru*	*quatuor*	vier

aber:

calu	*calu*	*caballus*	das Pferd
cale	*cale*	*callis*	der Weg
care	*care*	*qualis*	welche

u. s. w.

Dies letzte Wort zeigt eine Umwandlung des lateinischen *l*-Lautes, der in beiden Dialecten zum *r*-Laut wird, z. B.

čeru	*ceru*	*coelum*	der Himmel
gura	*gura*	*gula*	der Mund

mascuru	*mascuru*	*masculus*	das Männlein
paru	*paru*	*palus*	der Pfahl
peru	*peru*	*pilus*	das Haar
purečе	*purece*	*pulex*	der Floh
sare	*sare*	*sal*	das Salz

u. s. w.

Im istrischen Dialecte, einer Abweichung des Makedo-Rumänischen, wird das *n* zu *r*, z. B. *dumineca*, Sonntag, lautet im Istrischen *dumireca*; *farina*, das Mehl, lautet dort *farira*; *lana*, die Wolle, *lara* u. s. w. Aber das lateinische *monumentum*, Grabmal, lautet in beiden Hauptdialecten *mormintu*.

Vor *a* und *e* wird in beiden Dialecten das *e* zu *ea*, *ia*, das *o* zu *oa* gedehnt, oder diphthongisirt. Daher lautet das *video*, *vides*, *videt* im Rumänischen: *vedu*, *vezi*, *veade*. Beispiele:

eapa	*iapa*	*equa*	die Stute
dereapta	*deriapta*	*directa*	die Rechte
doamna	*doamna*	*domina*	die Frau
foame	*foamè*	*fames*	der Hunger
oameni	*oameni*	*homines*	die Menschen
(aber	*omu* *omu*	*homo*	der Mensch)
peatra	*kiatra*	*petra*	der Fels
peale	*kiale*	*pellis*	das Fell
moara	*moara*	*mola*	die Mühle
soare	*soare*	*sol*	die Sonne

u. s. w.

Der Wortschatz beider Dialecte enthält aber auch solche lateinische Wörter, deren Bedeutung in beiden Dialecten des Rumänischen eine andere geworden ist, z. B.

barbatu	*barbatu*	der Mann	*barbatus*
doru	*doru*	der Wunsch	*dolor*
inima	*inima*	das Herz	*anima*
sufletu	*sufletu*	die Seele	*subflatus*
lucru	*lucru*	die Arbeit	*lucrum*
leau	*liau*	ich nehme	*levo*
leareaminte	*loareaminte*	das Aufmerken	*animadversio*

orbu	*orbu*	der Blinde	*orbus*
sarutare	*sarutare*	das Küssen	*salutare*

u. s. w.

Natürlich haben beide Dialecte sehr viele Wörter, die nicht lateinischen Ursprunges sind, deren Herkunft wir hier unbeachtet lassen, als:

aruncu	*aruncu*	ich werfe
belescu	*belescu*	ich schäle
buza	*buza*	die Lippe
fečora	*ficora*	das Mädchen
fečoru	*ficoru*	der Knabe
folosescu	*felisescu*	ich nütze
galbenu	*galbenu*	gelb
graiu	*griaiu*	die Stimme, das Wort
grasime	*gresime*	die Fette
hranescu	*harnescu*	ich nähre
invetiu	*invetiu*	ich lehre
me invetiu	*me invetiu*	ich lerne
moaša	*moasa*	die Alte
padure	*padure*	der Wald
suta	*suta*	hundert
trupu	*trupu*	der Körper
lingura	*lingura*	der Löffel
mare	*mare*	gross

u. s. w.

Wir finden endlich Wörter in beiden Dialecten, welche dem Griechischen entnommen sind, wie:

dascalu	*dascalu*	der Lehrer	διδάσκω
dracu	*dracu*	der Teufel	δράκων
drumu	*drumu*	der Weg	δρόμος
ermu	*ermu*	die Wüste	ἔρημος
lipsa	*lipsa*	der Mangel	λεῖψις
lipsescu	*lipsescu*	ich ermangele	
pedepsa	*pedefsa*	die Strafe	παίδευσις

u. s. w.

Nun führe ich nur drei Eigenthümlichkeiten an, durch welche sich beide rumänischen Dialecte von den anderen romanischen Sprachen unterscheiden.

In dem Italienischen, wie in allen anderen romanischen Sprachen, hat das lateinische Pronomen demonstrativum *ille, illa* die Rolle des Artikels übernommen, welcher dann mit einigen Präpositionen die Declination bilden musste, nachdem die lateinischen Casusendungen ihre Wirkung verloren hatten. Dieser Artikel steht überall vor dem Nomen. Auch im Rumänischen hat das Pronomen demonstrativum die Rolle des Artikels übernommen, aber dieser wird, sonderbarer Weise, hinten an das Nomen angehängt, wodurch die rumänische Declination sich sehr verschieden von der der anderen romanischen Sprachen gestaltet, wie das Beispiel es zeigt.

Italienisch	Dako-Rumänisch	Makedo-Rumänisch	
il lupo	*lupu-lu*	*lup-lu*	der Wolf
del lupo	*a lupului*	*a luplui*	
al lupo	*a lupului*	*a luplui*	
i lupi	*lupi-li, lupii*	*lupli*	die Wölfe
dei lupi	*a lupi-loru*	*a luplor*	
ai lupi	*a lupiloru*	*a luplor*	
la donna	*doamna-a, doamn'a*	*doamn'a*	die Frau
della donna	*doamne-ei, doamn'ei*	*a doamni-li*	
alla donna	*doamne-ei, doamn'ei*	*a doamni-li*	
le donne	*doamne-le*	*doamni-le*	die Frauen
delle donne	*doamne-loru*	*a doamni-lor*	
alle donne	*doamne-loru*	*a doamni-lor*	

Das *loru, lor* des Rumänischen ist dem pluralen Genitiv und Dativ des Demonstrativums *elu, e'a (ela)* entnommen, das auch dem italienischen *di loro, a loro* entspricht. Uebrigens zeigt die rumänische Declination noch manch Schwankendes, so hiess eine Zeitung im Anfange ‚Gazeta de Transilvania', jetzt heisst sie ‚Gazeta Transilvaniei'. So lautet der Nominativ des Pronomen possessivum im Dako-Rumänischen: *alu mieu, a-mea,* der meine, die meine; *ai miei, ale mele,* die meinen. Im Makedo-

Rumänischen: *a-meu, a-mea; a-mei a-mele.* Hier scheint das *a* als Präposition ganz überflüssig; man müsste es als ein *a* prostethicum betrachten.

Auch die Bildung der compositen Zahlwörter weicht von den gewöhnlichen romanischen Zahlwörtern ab. So sagt der Italiener: *undici, dodici, tredici* und so fort bis *sedici*, dann aber *dieci sette, dieci otto, dieci nuovo.* Der Dako-Rumäne sagt: *un-spre-zeče (unum supra decem), doi-spre-zeče, trei-spre-zeče, patru-spre-zeče (quatuor supra decem* u. s. w.*), optu-spre-zeče, noue-spre-zeče.* Ebenso der Makedo-Rumäne: *un-spre zace, dao-spre-zace, trei-spre-zace, patru-spre-zace.*

Die multiplicirten Zahlwörter werden in dem Italienischen und anderen romanischen Sprachen durch die lateinischen Synthesen ausgedrückt, wie *venti* (20), *trenta* (30), *quaranta* (40); *vingt, trente, quarante* u. s. w. Die rumänische Sprache hat die lateinischen Synthesen aufgelöst, und der Dako-Rumäne sagt: *doue zeči* = zwei zehn, *trei zeči, patru zeči* u. s. w. Der Makedo-Rumäne sagt: *žinžici* (20, ein dunkles Wort, aber) *trei zaci, patru zaci* u. s. w. Auffallend ist es, dass die rumänische Sprache für hundert das unlateinische (slavische) *suta* in beiden Dialecten aufgenommen hat, während die anderen romanischen Sprachen das lateinische *centum* beibehalten haben.

Endlich weicht die rumänische Sprache in der Bildung des Futurums von ihren romanischen Schwestern ab. Diese haben sich eine neue Synthese des Verbums mit dem Hilfszeitwort *habeo* gebildet: hingegen die rumänische Sprache nahm das Verbum *volo* = ich will, zu dem Infinitiv des Verbums, wie wir an dem folgenden Beispiele sehen.

Italienisch	Dako-Rumänisch	Makedo-Rumänisch
loderò	*voliu lauda*	*voi lavdare*
loderai	*veri lauda*	*vrei lavdare*
loderà	*va lauda*	*va lavdare*
loderemo	*vomu lauda*	*vremu lavdare*
loderete	*vreti lauda*	*vreci lavdare*
loderanno	*voru lauda*	*voru lavdare.*

Um den *r*-Laut in dem rumänischen Hilfswort zu erklären, muss man sich erinnern, dass das lateinische *l* im Rumänischen zu *r* wird. Das lateinische *velle* lautet demnach im Rumänischen *vre* oder *vrere*. Das Präsens dieses Wortes hat im Dako-Rumänischen dreierlei Formen; im Makedo-Rumänischen nur eine.

Dako-Rumänisch.			Makedo-Rumänisch.
vreu	*voliu*	*oiu*	*voi*
vrei	*veri, vei*	*oi*	*vrei*
vre	*va*	*o*	*va*
vremu	*vomu*	*omu*	*vremu*
vreti	*vreti, veti*	*eti*	*vreci*
vreu	*voru*	*oru*	*va*

I.

Wo mag nun diese Sprache entstanden sein? Im Norden der Donau, und zwar in dem heutigen Siebenbürgen, dem berühmten alten Goldland, das den Mittelpunkt der gefürchteten dakischen Macht unter Dekebalus bildete, die aber der römische Kaiser Trajanus in den Jahren 101—104 n. Chr. vernichtete und Dakien zur römischen Provinz machte. So lautet die erste Antwort auf die Frage, wo die rumänische Sprache entstanden sein kann. Diese Antwort hatte den Beifall der vorigen Jahrhunderte, und gilt bei Vielen noch jetzt als historisch gut begründet. Wie Gibbon vor einem Jahrhundert in seinem berühmten Werke (Decline and fall of the Roman Empire, Chapter XI.), so nahm sie auch Leopold von Ranke in seiner Weltgeschichte (III. Band, I. Abtheilung, Leipzig 1883. Seite 452) als solche an.

Sie stützt sich auf das Zeugniss der Geschichte, dass in Dakien das römische Wesen eine hohe Entwickelung erreichte: was die vielen aufgefundenen und publicirten Inschriften, die Spuren römischer Strassen und die, leider sehr verschleppten Ueberreste römischer Bauten bestätigen. Sie stützt sich aber auch auf das Zeugniss der Gegenwart; denn Siebenbürgen hat eine rumänische Bevölkerung, welche jetzt die Mehrheit der dortigen Bewohner ausmacht, die demnach von den Colonisten, mit welchen Trajanus das durch den blutigen Eroberungskrieg menschenleer gewordene Land bevölkerte, abstammen können. Mit dieser allgemeinen Auffassung begnügen sich die landläufigen Lehrbücher, wie sich denn auch die bewunderten Gibbon und von Ranke damit begnügten, denen beiden es wohl sehr ferne liegen mochte, in diesem abseits liegenden dunkeln Winkel der Geschichte genauere Forschungen anzustellen.

Die rumänische Geschichtsschreibung, welche seit 1812 (damals erschienen Peter Major's Untersuchungen über das Erstehen des Rumänenthums — das allererste Werk dieser Art) sehr emsig arbeitet, hat aber die allgemeine Auffassung mit einem reichen stofflichen Inhalt ausgestattet. Sie, die rumänische Geschichtsschreibung, weiss, nach Peter Major's Entdeckung, dass die heutigen Walachen oder Rumänen Siebenbürgens, reines römisches Blut sind: soll doch Trajanus die Daker mit Stumpf und Stiel ausgerottet haben. Die neuen Colonisten kamen mit Weib und Kind in's Land; kein einziger heiratete ein barbarisches Weib, wie noch heutzutage, so behauptete Peter Major, der Rumäne sich nur mit einer Rumänin vermählt. Die rumänische Geschichtsschreibung weiss, dass das Christenthum unter den römischen Colonisten sehr begründet war, deswegen bildete sich daselbst eine christliche Hierarchie, so dass natürlicher Weise lateinisches Schriftenthum und lateinische Gelehrsamkeit im alten Dakien fortblühten. Sie weiss, dass diese gebildete römische oder romanisirte Bevölkerung unter der gothischen Herrschaft leidlichen Bestand hatte, auch humanisirte sie die rohen Gothen. Sie weiss es, wenigstens zum Theil, dass diese Bevölkerung mit den Hunnen, den Nachfolgern der Gothen, auf freundschaftlichem Fusse stand, soll doch den Hunnen die romanische Sprache ganz geläufig gewesen sein: zum anderen Theil findet sie zwar, dass die Hunnen eine wahre Teufelsbrut waren. Aber die Romanen, den Unholden ausweichend, zogen sich in die Berge und kamen, sammt ihren Herrschern, jedesmal in ihre früheren Sitze zurück, sobald die barbarischen Horden, die einander ablösten, das Land verlassen hatten. Dies geschah zumal, behaupten die rumänischen Geschichtsschreiber, um 800 n. Chr., nach dem Verfall des Avarenreiches. Von nun an blieben sie alleinige Inhaber des heutigen Siebenbürgens, und stifteten mehrere Staaten, deren Herrscher Gelou, Men-Marot und Glad waren, als die Magyaren erschienen. Diese mussten demnach jene Herrscher besiegen, als sie das Land in Besitz nehmen wollten, was ihnen aber nur zum Theile gelungen ist. Denn auch nachher hatten sich souveräne rumänische Fürstenthümer erhalten, namentlich das von Fogaras im Süden des Landes, dessen Herrscher, der schwarze Rudolf oder Gaudentius (Rad-Negr) 1290 aus Fogaras auszog und den walachischen Staat, das heutige Romanien begründete. Endlich führt die rumänische Geschichtsschreibung auch Traditionen, z. B. von der Trajan's Wiese, und die allgemeine Ueberzeugung des Volkes von dessen römischer Abstammung als Belege für ihre Behauptungen an.

Der stoffliche Inhalt, mit dem die rumänische Geschichtsschreibung die oben erwähnte allgemeine Auffassung ausstattet, ist wohl glaublich: ist er aber auch geschichtlich?

Die Geschichte muss vorerst den heutigen Rumänen das reine römische Blut absprechen. Trajanus hatte die Daker nicht mit Stumpf und Stiel ausgerottet, obwohl er ihre staatliche Macht für immer gebrochen hat. Dakische Hilfstruppen dienten auch nach Trajan's Tod in den römischen Heeren; und in der eigentlichen dakischen Provinz schlossen sich manche Daker dem römischen Wesen an, was viele Inschriften bezeugen. Eine Mischung der Colonisten mit fremdem Blute war daselbst ebenso allgemein, wie überall in den römischen Provinzen.

Was weiss aber die Geschichte von diesen Colonisten selbst? Sie weiss, dass sie nicht aus Italien stammten, also nichts weniger als Römer waren. Italien konnte zu Trajan's Zeiten keine Colonien abgeben, so sehr entvölkert war es bereits, oder vielmehr so sehr hatten die Latifundien überhand genommen, dass die Landbevölkerung fast nur aus Sklaven bestand. Die nach Dakien versetzte neue Bevölkerung kam zum allergrössten Theile aus Kleinasien, aber auch aus Noricum und Pannonien. Für den Goldbergbau wurden Pirusten aus Dalmatien gepresst. Nur nach Apulum, wo heute Karlsburg oder Weissenburg liegt, versetzte Decius um 252 Colonisten aus Apulien, und benannte es ‚Nova colonia Apulum'. Diese Colonisten waren gräcisirte Autochthonen, wenn sie auch schon lateinisch sprachen. Alles dies beweisen zahlreiche Inschriften. Die neue Bevölkerung der dakischen Provinz war ein Mischvolk, wie kaum in einer anderen Provinz des weiten römischen Reiches.

Von den dakischen Colonisten weiss noch die Geschichte dass sie, vor den Einfällen der Gothen, nach Mösien jenseits der Donau versetzt wurden, und dass Aurelianus auch die Militärmacht aus der trajanischen Provinz herauszog. Ob alle oder nicht alle Provincialen diese Provinz verlassen haben, ist eine irrelevante Frage. Gewiss zogen nicht alle fort, aber eben so gewiss ist es, dass durch diesen Exodus das romanische Wesen daselbst geschwächt, das barbarische hingegen sehr verstärkt werden musste.

Was weiss weiter die Geschichte von dem Christenthume im trajanischen Dakien? Gar nichts; denn die aufgefundenen Inschriften geben davon kein Zeugniss. Die Geschichte weiss nur, dass Decius, der sich ‚Restitutor Daciarum' nannte, unter allen Imperatoren der heftigste Verfolger der Christen war. Wir müssen demnach annehmen, dass zu seiner Zeit, um 250—252, in Dakien das Christenthum schwerlich so geblüht habe, um eine organisirte Hierarchie zu besitzen. Nach Decius aber beginnt schon der Verfall der Provinz, die sich um 260 der Gothen nicht mehr erwehren konnte. Die Geschichte weiss dann, dass zu den Gothen das Christenthum nicht aus Dakien, sondern aus Kleinasien gelangte, und dass selbst ein Theil der Gothen unter Athanarich die christlichen Gothen vertrieb, was den Zwiespalt unter den Gothen verursachte und den Sieg der Hunnen über sie erleichterte. Als dann Athanarich sich vor den Hunnen nach Siebenbürgen retten wollte, musste er dort Sarmaten verdrängen (extrusis Sarmatibus, wie es bei Ammianus Marcellinus XXXI, 4, 12 heisst). Um 370, also nur hundert Jahre nach dem Exodus der Provincialen aus Siebenbürgen, hören wir daselbst nichts mehr von romanischen Einwohnern, so wie auch der Daker

Name schon verschwunden war. In dieser, für das trajanische Dakien so traurigen Zeit, konnte sich daselbst eine christliche Hierarchie oder gar römische Gelehrsamkeit kaum erhalten haben.

Nun erscheint in dem Gesandtschaftsberichte des Priscus das positivste Zeugniss aus dem Jahre 448 über die ehemalige trajanische Provinz. Das sogenannte ungarische Banat zwischen der Donau, der Theiss, der Maros und dem heutigen Hunyader Comitat von Siebenbürgen hatte mit diesem Comitate und dessen nördlichen und östlichen Umgebungen den weitaus romanisirtesten Theil der römischen Provinz gebildet. Die griechische Gesandtschaft, nachdem sie die Donau überschritten, durchzog den ganzen Banat bis an die Maros, übersetzte unterhalb oder oberhalb Szegedins die Theiss, um an das Hoflager Attila's zu gelangen.

Nirgends fand Priscus eine Spur des ehemaligen römischen Wesens, er, der lateinisch (er nennt es ausonisch) verstand, Christ war, demnach die etwaigen christlichen Insassen wohl bemerken musste, er hört von einer solchen Bevölkerung des alten Dakiens nichts, dessen Eroberung durch Trajanus und Aufgeben durch Aurelianus ihm nicht unbekannt sein konnten.

Die Hunnenmacht zerfällt, und die Gepiden bleiben als Herren von Siebenbürgen da. Gegen diese knüpft Kaiser Justinianus sowohl mit den Utriguren und Kutriguren am Don und dem Asow'schen Meere, als auch mit den Longobarden in dem heutigen Ungarn Unterhandlungen an — so weit suchte er Verbündete — aber die sehr zahlreichen Nachkommen der dakischen Provincialen, die, nach der Behauptung der rumänischen Geschichtsschreibung, unter eigenen Herrschern in Siebenbürgen (ob neben oder unter den Gepiden?) leben sollten, und des Kaisers erwünschteste Verbündete hätten sein müssen, diese findet dessen herumspähende Politik nicht. Vielmehr lässt er in dem heutigen Serbien und Bulgarien längst der Donau eine Reihe von Fortificationen errichten gegen das Barbarenland am linken Donauufer. Justinianus und seine politische und militärische Umgebung hatten also keine Kunde von romanischen Einwohnern in dem Barbarenlande.

Nach der Besiegung der Gepiden und dem Abzug der Longobarden aus Pannonien herrschten die Avaren dritthalb hundert Jahre lang in dem heutigen Ungarn, Siebenbürgen und Romanien (Moldau und Walachei). Die vielen Kriege der griechischen Kaiser mit diesen neuen Nachbarn bieten vielfache Gelegenheit, die verschiedenen Völkerschaften des grossen Avarenreiches kennen zu lernen; so erfahren wir, dass neben den Avaren und Bulgaren die Slaven am zahlreichsten waren; wir hören auch von drei Gepidendörfern, gerade in der Gegend, die Priscus durchwandert hatte: aber von romanischen Einwohnern diesseits der Donau hören wir abermals nichts.

Das Avarenreich wird durch Karl des Grossen Armeen vernichtet. Nun sollen, nach der Behauptung der rumänischen Geschichtsschreibung, die Romanen alleinige Besitzer von Siebenbürgen geworden sein, so dass zur Zeit, als die Ungarn oder Magyaren erschienen, daselbst drei rumänische Fürsten: Gelou, Men-Marot und Glad, sowie zwischen der Theiss und der Donau in Ungarn der Bulgarenfürst Zalan geherrscht haben sollen. Die rumänisch-christliche Hierarchie und die lateinische Litteratur hätte sich demnach von 800—900 ganz frei erhalten und entwickelt. Die Ungarn kämpften zwar mit Erfolg gegen die genannten Fürsten, ohne jedoch die Rumänen zu besiegen, die vielmehr ihre Verbündeten wurden und noch lange Zeit hindurch souveräne Fürstenthümer, namentlich das von Fogaras, behielten. Die lateinische Schrift und Kirchensprache hätte unter den Rumänen Siebenbürgens, der Moldau und der Walachei bis zu dem florentinischen Concilium 1439 geherrscht, das, wie bekannt, die Union der orientalischen und occidentalischen Kirchen angenommen hat.

Diese letzteren Behauptungen der rumänischen Geschichtsschreibung unterstützen aber weder die gleichzeitigen griechischen und lateinischen Schriftsteller, noch die allbekannten Begebenheiten. Sie stehen aber auch im Widerspruche mit der Topographie Siebenbürgens, mit dem fremden Zeugniss der magyarischen Sprache und — was noch bedeutungsvoller ist — auch mit dem einheimischen Zeugniss der rumänischen Sprache selbst.

Der Prumer Abt Regino, Liutprand des deutschen Kaisers Gesandter in Constantinopel, die griechischen Kaiser Leo Sapiens und Constantinus Porphyrogenitus (alle vier Genannten sind Berichterstatter über die Kriege mit den erscheinenden Magyaren und deren Niederlassung), erhielten keine Kenntniss von rumänisch-christlichen Fürsten und Einwohnern Siebenbürgens oder von einem bulgarischen Zalan in Ungarn. Der deutsche Kaiser Arnulf, der mährische Fürst Svatopluk, und der mächtige Symeon, Herrscher der Bulgaren jenseits der Donau, mussten die auftretenden Magyaren als Feinde fürchten, und hätten sich gewiss die Mitwirkung der genannten, Gelou, Men-Marot, Glad und des Zalan verschafft, wenn diese historische und nicht erdichtete Persönlichkeiten gewesen wären. Umgekehrt, der anonyme ‚Bela regis Notarius', dem wir allein die genannten Persönlichkeiten verdanken, kennt seinerseits weder den Kaiser Arnulf, noch den mährischen Svatopluk, noch den bulgarischen Symeon. Die Erzählung des anonymen Notarius von der magyarischen Occupation des Landes hat nicht mehr historischen Boden als die Helden Ariosto's im Orlando furioso.

Byzantinische Berichte wissen, dass zwei ungarische Stammfürsten, Bolosudes und Gylas — in den ungarischen Chroniken Gyula — um 950 in Constantinopel die Taufe empfingen, und dass sie der Kaiser Constantinus Porphyrogenitus, der bei dem Taufact ihr Pathe war, mit der Patricierwürde auszeichnete. Sie erhielten auch einen Mönch, Hierotheus, den der Patriarch zum Bischof des zu bekehrenden Volkes geweiht hatte, und kehrten in ihre Heimat zurück. Bolosudes ward Apostat, und verlor sein Leben in der berühmten Schlacht bei Augsburg, 955; Gylas oder Gyula, blieb der neuen Religion treu, und lebte als Stammfürst in Siebenbürgen. Seine christliche Enkelin ward Gemalin des Grossfürsten Geisa und Mutter des heiligen Stephans, ersten Königs von Ungarn.

Dieser hatte als christlicher König mit den Stammfürsten zu kämpfen, namentlich auch mit Achtum, der zwischen der Donau, der Theiss und der Maros, also in dem romanisirtesten Theile der ehemaligen dakischen Provinz, hauste, und aus

Widdin (Bdyn) bulgarische Mönche berufen hatte. Nach seinem Falle setzte Stephan den italienischen Gerhard auf den neuen Bischofsstuhl von Csanád, allwo die bulgarischen Mönche bereits das Christenthum zu pflanzen begonnen hatten.

Weder Gylas oder Gyula, noch Achtum, hatten in ihrem Besitzthum romanische Christen und eine Hierarchie gefunden, sonst hätte jener nicht in Constantinopel die Taufe empfangen und von daher einen Bischof mitnehmen, und Achtum hätte sich nicht nach Widdin um Mönche wenden müssen. Endlich der italienische — nachher auch canonisirte — Gerhard, der seine Mühe mit den heidnischen Schülern so beredt erzählt, hätte gewiss mit Freuden die romanischen Christen in seinem neuen Sprengel begrüsst, mit denen er sich sogar in seiner Muttersprache hätte verständig machen können.

Werfen wir nun einen Blick auf die Topographie Siebenbürgens. Kein einziger dakischer oder romanischer Ortsname tritt uns hier entgegen. In allen andern römischen Provinzen, nicht nur in dem heutigen Deutschland, sondern auch in England, wo die römische oder romanisirte Einwohnerschaft seit mehr als tausend Jahren verschollen ist, haben sich römische Ortsnamen erhalten; in Siebenbürgen finden wir keinen einzigen Ortsnamen aus der Römerzeit. Diese auffällige Erscheinung ist nur dadurch erklärlich, dass in jenen Provinzen die ethnische Umwandlung nur langsam vor sich ging, so dass die schwindende romanische Bevölkerung die Ortsnamen der sich stets mehrenden neuen Bevölkerung überliefern konnte. In Siebenbürgen muss die ethnische Umwandlung überall plötzlich geschehen sein, so dass die Tradition so zu sagen mit einem Male unterbrochen wurde. Selbst in demjenigen Theile vom römischen Pannonien, der zu Ungarn gehört und in dem die römische Herrschaft um ein Jahrhundert früher begonnen und um mehr als zwei Jahrhunderte länger gedauert hat als in Siebenbürgen, selbst hier konnte sich, und zwar jenseits der Donau, nur ein Ortsname, Siscia (Sisek) und nur ein Gauname, Sirmium (Sirmien), erhalten. Es war demnach auch in diesem Theile Pannoniens die ethnische Umwandlung plötzlicher und durchschlagender als anderswo.

Was für Ortsnamen finden wir aber in Siebenbürgen? Lauter slavische; die ungarischen und deutschen Ortsnamen lagern sich gleichsam auf die ältere, slavische, Nomenclatur. Die Ungarn oder Magyaren fanden demnach, als sie das Land occupirten, nur eine slavische Bevölkerung vor; so wie sie auch in Ungarn nur Slaven fanden.

Dieses Factum bestätigt auch die magyarische Sprache. Diese strotzt nämlich von slavischen Wörtern, und zwar zeigt sie in ihrer ganzen geographischen Ausbreitung denselben slavischen Einfluss. Hätte sie ‚im Lande jenseits des Waldes' (dies ist die Bedeutung des Erdel, der ungarischen Benennung für Siebenbürgen) nicht eine slavische, sondern eine romanische Bevölkerung vorgefunden, die ja auch gebildeter hätte sein müssen, so würde sie unstreitig dort romanische Ausdrücke, und vielleicht noch in grösserer Menge, angenommen haben. Da aber die Sprache der Szekler, des östlichsten magyarischen Volksstammes in Siebenbürgen, dieselben Slavismen aufweist, welche wir hier in der österreichischen Nachbarschaft, auf der Donauinsel Schütt oder in dem Oedenburger Comitate finden: so steht es ausser allem Zweifel, dass Siebenbürgen, vor der Ankunft der Magyaren, nur eine slavische Bevölkerung hatte.

Aus allem diesen geht aber hervor, dass die romanische Bevölkerung des trajanischen Dakiens, die etwa nach dem Exodus zurückgeblieben war, während der gothischen Stürme verschwand; und dass die Slaven, die vielleicht schon im Avarenreiche die zahlreichste Völkerschaft gebildet hatten, zur Zeit der magyarischen Occupation die alleinigen Bewohner Ungarns und Siebenbürgens waren.

Doch nehmen wir die allgemeine Auffassung und deren stoffliche Ausstattung, wie wir sie gesehen haben, an, wird sie etwa durch die rumänische Sprache unterstützt? Dies führt uns zur Beleuchtung der zweiten Antwort auf die Frage: Wo kann die rumänische Sprache entstanden sein?

II.

Die zweite Antwort lautet so: Die rumänische Sprache ist sowohl in Siebenbürgen als auch im Süden, auf der Balkanhalbinsel, entstanden. Diese Antwort hat Xenopol, Professor der rumänischen Geschichte an der Universität zu Jassy, wenn auch nicht mit klaren Worten, doch mit der Behauptung gegeben, dass der nördliche Rumäne den südlichen, ohne Vorübung oder Vorstudium, nicht verstehen kann (sans une étude ou une habitude préalable, Seite 198 des ‚Une énigme historique. Les Roumains au Moyen-Âge‘. Paris, 1885); dass demnach die beiden Hauptdialecte des Rumänischen sich verschieden gebildet haben. Josef Ladislaus Pič drückt sich (in seinem neuesten Werke: ‚Zur rumänisch-ungarischen Streitfrage, Leipzig, 1886‘, Seite 38) über den Ursprung des Rumänischen folgendermassen aus: ‚Indem wir laut unserer Schlussfolgerung die Dako-Rumänen von den im trajanischen Dakien zurückgebliebenen römischen Colonisten und romanisirten Daken ableiten, die Makedo-Rumänen aber von den nach dem aurelianischen Dakien (nach Mösien) herübergegangenen Colonisten und romanisirten Dakiern, sowie von Bruchstücken romanischer Bevölkerung in Thrakien abstammen lassen: haben wir zugleich eine natürliche Erklärung des einheitlichen Ursprungs der beiden verbrüderten Volksstämme gegeben. Der Zeitpunkt ihrer Trennung wäre dann allenfalls in der Zeitperiode, wo das trajanische Dakien den Gothen als Beute belassen wurde (270—275), zu suchen; so dass man annehmen müsste, die Dako-Rumänen seien durch den Gotheneinfall in die Gebirge Transsylvaniens verschlagen, die Makedo-Rumänen aber etwa durch die Hunnen- oder Avarenstürme nach dem Pindosgebirge, Epirus und Makedonien, verdrängt worden, wo dann jede Berührung zwischen ihnen aufhören musste‘. Pič nimmt also wohl einen einheitlichen Ursprung an, muss aber doch eine verschiedene geschichtliche Entwickelung zugeben, da jede Berührung zwischen den Dako-Rumänen und Makedo-Rumänen, die ungefähr sechs geographische Breitengrade von einander trennen, aufgehört hat. Die unausbleibliche geschichtliche Entwickelung einverstanden, lautet demnach die zweite Antwort wirklich so: Die rumänische Sprache hat sich sowohl in Siebenbürgen, als auch auf dem Pindosgebirge, in Epirus und Makedonien gebildet. Kann nun die rumänische Sprache selbst diese Antwort mit ihrem untrüglichen Zeugniss unterstützen?

Die Sprache hat in beiden Dialecten eine grosse Menge solcher Wörter, welche der äusseren Form und der Bedeutung nach fast identisch mit den entsprechenden lateinischen Wörtern sind, trotz des grösseren oder geringeren Lautschwundes, selbst trotz der Lautwechsel *tsch* und *tz*, *f* und *v*, *h* und *j*, welche sich in der Mundsprache zeigen konnten, ohne von der Schriftsprache aufgenommen zu werden. Diese Wörter kann man ganz gut als gleiches romanisches Erbtheil sowohl in Siebenbürgen, als auch im Süden, auf der Balkanhalbinsel, ansehen, das sich sowohl hier als da gleicherweise erhalten hat.

Zweifelhaft muss aber erscheinen, dass der Lautwechsel des lateinischen Gutturalen zu dem rumänischen Labialen, des lateinischen *l*-Lautes zu dem rumänischen *r*-Laut, schon um 270 ausgebildet soll gewesen sein, so dass die nach Mösien gezogenen Colonisten sie mit sich hinüber nehmen, und bis auf den Pindos und nach Epirus u. s. w. verpflanzen konnten. Denn diesen Lautwechsel hätte schon die Schrift kaum unbeachtet lassen können, und wir müssten davon in den zahlreichen Inschriften einige Spuren entdecken. Wir finden aber, wenigstens meines Wissens, nirgends *limba* statt *lingua*, nirgends *patru*, *patror* statt *quatuor*, nirgends *care* statt *quale*, nirgends *sóre (soare)* statt *sol*, *sole*, nirgends *sare* statt *sal*, *sale* u. s. w.

Noch zweifelhafter muss erscheinen, dass nicht wenig lateinische Wörter in beiden, örtlich so weit von einander entfernten Dialecten, dieselbe neue Bedeutung erhalten konnten, so dass z. B. *dolor* in beiden Dialecten zu *doru* mit der Bedeutung ‚Wunsch', oder dass *anima*, *sufflatus*, jenes zu *inima*, dieses zu *sufletu*, in beiden Dialecten mit der Bedeutung ‚Herz', ‚Seele', hätten werden können.

Viel weniger glaublich ist es auch, dass dieselben nichtlateinischen Wörter in beide Dialecte mit gleicher Bedeutung hineingekommen sind. Diese Fremdwörter setzen nämlich dieselbe Umgebung voraus, die wahrlich Niemand in Siebenbürgen und auf der Balkanhalbinsel während der langen Periode von 270—1200 oder auch nur bis 900 anzunehmen wagen dürfte.

Um Anderes unberührt zu lassen, die Bildung des Futurums mit *volo* hat sich gewiss bis 270 nicht gemacht; sie kann erst nachher entstanden sein. Und auch diese hätte sich auf gleiche Weise sowohl in Siebenbürgen als auch in Epirus und in Makedonien u. s. w. entwickelt? Dies ist wohl höchst unglaublich.

Wie wir sahen, ist der postpositive Artikel dasjenige, was das Rumänische am auffälligsten von den andern romanischen Sprachen unterscheidet *(lupu-lu, lup-lu;* italienisch *il lupo;* französisch *le loup* u. s. w.). Wie ist diese Ausdrucksweise in das Rumänische gekommen? etwa durch einen der Sprache innewohnenden Hang dazu, oder durch eine fremde Einwirkung? denn einen dritten Grund dürfte wohl Niemand auffinden.

Einen der Sprache innewohnenden Hang, der sich in beiden Dialecten mit ganz gleicher Wirkung geäussert hätte, kann man darum nicht annehmen, weil wir ihn auch der lateinischen Sprache zuschreiben und dessen Wirkung nicht nur in ihr selbst, sondern auch in den andern romanischen Sprachen bemerken müssten. Da aber dies der Fall nicht ist, so können wir auch einen innewohnenden Hang zur Bildung des postpositiven Artikels der lateinischen Muttersprache nicht andichten. Was aber diese selbst nicht hatte, das konnte sie auch keiner Tochtersprache als Erbtheil überlassen. Das Erscheinen des postpositiven Artikels im Rumänischen muss demnach die Wirkung eines fremden Einflusses sein.

Dass aber sowohl in Siebenbürgen als auch auf der Balkanhalbinsel, deren beider Geschichte von 270 an bis 1200 himmelweit verschieden war, eine und dieselbe fremde Einwirkung hätte stattgefunden, das wird wohl Niemand auch nur denken wollen. Es ist folglich ausser allen Zweifel gestellt, dass die Erscheinung des postpositiven Artikels in dem Rumänischen nicht sowohl in Siebenbürgen als auch auf der Balkanhalbinsel, sondern entweder nur hier, oder nur dort zu Tage treten konnte, dass demnach das Entstehen der rumänischen Sprache nur Einer Gegend zugeschrieben werden muss. Wo trat nun der postpositive Artikel zu Tage, d. h. wo entstand die rumänische Sprache?

Soweit das rumänische Schriftenthum im Norden der Donau, namentlich in Siebenbürgen — das hierin den Reigen führt — sich zurückdatiren lässt, immer finden wir die kyrillische Schrift in ausschliesslicher Anwendung. Diese Erscheinung intriguirt ungemein die rumänische Geschichtsschreibung, welche die siebenbürgischen Rumänen als unmittelbare Descendenten der trajanischen Colonisten darstellt, die zur Zeit der magyarischen Occupation die alleinige lateinisch gebildete Bevölkerung sollen gewesen sein. Sie waren im Besitze einer römischen — christlichen — Litteratur; sie hatten eine ausgebildete Hierarchie, folglich, behauptet diese Geschichtsschreibung, musste bei ihnen lateinische Sprache und Schrift einheimisch gewesen sein. Freilich fand man im Anfang des XVIII. Jahrhunderts, als man die zur orientalischen Kirche gehörenden Rumänen in den Schooss der römisch-katholischen Kirche ziehen wollte, unter ihren Popen nicht die geringste lateinische Kenntniss und das rumänische Volk so ziemlich des Lesens und Schreibens unkundig; freilich wer damals rumänisch schrieb, bediente sich blos der kyrillischen Schrift; da die lateinische zum Ausdruck der rumänischen Laute damals noch unanwendbar schien.

Diesen Widerspruch zwischen der Wirklichkeit und der fingirten Geschichte trachtete man damit zu beheben, dass man erzählte, die lateinische Wissenschaft und Schrift hätte bis in das XV. Jahrhundert in Siebenbürgen, in der Moldau und Walachei geherrscht und der moldauische Metropolit hätte auch die Union der orientalischen und occidentalischen Kirche auf dem Florentiner Concilium 1439 mit unterschrieben. Allein der Epheser Marcus, der eifrigste Opponent der Union, wusste nach dem plötzlichen Tode des Moldauer Metropoliten auf dessen Sitz einen seiner Anhänger zu bringen. Diesem gelang es in dem Woewoden, in den Bojaren und in dem gesammten Volke einen solchen Hass gegen die römisch-katholische Kirche anzufachen, dass man alle lateinischen Bücher und Schriften zusammenraffte und verbrannte. Und, um die Union für alle Zeiten unmöglich zu machen, entschloss man sich, die slavische Liturgie in den Gottesdienst, und die slavische Sprache sammt der kyrillischen Schrift in das öffentliche und Privatleben einzuführen. Dem Beispiele der Moldauer folgten die walachischen und siebenbürgischen Rumänen nach. Somit hörte die lateinische Wissenschaft und Bildung unter den Rumänen auf und slavische ‚Finsterniss' und Unwissenheit lagerte sich auf sie.

Wer diese Fabel, die gewiss einzig in ihrer Art ist, erfunden hat, kann ich nicht angeben; sie wurde aber von den ersten Koryphäen der rumänischen Gelehrsamkeit, einem Šinkai, einem Major, nacherzählt und als geschichtliche Wahrheit verbreitet. Heute scheint sie nicht mehr allgemeinen Glauben zu finden, denn der schon erwähnte Jassyer Historiker, Xenopol, glaubt sie nicht. Er sucht vielmehr und findet eine andere historische Lösung des grossen Räthsels. ‚Das Verhältniss, welches zwischen der rumänischen Kirche der Moldau und Walachei und der Kirche der Bulgaren bestanden hat, beweist, dass die Einführung des slovenischen oder bulgarischen Ritus in die rumänische Kirche nur während der Dauer des ersten bulgarischen Reiches (680—1018) und nur bei den Rumänen im Norden der Donau stattgefunden haben kann. Die rumänische Kirche Siebenbürgens war hierarchisch immer der walachischen untergeordnet.' So schreibt Xenopol in dem bereits citirten Buche (les relations qui ont existé entre l'église roumaine tant en Moldavie qu'en Valachie, et celle des Bulgares, prouvent que l'introduction du rite slovène ou bulgare chez les Roumains n'a pu avoir lieu que du temps du premier royaume bulgare [680—1018] et que les Roumains n'ont pu le recevoir qu'au nord du Danube. L'église de Transylvanie a toujours été hiérarchiquement soumise à l'église valaque, S. 62).

Xenopol gibt sich nun alle mögliche Mühe zu beweisen, dass die Herrschaft der Bulgaren von 680—1018 sich auch im Norden der Donau, über die Walachei, die Moldau und über

Siebenbürgen erstreckt hat, und wir wollen dieses nördliche bulgarische Reich des rumänischen Historikers auch nicht zerstören: nur das bemerken wir, dass Xenopol damit die Resultate der rumänischen Geschichtsschreibung, welche nicht ein bulgarisches Reich, sondern rumänische Herrscher zu dieser Zeit in Siebenbürgen findet, über den Haufen wirft. Wir lassen also dieses nördliche bulgarische Reich bestehen und fragen: waren diese Bulgaren vor 890, nämlich vor dem Erscheinen der Magyaren, Heiden oder Christen? Der Bulgarenfürst im Süden der Donau, d. h. im heutigen Bulgarien, Bogor oder Boris, liess sich zuerst, um 864, taufen. Im August des Jahres 866 schickten die Bulgaren an den Papst Nicolaus I. 106 Fragen, wie sie als Christen ihre Lebensweise einzurichten hätten? ‚Im November desselben Jahres kamen zwei Bischöfe nach Bulgarien, welche die Antwort auf jene Fragen brachten. An und für sich haben diese ein sehr bedeutendes Interesse, indem wir daraus nahezu über das gesammte Leben des bulgarischen Volkes Belehrung entnehmen können. Insbesondere schöpfen wir daraus in unumstösslicher Weise die werthvolle Ueberzeugung, dass das herrschende nicht-slavische Bulgarenvolk damals mit den unterworfenen Slaven noch nicht verschmolzen war.‘ (Constant. Jos. Jireček, Geschichte der Bulgaren, Seite 156.) Es ist demnach klar, dass auch die vermeinten nördlichen herrschenden Bulgaren bis 866 weder Christen noch slavisirt sein konnten; dass diese demnach von 680—866 den vermeinten siebenbürgischen Rumänen den slovenischen oder bulgarischen Ritus, demnach die slovenische Kirchensprache, nicht mittheilen konnten.

Die Slavisirung der Bulgaren und das Entstehen der altbulgarischen Litteratur begann erst nach 885, nach dem Ableben des Methodius, dessen Schüler von Svatopluk aus Mähren vertrieben, in dem heutigen Bulgarien Aufnahme und einen Wirkungskreis fanden. Symeon, welcher von 893—927 herrschte, war ein Beförderer der bulgarischen Litteratur; unter ihm muss die Slavisirung der Bulgaren grosse Fortschritte gemacht haben. Aber derselbe Symeon, der zuerst besiegt von den Magyaren, dann im Bündniss mit den Petschenegen Sieger über jene wurde, konnte doch die Zerstörung des Mährenreiches und die Einnahme Pannoniens durch die Magyaren nicht verhindern. Und als diese Herren des Landes und die feindlichen Petschenegen in der heutigen Moldau und Walachei sesshaft geworden, da war kein Raum mehr einer Einwirkung der vermeinten nördlichen Bulgaren auf die vermeinten nördlichen Rumänen. Die Einführung des slovenischen oder bulgarischen Ritus in die vermeinte rumänische Kirche konnte vor Symeon's Zeit gar nicht geschehen; die Einführung der kyrillischen Schrift aber konnte noch weniger im Anfang der sich bildenden bulgarischen Litteratur stattfinden.

Fragen wir doch die Geschichte, welche Völker eine neue Schrift annehmen oder sich aufdrängen lassen? Und sie antwortet uns: Analphabetische Völker, die bis dahin keine Schrift hatten, und Völker, die zu einer neuen Religion bekehrt werden. Ueber die erstern ist es unnöthig auch nur ein Wort zur Erläuterung hinzu zu fügen. Ueber die andern kann bemerkt werden, dass diese sowohl analphabetisch als auch schriftkundig sein können; weiter, dass ihnen zu lieb auch eine eigene Schrift zusammengesetzt werden kann. Ob die Finnen oder Suomen, die Magyaren, die Türken u. s. w. irgend eine Schrift hatten, bevor sie zur christlichen oder zu der mohammedanischen Religion sich bekannten, das weiss ich nicht, aber gewiss ist, dass die Suomen, die Magyaren mit dem Christenthume die lateinische Schrift und die Türken mit dem Islam die arabische Schrift annahmen. Die Perser waren schriftkundig, aber der Islam brachte ihnen doch die arabische Schrift. Zur Bekehrung der Gothen, der Slaven wurden neue Schriften zusammengesetzt; und die Bulgaren nahmen mit dem Christenthume die slavische oder kyrillische Schrift an.

Die Rumänen haben auch die kyrillische Schrift angenommen: waren sie demnach analphabetisch, als sie das thaten? oder verliessen sie erst damals das Heidenthum? denn, dass nicht ihnen zu lieb die kyrillische Schrift erfunden wurde, ist ja allgemein bekannt. In Siebenbürgen hätten wohl, nach dem Exodus der römischen Provincialen, die schwachen Ueberreste analphabetisch werden und heidnisch bleiben können; allein hätten sie einmal dort das Christenthum angenommen, so wäre die lateinische Schrift zu ihnen gelangt und ihre Sprache hätte keinen postpositiven Artikel.

III.

Die Provinzen im Süden der Donau waren schon im Anfang unserer Aera längst vollständig römisch. Nachdem Trajanus Dakien unterworfen hatte, wurde eine Reihe neuer Städte zu den schon bestehenden gegründet, wie Ulpia Traiana (Arčar Palanka an der Donau), Nicopolis ad Istrum (Nikup) u. s. w. Und nach der Uebersiedelung aus dem trajanischen Dakien wurde Mösien ‚aurelianisches Dakien' genannt, und in ‚Ufer-Dakien' (Dacia ripensis) und ‚Mittel-Dakien' (Dacia mediterranea) getheilt. Weiter lag Dardanien, allwo Naïssus (heute Niš) entstanden war, der Geburtsort des nachherigen Kaisers Constantinus. Sardica (heute Sophia), das seine Blüthe dem Kaiser Aurelius verdankte, lag in Mittel-Dakien.

Das Christenthum verbreitete sich bald in diesen Provinzen; und nachdem Constantinus die neue Religion zur Staatsreligion, und das alte Byzanz zur neuen Residenzstadt ‚Constantinopolis' erhoben hatte, musste die Halbinsel eine grosse christliche Provinz und zugleich der Schwerpunkt des römischen Reiches werden, während das ehemalige trajanische Dakien, als Barbarenland, dem römischen Einfluss völlig entzogen blieb. Auf den Bischofssitzen dieser Gegenden sehen wir im IV. Jahrhundert lateinisch schreibende Männer, die wohl auch lateinisch werden gepredigt haben. Das zweite christliche Concilium wird in Sardica abgehalten, 347. Das Verzeichniss der lateinischen Bischöfe (denn die Orientalen oder die griechischen Bischöfe hatten sich in Philippopolis versammelt) zeigt, dass die wichtigsten Städte der thrakischen und dakischen Diöcese durch Bischöfe vertreten waren. Sirmium, das oft der Aufenthaltsort der Kaiser war, sah in seinen Mauern dreimal das Concilium versammelt, 351, 357, 358. Das von der kaiserlichen Autorität unterstützte Christenthum musste also auch unter der Landbevölkerung, den

Thrakern verschiedener Namen, herrschend werden und sie immer mehr und mehr romanisiren.

Nach den Gothen- und Hunnenstürmen, und auch schon zugleich mit ihnen, drangen Slavenscharen aus dem jenseitigen bereits slavisirten Dakien in diese romanisirten Provinzen und wurden als Colonnen sesshaft gemacht. Es erfolgten auch selbstständige Slavenzüge, die das ganze aurelianische Dakien in Besitz nahmen, aber die Oberherrschaft der byzantinischen Kaiser anerkannten, deren Reich sich noch immer bis an die Donau erstreckte.

Durch diese Slaveneinfälle und durch ihre bleibenden Niederlassungen wurde das alteinheimische thrakische Volk, das seit seiner Romanisirung mit Recht thrako-romanisch genannt werden konnte, in die Berge gedrängt, und wo es sitzen blieb, musste es mit den Slaven in vielfache Berührungen kommen, welche eine neue Amalgamisirung veranlassten. Die Städte des Binnenlandes verödeten; ihre Bewohner suchten und fanden Unterkunft in den Seestädten.

Nun kamen um 680 die Bulgaren, eine neue Volksschichte, die sich über die Slaven und Thrako-Romanen ausbreitete und die byzantinische Herrschaft von der Donau weg in sehr enge Grenzen drängte. Aber noch vor dem Entstehen der bulgarischen Macht hatte sich in diesem römischen Reiche eine ethnische Wandlung vollzogen.

Die obere Gesellschaftsschichte auf der Balkanhalbinsel, selbst den südlichen griechischen Theil abgerechnet, war doch nie so ganz lateinisch, wie in Italien. Der lateinischen Sprache und Wissenschaft trat hier die christliche Theologie entgegen, welche sich ausschliesslich in der griechischen Sprache entwickelte und die Geister in übergrossem Maasse beherrschte. Kaiser Justinianus musste zwar das römische Recht in der lateinischen Sprache codificiren lassen, aber seine eigenen Edicte erschienen schon griechisch, sowie seine Regierung, seine Bauten, seine Kriege nur einen griechischen Erzähler (Prokopios) fanden. Zu Phoka's Zeiten (602—610) scheint das lateinische Rechtsprechen auch da aufgehört zu haben, wo es bis dahin gebräuchlich war. Unter Heraklios (610—641) war schon Administration, Rechtspflege, Heeresführung, alles griechisch.

Die regierende und bürgerliche Gesellschaft, obwohl sie griechisch sprach und schrieb, behielt aber doch den römischen Namen und nannte sich Romäer (ῥωμαῖοι), dadurch sich von den eigentlichen Griechen, die man Hellenen nannte, unterscheidend. Und als in späteren Zeiten das alte römische Reich auf die Provinz Thrakien eingeschrumpft war, überlieferte dies den römischen Namen auch den Türken, die es Rum-ili (Rum-Provinz) nannten, woher der heutige Name ‚Rumelien'.

Aber unter der Schichte der romäischen Gesellschaft, sowie auch unter der Schichte der bereits slavisirten Bulgaren, hatten sich doch zerstreut lebende Ueberreste der thrako-romanischen Bevölkerung erhalten, die man Blaken, Wlachen (βλάκοι, βλάχοι) nannte. Dieser Name war vielleicht schon unter den Slaven aufgekommen, die vor den Bulgaren die Balkanhalbinsel überfluthet hatten, und wurde nachher sowohl von diesen, als auch von den Romäern oder Byzantinern angenommen. Er wird zuerst um 976 erwähnt, taucht aber bald in vielen Gegenden auf. Als Kaiser Basilios Bulgarien erobert hatte, constituirte er 1019 die bulgarische Kirche, die von nun an keinen Patriarchen, aber doch einen Erzbischof in Ochrida haben sollte. Diesem Erzbischof ordnete er alle Walachen ganz Bulgariens unter.

Aber auch anderswo finden wir Walachen. Niketas Choniates, den wir bald noch einmal erwähnen werden, sagt uns, dass zu seiner Zeit Thessalien ‚Gross-Wlachien' (μεγάλη Βλαχία) geheissen habe. So war in Alt-Aetolien und Akarnanien ‚Klein-Wlachien' (μικρὰ Βλαχία) und im südöstlichen Epirus ‚Ober-Wlachien' (Ἀνωβλαχία). Die Benennung dieser Gross-, Klein- und Ober-Wlachien beweist, dass in diesen Gegenden die Wlachen sehr zahlreich gewesen sein müssen. Sie erscheinen meistens als Hirten, die ein nomadisirendes Leben führen; sie dienen aber auch in den kaiserlichen Heeren und besorgen auf ihren Lastthieren den Tauschhandel zwischen den adriatischen Uferstädten und dem Binnenland.

Diese Walachen oder Wlachen waren wohl seit der Bekehrung der Thrakier, d. h. der Mösier, Bessen u. s. w. Christen, konnten aber nirgends eine eigene Eparchie bilden und einen eigenen walachischen Clerus haben. Die bulgarischen Walachen verehrten ihr kirchliches Oberhaupt in den Erzbischöfen von Ochrida; ihre Priester waren nur Bulgaren, welche die slovenische Kirchensprache hatten und auch die Messe slovenisch absangen, so wie sie von Methodius einst in Mähren und Pannonien eingeführt wurde. Die Walachen in Thessalien, Aetolien, Akarnanien, in dem Epirus hatten einen griechischen Clerus, dessen Kirchensprache natürlich die griechische war. Alle genannten Walachen insgesammt waren analphabetisch; denn, wenn sie auch eine romanische Volkssprache redeten, so schrieb doch damals keine Seele walachisch. Ihre Schriftkundigen, ihre Priester, schrieben nur bulgarisch, d. h. slovenisch oder griechisch.

Dieser culturelle Zustand wurde auch durch die Entstehung des neuen oder zweiten Bulgarenreiches nicht verändert.

Als Kaiser Isaak Angelos nach dem Tode seiner Gemalin die Tochter des ungarischen Königs Béla III. (Οὐγγρίας ῥήξ Βελάς) heiratete, so erzählt es der oben erwähnte Niketas Choniates, war für die grossen Ausgaben der Hochzeitsfeier kein Geld vorhanden. Der Kaiser liess demnach aus den Provinzen und Städten Steuern eintreiben und machte sich dadurch die in dem Hämus (Balkan) wohnenden Barbaren, die man vordem Mösier genannt hatte, nun aber Vlachen heissen (οἱ Μυσοὶ πρότερον ὠνομάζοντο, νυνὶ δὲ Βλάχοι κικλήσκονται) und durch unzugängliche Berge geschützt waren, zu grossen Feinden. Und als sie sahen, dass man ihr Vieh wegtrieb, empörten sie sich. Ihre Anführer waren zwei Brüder, Petrus und Asan, aus demselben Volke (ὁμογενεῖς καὶ ταυτόσποροι). Um einen sichtbaren Vorwand zur Empörung zu haben, gingen sie beide zum Kaiser und baten in die Armee aufgenommen zu werden, zur Belohnung aber verlangten sie ein kleines Besitzthum im Hämus, das ihnen durch ein kaiserliches Diplom (διὰ βασιλείου γράμματος) zugesichert werde. Dies wurde ihnen abgeschlagen und als sie darauf ungebührliche Reden führten, gab der Sebastokrator Johann dem Asan einen Backenstreich. Nun hatten sie den Vorwand. Die

Vlachen zeigten aber nicht Lust eine Empörung zu wagen. Da ersannen die Brüder ein sonderbares Mittel, das Volk aufzuregen. Sie bauten ein hölzernes Haus, widmeten es dem heiligen Märtyrer Demetrios von Thessalonika und gaben vor, dass dieser Heilige Thessalonika verlassen und hieher in das Haus gekommen sei; Gott selbst will also die Befreiung der Bulgaren und Vlachen (τοῦ τῶν Βουλγάρων καὶ τῶν Βλάχων γενοῦς). Es fehlte auch nicht an Propheten und Prophetinnen, die mit blutgetränkten Augen und schäumendem Munde das Volk zum Aufstand anfeuerten. Petrus setzte sich eine Krone auf, zog purpurne Schuhe an und zeigte sich dem Volke als Kaiser. — Isaak überraschte sie in ihren Bergen; allein Petrus und Asan entflohen zu den Kumanen in der heutigen Walachei. Der Kaiser durchzog ganz Mösien, verbrannte hie und da die Getreidevorräthe und liess sich von den abbittenden Vlachen zur Rückkehr bewegen.

Nun kamen die Brüder mit kumanischer Hilfe zurück und die Befreiung gelang um so leichter, als damals auch die Franken Constantinopel bedrängten, das sie auch bald einnahmen. Obgleich Asan und Petrus ermordet wurden, folgte doch der dritte Bruder Kalojan (der schöne Johann, auch Joannitzins = Hänschen), als Herrscher (1197—1207) nach und wusste sich mit Hilfe der Kumanen — er selbst hatte eine kumanische Frau — einstweilen zu behaupten. Da aber der lateinische Kaiser Balduin sein freundschaftliches Anerbieten zu einem Bündniss mit dieser stolzen Antwort: Kalojan darf mit den Franken nicht wie ein König mit Freunden, sondern nur wie ein Sclave mit seinen Herren verkehren, abgewiesen hatte, wendete sich Kalojan an den Papst Innocenz III., bot sich zur kirchlichen Union mit Rom an, verlangte aber für sich eine Krone und für seinen Erzbischof die Patriarchenwürde. Beides erlangte er und der Cardinal Leo, als päpstlicher Legat, weihte am 7. November 1204 den Erzbischof Vasil zum Primas von Bulgarien und krönte Tags darauf den Kalojan zum König. Der Papst beschwichtigte damit den König von Ungarn, Béla III., der Einwendungen gegen diese Erhebung gemacht hatte, dass Peter und Johannes

Asan von den vorigen Königen abstammen und das Land ihrer Vorfahren nicht erobert, sondern nur wieder in Besitz genommen haben (de priorum regum prosapia descendentes terram patrum suorum non tam occupare quam reoccupare coeperunt). Andererseits schmeichelte der Papst dem Kalojan, dass das Volk seines Landes sich rühme vom römischen Blute abzustammen (populus terrae tuae, qui de sanguine Romano se asserit descendisse); und Kalojan dankt, dass Gott seine Niedrigkeit an seine Vorfahren erinnerte (multas agimus gratias omnipotenti Deo, qui respexit humilitatem nostram et reduxit nos ad memoriam sanguinis et patriae nostrae, a qua descendimus). Was Kinnamos, ebenfalls wie Niketas Choniates, ein gleichzeitiger byzantinischer Historiker, meinte, dass die Walachen Abkömmlinge alter Colonisten aus Italien seien, das war gewiss auch in Italien und am päpstlichen Hofe bekannt und darauf stützte sich das päpstliche Compliment an Kalojan und dessen Danksagung zu Gott.

Aber dies Alles brachte doch keine Aenderung in dem culturellen Zustande der Walachen hervor. In dem neuen bulgarischen Reiche, das unter Johannes Asan II. (1218—1241), der ein Schwager des ungarischen Königs Béla IV. war, die höchste Blüthe erreichte, erhob sich wohl das bulgarische Kirchenwesen und die bulgarische Cultur im Allgemeinen, aber von walachischer Cultur ist keine Rede. Die Bogomilen, die damals eine grosse Rolle in Bulgarien spielten, erzeigten auch eine eigene Litteratur, die aber ebenfalls slavisch war. Die Walachen blieben auch unter den Asaniden dem bulgarischen Clerus, dessen Patriarch nun in Trnovo residirte, unterworfen.

Dasselbe Los hatten die Walachen in Serbien, wo sie auch als Hirten auftraten und von den serbischen Fürsten häufig an Klöster vergabt wurden. Die walachischen Dörfer im Gebirge nannte man Katunen und ihre Richter oder Häuptlinge Knez. Wenn sie eigene Heerden hatten, zahlten sie den Grundherren jährlich von 50 Schafen ein Schaf und ein Lamm, und von 50 Kälbern eines. Für das Weiden fremden Viehes erhielten sie entweder einen Antheil an der Heerde oder monatliche Bezahlung. Die nicht als Hirten verwendet wurden, mussten ihren

Grundbesitzern Heu mähen, Wolle reinigen, Felder hüten, mit einem Worte, gewisse bestimmte Dienste leisten. Das neue entstandene Volk der Walachen hatte demnach, wie wir sahen, im Süden der Balkanhalbinsel, wo das alte Hellenenthum herrschte, griechische Priester, griechische Kirchensprache und eine griechische Liturgie; im Norden aber und in der Mitte der Balkanhalbinsel, soweit sich das Bulgarische und Serbische erstreckte, hatte das Walachenvolk nur bulgarische und serbische Priester, folglich die slovenische Kirchensprache, die beiden, den Bulgaren und Serben gemeinschaftlich war, und eine slovenische Liturgie.

Die Petschenegen und die sie ablösenden Kumanen waren seit dem X. Jahrhundert im Besitze der heutigen Moldau und Walachei. Beide Völker machten häufige Einfälle in die heutige Bulgarei und in das heutige Serbien, die von 1018 an wieder unter der byzantinischen Herrschaft standen. Diese Einfälle geschahen nie ohne Wegschleppung gefangener Einwohner, die auch walachische Hirten und walachische Krieger der byzantinischen Armeen sein konnten. Und walachische Hirten, die freiwillig hinüberzogen, mochten den Kumanen in den mit Weideland reich begabten Gegenden gerne gesehene Ankömmlinge sein. Wir sahen, dass der bulgarisch-walachische Aufstand von 1185 nur mit kumanischer Hilfe zu Stande kam und es ist gewiss, dass sich das zweite Bulgarenreich nur mit dieser Hilfe nicht nur gegen die griechischen, sondern auch gegen die lateinischen Kaiser von Constantinopel behauptete. Durch dieses Eingreifen der Kumanen in die balkanischen Verhältnisse musste die Einwanderung der beweglichen walachischen Hirten in das reiche Weideland im Norden der Donau sehr befördert werden. Und wie die siebenbürgischen Schafhirten, die Mokanen, noch bis in die neueste Zeit im Herbst in die Moldau und Walachei zogen und nachdem sie bei Giurgevo, Kalaraš, Gura Jalomnitza, Braila und Galatz die Donau übersetzten, in der Dobrudša, zwischen Tuldša und Warna zu überwintern pflegten, ebenso konnten die walachischen Hirten im XII. und XIII. Jahrhundert weite Wanderungen mit ihren Heerden, und zwar noch viel leichter, unternehmen, als ja damals die Bevölkerung überall sehr geringe war und der Pflug die Triften noch nicht aufgeackert hatte.

In Siebenbürgen erwähnt das Diplom des Andreas II. von 1222, welches den deutschen Rittern oder den Brüdern des heiligen Marienspitals in Jerusalem das Burzenland (terram desertam et inhabitatam de Borza), das heutige Kronstädter Comitat in Siebenbürgen, zur Vertheidigung gegen die Kumanen der heutigen Walachei übergibt, zum allerersteumal der Walachen, die also schon im Kumanenland oder an dessen Grenze, und zwar mit königlicher Bewilligung wohnten. Denn das genannte Diplom gestattet den Rittern freien tributlosen Durchzug sowohl durch die Sitze der Szekler als auch die der Walachen (quod nullum tributum debeant solvere, nec populi eorum, cum transierint per terram Siculorum aut per terram Blacorum). Zwei Jahre darauf, 1224, gab Andreas das berühmte Privilegium den siebenbürgischen Sachsen, die ‚hinterwaldige teutonische Gäste = hospites Teutonici Ultrasilvani' benannt wurden, in welchem diesen auch ‚der blakische und bissenische Wald zur gemeinschaftlichen Benützung mit den Wlachen und Bissenen übertragen wird' (silvam Blacorum et Bissenorum cum aquis usus communes exercendo cum praedictis scilicet Blacis et Bissenis eisdem contulimus). Bissenen oder Petschenegen waren schon früher und auch anderswo eingewandert; hier finden wir einige von ihnen in dem concedirten Besitze eines Waldes, in welchen auch Walachen aufgenommen wurden. Der König übergibt nun diesen Wald den Deutschen, ohne die Walachen und Bissenen zu versetzen, wie er es ein Jahr früher mit einer Schenkung an das Kloster Kertz (de Candela), in der Nachbarschaft von Cibin, gethan hatte, aus welcher er die Walachen versetzte (exemtam de Blacis). Die Walachen wurden sämmtlich, sowie in Serbien, als Eigenthum der Krone betrachtet, mit denen diese frei schaltete, was wir bald genauer erfahren.

Der neuerrichtete Prädicanten-Orden (oder die Dominikaner) hatte sich die Bekehrung der Kumanen zur Aufgabe gemacht. Namentlich war Robertus, Primas von Ungarn, durch die Taufe vieler vornehmer und gemeiner Kumanen berühmt.

Zum päpstlichen Legaten ernannt, errichtete er 1228 das kumanische Bisthum, zu dessen Bischof er den Dominikaner Theodorich ernannte. Die Gläubigen waren die Szekler am Seret, die bekehrten Kumanen und die unter und mit diesen wohnenden Walachen. Die Szekler protestirten aber gegen die Benennung ‚Kumanisches Bisthum', die eine Umänderung des früheren Namens war. Theodorich belehrte sie, dass durch die Namensumänderung ihr Verhältniss zum Bisthum keinen Nachtheil erleidet (quid vobis officit nominis mutatio, eadem manente episcopatus erga vestram nationem ratione et virtute?). Warum könnten Szekler, Kumanen und Walachen sich in einem Bisthum nicht vertragen, da doch in der Kirche Christi der Wolf neben dem Lamm weiden soll? (quidni etiam Siculum cum Cumano Vlachoque?). — Papst Gregor IX. schrieb aber 1234: ‚Wir hören, dass es im kumanischen Bisthume Leute gibt, die sich Vlachen nennen und dem Namen nach wohl Christen sind, aber sonderbare Gebräuche beobachten, die dem Christenthume zuwider laufen. Sie verachten die römische Kirche und nehmen die Sacramente nicht von dem kumanischen Bischof an, sondern suchen griechische Bischöfe auf, ja sie verleiten sogar auch Ungarn, Deutsche und andere Rechtgläubige, dasselbe zu thun'. Der Papst bevollmächtigt demnach den kumanischen Bischof, einen geeigneten (d. h. der Sprache mächtigen) Vicar zu ernennen, damit die Leute keinen Vorwand haben, sich an schismatische Bischöfe zu wenden. Den König Béla aber, der als ‚rex junior' schon 1233 den Titel ‚König von Kumanien = rex Cumaniae' angenommen hatte, forderte er auf, die Vlachen zu zwingen, denjenigen Bischof anzuerkennen, den die Kirche bestellt.

Aus diesen Daten ersehen wir, dass die Walachen sich wohl zur römischen Kirche bekannten, wenn sie mussten, aber doch lieber schismatische, d. h. orientalische Bischöfe aufsuchten und von diesen die Sacramente annahmen. Die Sprache gab den Vorwand gegen den lateinischen Bischof, der hier kumanischer genannt wird; der Vorwand soll durch einen geeigneten, der Sprache kundigen Vicar benommen werden. Es handelte sich hier um die slovenische Kirchensprache, denn die schismatischen Bischöfe amtirten eben in der slovenischen Kirchensprache. Uebrigens war wohl die Zehentabgabe, welche die schismatischen Bischöfe nicht beanspruchten, die römisch-katholischen Bischöfe aber überall eintrieben, der Hauptgrund, warum die Walachen den lateinischen Bischof nicht mochten und warum auch Ungarn und Deutsche sich gerne an orientalische Bischöfe hielten.

Der Mongolen-Einfall verheerte auch Siebenbürgen und das Kumanenland. Nach ihrem Rückzug 1242 war die Wiederbevölkerung des Landes die Hauptsorge. König Béla IV. übergab den Johanniterrittern 1247 nicht nur Severin, d. i. die kleine Walachei bis an den Altfluss, sondern auch Kumanien, d. i. die grosse Walachei vom Altfluss und dem siebenbürgischen Gebirge bis an das Meer und an die Donau unter bestimmten Bedingungen, von denen zwei hervorragen: die Vertheidigung und die Bevölkerung des Landes. Diese bedeutende Donation erwähnt in Severin drei Kenezate, von denen zwei in die Schenkung eingerechnet werden, eines aber den Walachen belassen wird, sowie sie es bisher inne hatten (quam [terram] Vlacis relinquimus, prout iidem hactenus tenuerunt); in Kumanien erwähnt sie Szeneslaus' Landstrich, der ebenfalls den Walachen verbleibt. Doch behält sich der König die Hälfte aller Einkünfte von Severin, auch von den genannten Kenezaten, die Einkünfte von Kumanien aber übergibt er auf 25 Jahre ganz dem Orden, ausgenommen den Landstrich des Szeneslaus, von dem nur die Hälfte des Einkommens dem Orden gebührt. Hier treffen wir zuerst auf Knezen diesseits der Donau; in Serbien haben wir schon früher solche gesehen. Sie sind Richter oder Häuptlinge der Walachen, deren Wohnort oder Wohnörter ein Kenezat, Knezenbezirk, bildete.

Der Orden übernahm die Verpflichtung, das Land zu bevölkern, nur durfte er keine Einwohner aus des Königs Landen ohne besondere Erlaubniss aufnehmen. (Curam dabit et operam ad populandum non solum dictas terras nostri regni, et quod rusticos de regno nostro cujuscunque conditionis et nationis ac

Saxones vel Teutonicos de nostro regno non recipiant, nisi de licentia regia speciali.) Damit war natürlich ausgesprochen, dass die neuen Ansiedler vorzüglich in Bulgarien und Serbien zu suchen seien. Walachische Hirten, bulgarische und serbische Bauern waren demnach willkommene Ansiedler.

In Siebenbürgen war dieselbe Menschenleere. Der siebenbürgische Bischof klagte 1246, dass durch die tatarische Verwüstung (hostili persecutione Tartarorum) — so nannte man den Mongoleneinfall — der bischöfliche Sitz Weissenburg und seine hergezählten Besitzungen menschenleer geworden sind. Er bat demnach den König, dass es ihm gestattet sei, durch Privilegien und Freiheiten sich neue Bewohner zu verschaffen. So hören wir 1252, dass der Landstrich Szék (terra Szék) seit der Tartarenverwüstung ohne Einwohner sei (per devastationem Tartarorum vacua). Dies nur als Beispiele.

Ein merkwürdiges Document des Andreas III. von 1293 lautet folgendermassen: ‚Auf den Rath unserer Barone sind wir durch die Bedürfnisse der Regierung gezwungen, gesammte Vlachen von den Besitzungen der Edelleute und Anderer auf unser königliches Prädium Székes zurückzufordern, selbst wenn es mit Gewalt gegen die Widerstrebenden geschehen müsste (reduci et etiam compelli redire invitos, si forte nostrae in hac parte non acquiescerent parere jussioni). Da aber König Ladislaus, unser Vetter (Enkel des Béla IV.), zum Heile seiner Seele, dem Weissenburger Capitel in Siebenbürgen 60 vlachische Familien (sexaginta mansiones Vlacorum) auf die Capitulargüter aufzunehmen, und dass sie da verbleiben könnten, gestattet hat, ohne eine königliche Steuer, wie das Fünfzigstel (quinquagesima) oder Zehnten zahlen zu müssen: so bestätigen wir dem Capitel diese Schenkung von 60 Vlachenfamilien und befehlen, dass kein königlicher Steuereinheber von den besagten Vlachen das Fünfzigstel, Zehntel oder sonst eine Gebühr abverlange.‘

Dies Document belehrt uns, dass die Krone die Walachen als ihre Hörigen betrachtete, die man nur mit königlicher Erlaubniss auf Privatgüter ansiedeln konnte. Es zeigt uns aber auch die Einkünfte der Krone von den Walachen, nämlich das

Fünfzigstel, die quinquagesima, vom Vieh, Schafen und Rindern, was wir schon in Serbien sahen, und den Zehnten von Bienen u. s. w. Das besagte Fünfzigstel musste später auch von den Walachen der Edelleute oder andern Besitzern der Krone eingeliefert werden; dies war die Walachensteuer, als Einkunft der Krone in Siebenbürgen, bis in die Mitte des XVI. Jahrhunderts.

Wir beschränken uns auf die wenigen angeführten Daten, denn wir können hier keine Geschichte des walachischen Incolats in Siebenbürgen geben und kehren zu unserem besonderen Gegenstand zurück.

Die einwandernden Walachen brachten, ohne Zweifel, die Sprache, in welcher sie geboren waren; ihre Popen, ob Bulgaren oder Serben, hielten den Gottesdienst nur in der slovenischen Kirchensprache und administrirten die Sacramente in derselben Sprache, und wenn sie etwa schrieben, bedienten sie sich der kyrillischen Schrift. Brachten aber die im XIII. Jahrhundert einwandernden Walachen in ihrer Sprache auch den postpositiven Artikel nach Siebenbürgen mit?

Wir mussten behaupten, dass der postpositive Artikel nur durch fremden Einfluss in die rumänische Sprache kommen konnte. Wo finden wir nun diesen fremden Einfluss? ‚In allen Sprachen der Balkanhalbinsel finden sich philologische Eigenheiten, welche weder griechischen noch romanischen noch slavischen Ursprungs sind. Blos im Albanesischen scheinen sie ursprünglich zu sein und da diese Sprache auf der Halbinsel die älteste ist, so ist der Schluss berechtigt, dass sie unzweifelhaft aus einem ihr verwandten Elemente stammen, nämlich aus dem alteinheimischen, jetzt verschollenen Thrako-Illyrischen. Das Thrako-Illyrische bildet die Grundlage, durch welche die darüber gelagerten Sprachschichten überall auf gleiche Weise modificirt worden sind.‘ So urtheilt Constantin Jos. Jireček in seiner ‚Geschichte der Bulgaren‘ (Prag 1876, Seite 114) und man muss ihm beistimmen, wenn er so fortfährt: ‚Derlei Eigenheiten sind vor Allem die merkwürdige Futurbildung und der dem Nomen hinten angehängte Artikel im Albanesischen, Rumänischen und Bulgarischen‘ u. s. w. ‚Beachtenswerth ist es auch, dass die Bulgaren bei den Albanesen Škjan (Bulgarien Škjenia) und bei den Rumänen ganz ähnlich heissen.' An einer andern Stelle (pag. 441) sagt Jireček, dass die bulgarische Sprache während der Periode des zweiten Bulgarenreiches (1186—1398) grosse Veränderungen erlitt. Ueberall drängen sich in die slovenische Schriftsprache Eigenthümlichkeiten der Volksmundart ein. Im XIV. Jahrhundert taucht auch der postpositive Artikel sporadisch auf. — Jagič hält den postpositiven Artikel im Rumänischen aus bestimmten Gründen für älter als den bulgarischen und glaubt, dass er der bulgarischen Sprache als ermunterndes Vorbild gedient habe. (Ueber die Sprache und Litteratur der heutigen Bulgaren. Deutsche Rundschau, 1880, Juli, pag. 61.)

Folgendes steht ausser allem Zweifel: dass das Thrako-Illyrische die Grundlage aller darübergelagerten Sprachschichten auf der Halbinsel bildet; dass das Albanesische die älteste Sprache auf derselben ist, und dass wir den postpositiven Artikel im Albanesischen, Rumänischen und in dem Neubulgarischen vorfinden. Jagič glaubt, dass die Erscheinung des postpositiven Artikels im Rumänischen älter sei, als in dem Neubulgarischen, in welchem sie erst im XIV. Jahrhundert sporadisch bemerkt wird. Schade, dass die rumänische Sprache aus dem XIII. und XIV. Jahrhundert keine schriftlichen Sprachproben aufweisen kann: man könnte in diesen Jahrhunderten nur rumänische Eigennamen aus den serbischen und ungarländischen Urkunden zusammenstellen, um, wenn möglich, aus diesen auf das Vorhandensein des postpositiven Artikels zu schliessen. Aber da die rumänischen Einwanderungen in die nördlichen Donauprovinzen, also auch nach Siebenbürgen, vor der Bildung der neubulgarischen Schriftsprache begonnen hatten, so glaube ich annehmen zu müssen, dass der postpositive Artikel schon in der Sprache der ältesten Einwanderer geherrscht habe, weil er sich später, nach und nach kaum hätte einnisten können, da eine litterarische Verbindung zwischen den südlichen und nördlichen Rumänen nie stattgefunden hat und auch in Siebenbürgen erst durch die Reformation die allerersten walachischen Drucke veranlasst wurden, von denen wieder nicht die geringste Kunde zu den südlichen Rumänen im XVI. und XVII. Jahrhundert gelangte. Es drängt sich uns also der Gedanke auf, dass der postpositive Artikel im Rumänischen eine unmittelbare Einwirkung des Thrako-Illyrischen auf die lateinische Volkssprache in der Halbinsel gewesen sei.

Damit wird zugleich das enge Verhältniss zwischen dem Albanesischen und Rumänischen anerkannt, was auch folgendes Factum bestätigt. Die evangelische Stadtpfarrkirche in Kronstadt wurde nach Lucas Jos. Marienburg (Geographie des Grossfürstenthums Siebenbürgen, II. Hermannstadt, 1813, Seite 333) in den Jahren 1383 oder 85—1424 erbauet. Um als Handlanger bei dem weitläufigen Bau sich Brod zu verdienen, kamen viele Arbeiter aus Bulgarien nach Kronstadt und der Magistrat wies ihnen oberhalb der Stadt Wohnplätze an, wo sie dann auch nach der Vollendung des Baues blieben. So bildete sich zum Theil auf Bergen und in Thälern die Vorstadt, die man ungarisch Bolgárszeg, d. h. Bulgarenwinkel, rumänisch aber Schkei nennt. — Wir finden also dieselbe Benennung der Bulgaren auch bei den Kronstädtischen Rumänen. Heute ist die ganze grosse Vorstadt rumänisch, nicht mehr bulgarisch.

Den postpositiven Artikel im Neubulgarischen schreibt man gewöhnlich der Einwirkung des Albanesischen zu und Jagič will den Vorgang der rumänischen Sprache als ermunterndes Beispiel für das Bulgarische ansehen. Mir scheint Beides nicht hinreichend zur Erklärung des postpositiven bulgarischen Artikels. Hätte das Albanesische eine solche Wirkung auf das Bulgarische äussern können: so entsteht die Frage, warum traf dieselbe Wirkung nicht auch das Serbische, das geographisch nicht entfernter lag, als das Bulgarische? Auch das ermunternde Beispiel des Rumänischen kann kaum eine bedeutende Wirkung gehabt haben, da dieses eine zu geringe sociale Stellung in Bulgarien schon im Anfang des XIII. Jahrhunderts behauptete. Sollte etwa die Wirkung des einheimischen Thrako-Illyrischen, die wir für das Thrako-Romanische annehmen, durch das älteste Slavische hindurch, sich auch bei den slavisirten Bulgaren geltend gemacht haben, ohne von der slovenischen Schriftsprache beachtet worden zu sein? Oder würde man sehr fehl greifen, wenn man eine Neigung zur Bildung dieses Artikels in der ursprünglichen bulgarischen Sprache selbst suchen würde?

Allgemein glaubt man, und es gibt kaum einen historischen Grund dagegen, dass die südlichen Bulgaren Stammverwandte derjenigen Bulgaren waren, die an der mittleren Donau das sogenannte Grossbulgarien bildeten. Grossbulgarien ist wohl längst verschwunden: aber in seinen Landstrichen leben noch heute Mordvinen, ein ugrisches Volk, dessen Sprache wir kennen. Wäre es denn nicht gestattet anzunehmen, dass die Mordvinen Ueberbleibsel der wolgaischen Bulgaren sind, so wie ich aus Sprachgründen (die hier unerörtert bleiben müssen) die Čuvašen (Tschuwaschen) für Ueberreste der alten bekannten Chasaren halte? Nun, die Mordvinensprache hat den postpositiven Artikel, wie ihn das Vogulische und das Ostjakische hat: wie, wenn das eigentliche Bulgarische, das man für eine finno-ugrische Sprache ansieht, etwa eine Mordvinensprache war? Dann wäre der postpositive Artikel natürlich in der alten Bulgarensprache heimisch gewesen, und er wäre, wie das Oel eines ölgetränkten Blattes durch obere ungetränkte Blätter durchschlägt, durch das Kirchlich-Slovenische hindurch in die bulgarische Volkssprache gedrungen, die nun die neubulgarische heisst. Doch dem sei wie ihm wolle: die rumänische Sprache konnte den postpositiven Artikel nur auf der Balkanhalbinsel erlangen, allwo ihre Priester in der slovenischen Kirchensprache erzogen, die kyrillische Schrift allein gebrauchten, wenn sie ja schrieben.

— —

Die rumänische Sprache ist auf der Balkanhalbinsel unter romanisirten christlichen Thrakern entstanden und hat sich unter überwiegend slavischem Einflusse gebildet, was unter der Herrschaft der slavischen Kirchensprache und Schrift ganz natürlich war. Ich erwähne hier mit besonderem Accente die kyrillische Schrift, weil diese den Lauten der Sprache viel besser angepasst ist, als die lateinische angepasst werden kann. — Der griechische Einfluss ist ebenfalls sichtbar. War doch der südliche Theil des

Rumänenthums immer griechischen Eparchien unterordnet; und hat sich doch die slovenische Kirchensprache durch Uebersetzungen griechisch-christlicher Bücher gebildet, was eben mittelst der slovenischen Kirchensprache auch auf das ganze nördliche Rumänische einwirken musste.

Die mit Slavismen getränkten Rumänen, die man bis zu dem Ende des vorigen Jahrhunderts nur Walachen nannte, zogen immer mehr und mehr in die nördlichen Provinzen der Donau; es zogen aber auch Bulgaren und Serben dahin und zwar mehr als Ackers- und Kaufleute, denn als Hirten. Das Hirtenwesen war anfangs überall die Hauptbeschäftigung der Walachen. Das alte Kumanien (die grosse Walachei) nannten die Byzantiner schon im Anfange des XIV. Jahrhunderts ‚Ungrovlachien', was seinen politischen Grund hatte; die östlich-nördliche Provinz erhielt, nach dem Verschwinden der Kumanen, den Namen ‚Moldau'. Sowohl in Ungrovlachien als auch in der Moldau bildeten sich anfangs, unter der Suzeränität der ungarischen Krone, walachische Woiwodschaften, deren Würden, Namen und politische Ordnung einen bulgarischen Anstrich hatten, wie auch ihre politische und Kirchensprache die slovenische blieb. Woewoden, Bojaren, Priester und Mönche sprachen und schrieben slavisch: nur der walachische Bauer sprach walachisch, der aber niemals schrieb, denn er war des Schreibens unkundig. So weit entfernt war man da sich des Römerthums zu rühmen, dass man im XVI. und XVII. Jahrhundert den frohnenden, an die Scholle gebundenen Bauer, ob er Walache oder nicht Walache war, Rumunen und diesen Bauernstand Rumunenschaft (Rumunia) nannte. (Siehe ‚Neuere Erscheinungen der rum. Geschichtsschreibung' besprochen von P. H. Wien und Teschen, bei Prochaska, 1886, S. 179—193.)

In Siebenbürgen fanden die einwandernden walachischen Hirten, die Bulgaren und Serben andere Zustände; hier war der gesammte Boden im Besitze von Ungarn, Szeklern und Deutschen, die sich schon zu Ende des XIV. Jahrhunderts als politische Körperschaften fühlten und in der ersten Hälfte des XV. Jahrhunderts eine ähnliche Union bildeten, wie die Schweizer

Cantone im XIV. Jahrhundert, nur dass hier der ungarische König, als Souverän und Ertheiler aller Privilegien und Gerechtsamen, unangefochten blieb. Die einwandernden Walachen, mit Slavismen getränkt, um so mehr die Bulgaren und Serben, konnten mit den vorgefundenen Slaven viel leichter zusammenschmelzen als mit den Ungarn und Szeklern, die einer Sprache waren und sind, oder als mit den Deutschen. Daher nahmen sie auch die slavische Nomenclatur an. Von dem alten berühmten Sarmizegetusa, dem nachher römischen Ulpia Traiana Augusta, waren nur Ruinen übrig, welche die Magyaren ‚Várhely = Burg-Ort', die Slaven aber ‚Gredistje', d. h. Stadt, russisch Gorodischtsche, nannten. Die Walachen eigneten sich die slavische Benennung zu. Das ungarische Fejér-Vár = Weissenburg, seit Karl's Regierung ‚Karlsburg', ward der Sitz des katholischen Bischofs, nachher der Fürsten in Siebenbürgen. Es heisst slavisch Belgrád und diese Benennung nahmen auch die Walachen an, sowie die ersten walachischen Gelehrten, Šinkai, Peter Major u. s. w. ihn beibehielten. Heute nennen freilich die rumänischen Historiker diese Stadt ‚Alba Julia'.

Die Namen der grossen Flüsse haben ein zähes Leben, sie wandern von Volk zu Volk. Die Namen: Theiss, Maros, Samos, Aluta = Olt fanden die Römer vor; sie behielten sie und sie existiren noch heute. Kleinere Flüsse, deren Ruf nicht über ihre engeren Grenzen gelangt, werden von neueren Bewohnern umgetauft. So entstanden die slavischen Flussnamen: Krasna, Bistritza, Černa, Trnava u. s. w. Die Ungarn tauften einige um, von andern behielten sie die slavischen Namen. Sie umtauften die Trnava = Dornbach in ‚Kükülló = Külkül-jó', was auch Dornbach bedeutet. Die Walachen behielten aber den slavischen Namen und nennen ihn Tirnava. Černa oder Černa voda bedeutet ‚Schwarza', ‚Schwarzwasser'. Wir haben einen grössern Fluss dieses Namens im Szeklerland, den die Slaven Černa-Voda, die Deutschen Schwarzwasser benannten. Die Ungarn umtauften ihn in ‚Fekete-Ügy', d. h. Schwarzwasser; die Walachen behielten auch hier den slavischen Namen. In den allerletzten Zeiten nennen ihn freilich die rumänischen Schriftsteller

‚Valea nigra'. Einen kleineren Fluss dieses Namens haben wir im Hunyader Comitat. Die Ungarn umtauften ihn in Eger-ügy, zusammengezogen ‚Egregy', d. h. Erlenwasser, weil die Erle schwarz färbt. Die Walachen behielten den slavischen Namen Černa. (Von der Erle ist auch die Bischofsstadt Erlau = Erlenau, ungarisch ‚Eger' bekannt.) Die slavischen Flussnamen Krasna, Biala (Bela), Bistritza u. s. w. behielten auch die Ungarn.

Dass die einwandernden Walachen die römischen Traditionen nicht fortsetzen konnten — von denen sie übrigens gar keine Ahnung hatten — liegt auf der Hand. Und doch berufen sich die rumänischen Geschichtsschreiber auf solche Traditionen, was ihnen andere nachschreiben. — Bekanntlich hatte die lateinische Cultur in Mathias Corvinus einen grossen Patron. Damals war es gelehrte Sitte, alles Mögliche von den Römern abzuleiten; man lese nur das erste Buch des Antonii Bonfinii ‚Rerum Ungaricarum decadis primae'. Bonfinius war von Mathias zum Geschichtsschreiber aufgenommen. Im XVI. Jahrhundert fing man an auch die Inschriften in Siebenbürgen zu bemerken. Die Erinnerung an die römische Herrschaft erwachte und man forschte nach den Localitäten der Begebenheiten, die man damals und im XVII. Jahrhundert leichter aufzufinden glaubte, als heute, wo unsere Kenntniss von allem viel sicherer und genauer ist. Zur Erläuterung des Gesagten soll die Trajan's Wiese oder das Trajan's Feld, die Stelle, auf welcher Dekebalus besiegt worden sein soll, dienen.

Martin Opitz, der schlesische deutsche Dichter, lehrte um 1622 an der Bethlen'schen Akademie in dem siebenbürgischen Weissenburg (Fejér-Vár, Belgrad) und fand in Zalatna solches Behagen, dass er ein Gedicht: ‚Zalatna oder von der Ruhe des Gemüthes' schrieb. Darin heisst es:

‚Dann Zlato heisst das Gold auf wendisch, da die Stadt,
Zwar kleine, doch nicht arm, davon den Ursprung hat.
Die Römer wussten schon, was hier sei zu erlangen.
. . . .
. . . .
Wo will ich aber hin? ich soll von Zlatna schreiben,

Das den Verdruss der Zeit mir kann sowohl vertreiben
Mit seiner grossen Lust. Ich suche, was ich will,
So find' ich da genug, ja mehr noch als zu viel.
Geliebet dir ein Berg? Hier stehen sie mit Haufen;
Ein Wasser? Siehe da den schönen Apul laufen;
Ein schönes, grünes Thal? Geh' auf Trajani Feld;
In Summa, Zlatna ist wie eine kleine Welt.'

Opitz befand sich auf einer Stelle, die der Goldgruben wegen den Römern wichtig war. Das von Opitz erwähnte Wasser hiess bei den Colonisten Ampela, heute nennt man es Ompoly. Das etwa sechs Stunden Wegs entfernte Karlsburg liegt, wo das römische Apulum war. Opitz hatte vielleicht von diesem keine Kunde, er kennt nur den Fluss Apul. Auch hier sehen wir, dass sich der Flussname erhalten hat, während das Andenken an die Stadt Apulum verschwunden ist, obgleich auf einer Inschrift des Jahres 252 Decius nicht nur als Restitutor Daciarum, sondern auch als Gründer der ‚Nova Colonia Apulum' gefeiert wird. Wie sollte sich die Erinnerung an Trajan's Feld erhalten haben?

Im verflossenen Sommer sah ich bei Zalatna die anmuthige Berglehne, die man Trojan nennt, wenn man sagt: mergemu la Trojan = gehen wir auf das Trojan (ein Belustigungsort für Majalese u. s. w. Weder Feld noch Wiese wird dabei miterwähnt. — In dem Ofener ‚Lexicon Valachico-Latino-Hungarico-Germanicum' von 1826, das die ausgezeichnetsten siebenbürgischen Rumänen, unter ihnen auch Peter Major, verfasst haben, steht der Artikel ‚Troianu, mit kyrillischen Lettern trojun, pratum amplum, ‚eine weite Wiese'. Die Verfasser des Lexicons waren voll der römischen Ideen: sie erklärten aber das trojanu weder mit ‚Trajan's Feld' noch mit ‚Trajan's Wiese'. Das Trajan's Feld erscheint demnach nur als eine willkürliche Schöpfung des Dichters, den der Ausdruck trojan oder trojun an den römischen Imperator Traianus erinnerte.

Nun will man Trajan's Wiese in Keresztes bei Torda finden. Der Jassyer Historiker Xenopol erzählt in dem schon citirten Werke (Seite 93), dass man in einem Document von 1176 eine Ebene mit dem ungarischen Namen Keresztes, nicht aber mit dem rumänischen Namen ‚Pratul lui Traian' findet, den sie unter der rumänischen Herrschaft (die sich Xenopol einbildet) geführt hatte (qu'elle portait encore au temps de la domination roumaine); denn, fügt er hinzu, die Ungarn haben mit Bedacht alles magyarisirt (de tous temps les Hongrois se sont efforcés de magyariser tout ce qui les environne). Die Ungarn haben wirklich die Ortsnamen nicht magyarisirt, was hundert und hundert slavische Ortsnamen in Siebenbürgen und Ungarn beweisen. Ich habe auf meiner Reise Keresztes nicht berührt, habe also nicht erfahren, ob das ‚pratul lui Traian' auch wirklich im Volksmunde lebt. Aber so viel habe ich erfahren, dass das Wort *prat* (pratum = Wiese) in der Volkssprache nicht existirt, die nur das slavische *lunka* und das magyarische *rit, rét* für Wiese kennt. Auch das Ofener Lexicon hat dies Wort nicht; sowie auch das rumänisch-französische Dictionarium des Raoul Pontbrian, welches die Bukarester Schul-Ephorie 1862 der studirenden Jugend empfahl, es nicht hat. Das ‚pratul lui Traian' ist nur ein Product der Gelehrsamkeit, die den gelehrten Zopf des XVI. und XVII. Jahrhunderts nicht abgelegt hat. Jetzt paradirt es wohl in den Büchern. Auch das ‚Dictionnaire d'étymologie daco-roumaine. Éléments latins' des A. de Cihac (Francfort s. M. 1870, p. 215) nimmt das Wort *prat* auf, begleitet mit den entsprechenden Benennungen aller romanischen Sprachen: allein zum Beweis seiner wirklichen Existenz im Rumänischen führt es nur das gemachte ‚pratul lui Traian' und das ‚Cintea pratului', eine ebenfalls fabricirte botanische Benennung des ‚Lathyrus sativus' an.

Wie sich in spätern Zeiten, namentlich in dem XVI. und XVII. Jahrhundert, die Traditionen gebildet haben, so bildete sich durch die ungarische Geschichtsschreibung seit 1746, als der Anonymus regis Belae Notarius in Schwandtner's ‚Scriptores rerum Hungaricarum' zum erstenmal erschienen ist, die allgemeine Ueberzeugung des rumänisch schreibenden und lesenden Publicums, dass die Rumänen vor dem Erscheinen der Magyaren alleinige Besitzer Siebenbürgens waren; dass sie auch nach der magyarischen Occupation einige souveräne Fürstenthümer inne hatten; endlich, dass aus einem dieser Fürstenthümer, aus Fogaras, Rad Negr als ein zweiter Aeneas im Jahre 1290 auszog, um die walachische Woiwodschaft zu gründen. Im Lichte der Geschichte verschwinden alle diese Einbildungen.

Von der andern Seite muss die Geschichte es hervorheben, dass die rumänische Cultur in Siebenbürgen durch den Einfluss der Reformation im XVI. Jahrhundert begonnen und durch die Union mit der römischen Kirche im Anfang des XVIII. Jahrhunderts weiter befördert worden ist. Die Geschichte muss es bekennen und anerkennen, dass die siebenbürgischen calvinischen Fürsten Bethlen und Georg I. Rákóczi die erste walachische Buchdruckerei, natürlich mit kyrillischen Lettern, herstellen und das Neue Testament in's Walachische übersetzen liessen; die Geschichte muss es bekennen und anerkennen, dass dieser Georg Rákóczi um 1642 den Bann der slovenischen Kirchensprache aufhob, indem er befahl, dass der Gottesdienst und andere religiöse Verrichtungen in der walachischen Sprache gehalten und geschehen sollen. In Siebenbürgen entstanden und erwachsen, verbreitete sich die walachische Cultur und Wissenschaft auch nach der Moldau und Walachei. Diesem Umstand sind die zahlreichen magyarischen Ausdrücke, ja sogar magyarische Bildungssilben sowohl an rumänischen als an slavischen Wörtern, zu verdanken, die sich in der rumänischen Schriftsprache vorfanden und noch vorfinden, trotz des gewaltigen Purismus, der das Lateinische und Italienische mit leichter Mühe mit rumänischen Lauten ausdrückt. Aus Siebenbürgen stammen die bedeutenderen rumänischen Gelehrten; siebenbürgische Rumänen haben die ersten Gelehrtenschulen in der Walachei und Moldau in's Leben gerufen.

Anhang.

I.

Anonymus Belae regis Notarius.

In der kaiserlichen Hofbibliothek befindet sich ein Codex aus dem Ende des XIII. oder dem Anfang des XIV. Jahrhunderts, der so beginnt: ‚Incipit prologus in gesta hungarorum. P. dictus magister ac quondam bone memorie gloriosissimi Bele regis hungarie notarius. N. suo dilectissimo amico viro venerabili et arte literalis scientie imbuto salutem et sue petitionis affectum‘. Der Magister, den man kurzweg ‚Anonymus Notarius‘ nennt, hatte als Studirender, wie er in seinem Prologus erzählt, die trojanische Geschichte nach dem Vortrag seiner Lehrer und nach Dares Phrygius verfasst, welche seinem ‚dilectissimus amicus‘ so sehr gefiel, dass dieser ihn aufforderte auch die Geschichte der Ungarn und ihrer edlen Geschlechter zu schreiben. Das that er.

Unser Magister überträgt die ethnographischen, politischen und adeligen Besitzverhältnisse seiner Zeit auf das Ende des IX. Jahrhunderts und macht den Heerführer Árpád zu einem Herrscher, der, wie des Magisters König, Donationen seinen Getreuen ertheilt. Aus Ortsnamen bildet er Geschichten, indem er ihre eponymen Besitzer als Helden des Árpád's darstellt. — Er scheint in der Erlauer Diöcese heimisch gewesen zu sein, denn deren Localverhältnisse kennt er am genauesten.

Weil er die Kumanen, die unmittelbar vor dem Mongoleneinfall Sitze in Ungarn fanden und nachher Hauptstützen der Könige wurden, verherrlicht, so nehme ich an, dass er Notar Bela des IV. war und seine ‚Gesta Hungarorum‘ in den Tagen des Stephan V. und des Ladislaus III. (IV.), also im letzten Viertel des XIII. Jahrhunderts schrieb. (Vergleiche meine ‚Rumänen und ihre Ansprüche.‘ Wien und Teschen, bei Prochaska. 1883. Seite 241—250.)

II.

Die siebenbürgischen Schafhirten.

Der Kronstädter Joseph Franz Trausch erhielt am 19. October 1834 eine Privat-Audienz bei Franz I. Bei dieser Gelegenheit sagte Trausch unter Anderem Sr. Majestät: ‚Eine hier in Wien vernommene Nachricht hat in mir grosse Besorgnisse erregt, die nämlich, dass der jetzige Hospodar der Walachei der

Gesandtschaft Euer Majestät in Constantinopel eine Note zugeschickt habe, deren Inhalt zu Folge derselbe den siebenbürgischen Viehökonomen in Rücksicht des vermöge Tractat zu Ende gegangenen Termins und weil die Bojaren der Walachei ihre Triften zur eigenen nun ausgebreiteter zu betreibenden Wirthschaft behalten wollten, die Benützung der Triften für ihr Vieh in Zukunft nicht mehr gestatten wolle. Geschähe nun dieses wirklich, so müssten die siebenbürgischen Viehökonomen, welche an der Grenze der Walachei wohnen und den grössern Theil des Jahres hindurch ihr Vieh in der Walachei erhalten, besonders die aus dem Kronstädter District, wegen Mangel an eigenen Weiden, den bei weitem grössten Theil ihres Viehes verkaufen, selbst aber zu Grunde gehen, wodurch auch unter unsern übrigen Einwohnern eine grosse Noth entstehen würde'.

Sr. M.: ,Es ist mir lieb, dass Sie mir das gesagt haben. Ich werde es mir anmerken und mich erkundigen, dann will ich mich in der Sache schon verwenden'. (Siehe den Bericht über diese Audienz im Archiv des Vereines für siebenbürgische Landeskunde. Neue Folge. Zwölfter Band, I. Heft. Hermannstadt. 1874. S. 26—36.)

Schon unter dem Fürsten Georg I. Rákóczi wurden in Angelegenheit der in der Walachei weidenden siebenbürgischen Schafhirten Verträge geschlossen. Wie wir sehen, sollte im Jahre 1834 ein solcher Vertrag ablaufen, wurde aber wieder 1835 erneuert. Das siebenbürgische Vieh wanderte auch über die Donau in die Bulgarei. Im Winter 1846/7 waren in Bulgarien 250.000 Stück Schafe, welche im Frühling 332.000 Oka (das Oka zu $2^1/_4$ Wiener Pfund) Wolle lieferten, wovon 312.000 Oka nach Kronstadt gelangten. — Am 1. Juli 1855 schloss das k. k. Ministerium des Auswärtigen den letzten Vertrag mit der Pforte, welcher im Jahre 1865 ablief. (Vergleiche auch mein obenerwähntes Werk ,die Rumänen und ihre Ansprüche', S. 192—194.)

I Návagvāḥ e i Dáṣagvāḥ del Ṛigveda.

Da

Giacomo Lignana.

Fra gli inni funebri del Ṛigveda molto importante è senza dubbio il XIV del X *maṇḍala*. Nelle prime strofe si celebra il Dio dei morti, il Re *Yama*, figlio di *Vivasvat*, che primo raccolse, e riunì assieme gli uomini *Vaivasvatáṃ saṃgámanaṃ jánānāṃ Yamáṃ rájānam,* e primo trovò la via della immortalità, che nello stile patriarcale della prima vita pastorizia è chiamata *gávyūti*, dove poi egli fu seguito dai primi padri *yátrā naḥ pū́rve pitáraḥ pareyúḥ.*

Yama è invitato a discendere dalla regione della felicità immortale e sedere assieme coi padri *Añgiras, Añgirobhiḥ pitŕbhiḥ* sul *prastara* prendendo parte al sacrificio funebre, e il Dio viene e si inebbria al sacrificio assieme cogli *Añgiras* che sono chiamati *Vairūpa*, cioè figli di *Virūpa* patronimico che il commentatore spiega col seguente predicato *vividharūpayuktairvairūpasāmapriyairvā.*

Nella seguente strofa gli *Añgiras* sono invocati un'altra volta nel seguente ordine: *Añgiraso naḥ pitáro návagvaḥ* etc.; quindi si accompagna con preghiere ed augurii il trapassato, affinchè scevro di ogni colpa *hitvā́yāvadyám,* e col frutto delle buone opere, che non saranno state solamente quelle comprese nella definizione *ṣrautasmārtadānaphalam* del commentatore teologo, e con raggiante figura *tanvá suvárcāḥ* ed evitando i due cani di Sārama custodi del passo, si ricongiunga con Yama, e gli altri padri nell' alto dei cieli *paramé vyòman* pieno di luce, d'acque e di ogni bellezza *áhobhir adbhír aktúbhir vyàktam.*

Le idee contenute in quest' inno sono in gran parte communi ai popoli Indo-europei. I morti diventano compagni degli Dei e genii protettori dei superstiti; così nelle opere e i giorni di Esiodo V, 120:

> Αὐτὰρ ἐπειδὴ τοῦτο γένος κατὰ γαῖα κάλυψεν
> τοὶ μὲν δαίμονές εἰσι Διὸς μεγάλου διὰ βουλὰς
> ἐσθλοί, ἐπιχθόνιοι φύλακες θνητῶν ἀνθρώπων·

e nel verso 125:

> ἠέρα ἑσσάμενοι πάντῃ φοιτῶντες ἐπ' αἶαν

è indicata un' idea molto affine a quella espressa colla parola *vairūpa* del nostro inno, e che è spiegata da *sāyaṇācārya* per *vividharūpayukta* cioè moltiforme.

Il cielo pieno di luce e di bellezza in cui i padri assieme con *Yama* si inebbriano di felicità *yaména sadhamádam mádanti* è precisamente come l'Olimpo di Omero Odis. VI, verso 46:

> τῷ ἔνι τέρπονται μάκαρες θεοὶ ἤματα πάντα

il quale Olimpo non è mai scosso dai venti, nè bagnato dalle pioggie, nè coperto di neve, e dove il sereno si distende senza nube alcuna ἀνέφελος. È l' isola descritta da Pindaro nella II olimpica, dove spirano sempre le aure oceanine, vi splendono fiori d' oro, coi quali i beati intrecciano alle loro mani, ed ai loro capi monili: Ὅρμοισι τῶν χέρας ἀναπλέκοντι καὶ κεφαλάς.

Il cerbero poi dei Greci, come già ha dimostrato il Benfey, non è altro che *ṣarvara*, e secondo la forma, che si legge nel nostro inno *ṣabala*, predicato dei cani di *Sārama.*

In mezzo a queste rappresentazioni proethniche intorno alla vita oltremondana che cosa significano i Návagvāḥ? Appartengono essi solamente al ciclo delle rappresentazioni funebri degli Ariani dell' India, oppure trovano il loro riscontro nelle rappresentazioni degli altri popoli della medesima origine?

A nostro avviso i Návagvāḥ non recorrono isolati nella poesia vedica, ma si collegano colle primitive e communi rappresentazioni funebri degli altri popoli Ariani e specialmente dei Greci e degli Italici.

Sia che essi debbano considerarsi identici cogli Añgiras oppure distinti, non vi ha dubbio, che essi rappresentino, come risulta dall' inno precedente, un gruppo degli Dei Mani; essi abitano con Yama e gli altri padri nell' alto dei cieli, assistono con esso ai sacrifici funebri, e proteggono le generazioni superstiti. In alcuni inni sono poi descritti come compagni di Indra, e prendono parte alle sue imprese, Ṛigv. I, 33, 6. Vṛitra e i suoi seguaci assalgono l' esercito di Indra che è detto irreprensibile cioè senza difetto, e i Návagvāḥ si riuniscono e resistono, e i nemici fuggono precipitosamente come *snervati* confessando la propria impotenza:

áyuyutsann anavadyásya sénām áyātayanta kshitáyo návagvāḥ ‖
vṛshāyúdho ná vádhrayo nírashṭāḥ pravádbhir indrāc citáyanta āyan ‖

Sāyaṇācārya propone due spiegazioni etimologiche del nome dei Návagvāḥ cioè *navanīyágatayaḥ, stotavyacaritrāḥ* oppure *Añgirasāṃ satramāsīnānāṃ madhye ye navabhirmāsairavāptaphalā utthitās teshāṃ navagvā iti;* cioè da *náva* lodare oppure da *návan* nove. Vedremo in appresso quale debba essere il vero etimo di questo nome. In un' altro inno I, 62, 4, Indra rumoreggiando con grande scroscio assieme coi sette Víprāḥ, i *Návagvāḥ*, e i Dáṣagvâḥ squarcia la nuvola, cioè il nascondiglio di *Vṛitra*

sá sushṭúbhā sá stubhā saptá vípraiḥ svarénādrim svaryó návagvaiḥ ‖

L' apparire dei Dáṣagvāḥ assieme coi Návagvāḥ non lascia più alcun dubbio sull' origine etimologica del nome di questi ultimi, che sono i nove, come i primi sono i dieci, e così spiega il sayaṇācārya senza alcuna esitanza: *ye navabhirmāsaiḥ samāpya gatāste navagvāḥ, ye tu daṣabhirmāsaiḥ samāpya jagmuste daṣagvāḥ.*

Con questi dieci Dáṣagvāḥ, e con questi nove Návagvāḥ propizii Indra ha trovato il sole, che giaceva nascosto nella tenebra; III, 39, 5,

sūryaṃ viveda támasi kshiyántam.

I Návagvāḥ e i Dáṣagvāḥ spremendo il soma celebrano Indra cogli inni V, 29, 12,

Návagvāsaḥ sutásomāsa índram Daṣagvāso abhy árcanty arkaíḥ |

Celebrano Indra gli antichi padri Návagvāḥ e i sette Saggi lo eccitano all'opera: VI, 22, 2,

tám u naḥ pūrve pitáro návagvāḥ saptá víprāso abhí vājáyantaḥ ‖

La storia dell'aurora si intreccia con quella dei Navagvāḥ e dei Dāṣagvāḥ: IV, 51, 4,

kuvít sá devīḥ sanáyo návo vā yámo babhūyád ushaso vo adyá ‖

yénā návagve áñgire dáṣagve saptásye revatī revád ūshá ‖

Il che ricorda la connessione già da molti avvertita delle due parole latine *mane* e *manes.*

Le fiamme di Agni quando agitate dal vento consumano le selve sono paragonate pel loro impeto ai Návagvāḥ che accompagnano Indra alla battaglia. Nel libro IX, 108, 4 si fa il nome di uno di questi Návagvāḥ ed è *Dadhyāñk* e se ne racconta la impresa *yénā návagvo dadhyáññ aporṇuté* etc. etc. la quale impresa è quella stessa che per solito è attribuita ad Indra, cioè *Dadhyañk* apre la porta della caverna dove stanno nascoste le vacche rubate dai Paṇi, il che è spiegato dal commentatore *dvāram aporṇuté 'pācchādayati, vivṛitamakārshīt.*

In quest' inno adunque la impresa, che è compiuta colle forze riunite dei Návagvāḥ è attribuita ad uno solo di essi, cioè a *Dadhyañk.* Così pure X, 62, 6, i Návagvāḥ e i Dáṣagvāḥ vengono riassunti in una sola personalità per mezzo di un superlativo *āñgirastamo*, che sarebbe, se così si potesse dire un' *Angirasissimo*

yé agnéḥ pári jajñiré vírūpāso divás pári |
návagvo nú dáṣagvo āñgirastamo sácā devéshu mañhate. ||

nacquero da Agni, nacquero dal cielo i Virūpas; il nono, il decimo, l'Angirasissimo grandeggia fra gli Dei.

Ed anche qui i nomi sono spiegati dal commentatore in relazione col numero dei mesi: *kecana navasu massu karma kritvodatishṭhan kecana daṣasu massviti.* Il poeta di quest' inno chiama se stesso *Mānavám*, figlio di Manu, cioè figlio dell' uomo, e le imprese che egli celebra sono quelle degli uomini, i quali, poichè sono diventati immortali *amṛitatvám ānaṣuḥ* assieme con Indra, ed hanno secondo l'ordine fatto uscire il sole nel cielo *riténa sū́ryam árohayan*, hanno dilatata la madre terra *áprathayan prithivī́m mātáram*, hanno ricuperato il tesoro rapito dai Paṇi *udājan pitáro gomáyam*, e compiuto l' anno misero in rotta il demone Vala *ábhindan parivatsaré valám*.

Dopo tutti questi passi, e i seguenti del Maṇd. X, 14, difficilmente può essere ancora dubbiosa la significazione dei *Návagvāḥ* e dei *Daṣagvāḥ*. Essi sono i padri *pitáro* trapassati all'altra vita per quel cammino, che fu prima trovato da Yama. *yamó no gātúm prathamó viveda*, e da lui fu indicato ai molti, che vennero dopo *bahúbhyaḥ pánthām anupaspaṣānám*. All' ingresso di quel cammino, che conduce alla vita oltremondana stanno come nella divina comedia di Dante Alighieri le fiere selvaggie, che vorrebbero impedire il fatale andare, i due cani della Sarámā con quattr' occhi e dalla gaietta pelle *sārameyaú ṣvánau caturakshaú ṣabálau sādhúnā pathā́*, oltrepassati i quali si apre ai defunti la contemplazione di Yama e Varuṇa, e deposta ogni colpa, e colle membra raggianti, si uniscono nel supremo dei cieli *páramé vyòman* cogli altri padri e gli Dei, inondati di luce, fra dolci e fresche acque eternamente beati.

Nell' Egitto i defunti si identificano pure con Osiri riposano fra i rami dei sicomori, si uniscono coi raggi del sole, prendono diverse forme, e sono come i Virūpas dell' India secondo il senso attribuito a questa parola da *Sāyaṇācārya*, e si rinnovano per tutta la eternità *er ḥeḥ t'et.*

Qualunque però possa essere l'opinione intorno a una possibile connessione preistorica dell'India e dell'Egitto, la quale, considerato il tipo flessivo delle due lingue potrebbe anche non essere solo una ipotesi, importante per ora si è il notare, come le precedenti rappresentazioni Vediche si riscontrino pure fra i popoli, che siamo soliti a chiamare classici.

I numeri nove e dieci sono sacri ai Greci, e la strage che Apollo fa degli Achivi per l'insulto fatto al sacerdote, cui non fu restituita la figlia dura nove giorni. Il. 1, 53,

Ἐννῆμαρ μὲν ἀνὰ στρατὸν ᾤχετο κῆλα θεοῖο

e al decimo giorno vien convocata l'assemblea da Achille

τῇ δεκάτῃ δ' ἀγορήνδε καλέσσατο λαὸν Ἀχιλλεύς

Nove sono i bovi, che si sacrificano a Poseidon, Od. III, 8,

. . . . . . καί προὔχοντο ἑκάστοθι ἐννέα ταύρους

Iliade VI, 169 Bellerofonte che portava le tavolette dove erano scritte molte cose fatali θυμοφθόρα πολλά è ospitato nove giorni dal Re di Licia, che sacrifica nove bovi

Ἐννῆμαρ ξείνισσε καὶ ἐννέα βοῦς ἱέρευσεν

e solamente quando al decimo giorno appare l'Aurora delle rosee dita

ἀλλ' ὅτε δὴ δεκάτη ἐφάνη ῥοδοδάκτυλος Ἠώς

è interrogato dal Re, e mandato al combattimento contro la Chimera.

Eguale importanza hanno questi due numeri sacri nella Teogonia di Esiodo. La stessa distanza che vi ha fra il cielo e la terra vi ha pure fra questa e il Tartaro, il che è espresso permezzo della imagine della incudine di bronzo che dalla terra nel Tartaro impiegherebbe nove giorni e nove notti nella caduta per giungere solamente nel decimo giorno al sito: Teog. 724.

ἐννέα δ᾽ αὖ νύκτας τε καί ἤματα χάλκεος ἄκμων
ἐκ γαίης κατιὼν δεκάτῃ δ᾽ ἐς Τάρταρον ἵκοι.

L'onda Stigia che nasce dal sacro fiume Oceano bagna per nove parti la terra, e per una decima il Tartaro. Teog. 789,

. . . . . . δεκάτῃ δ'ἐπὶ μοῖρα δέδασται.

Iri la figlia di Thaumante mandata da Giove a riempiere di questa fredda e celebre acqua del Tartaro un vaso d'oro afine di procare la veracità del giuramento degli Dei impiega nove giorni, e siccome anche gli Dei giurano talvolta il falso restano esclusi per nove anni dal concilio e dalle imbandigioni celesti e non vi possono di nuovo prender parte che al decimo anno. Teog. 801, 802, 803,

εἰνάετες δὲ θεῶν ἀπομείρεται αἰὲν ἐόντων
οὔδέ ποτ'ἐς βουλὴν ἐπιμίσγεται οὐδ ἐπὶ δαῖτας
ἐννέα πάντ' ἔτεα · δεκάτῳ δ'ἐπι μίσγεται αὖτις

Una reminiscenza dei poeti greci sono certamente i versi di Vergilio, Libro VI, 38, 39.

. . . . . . *palus inamabilis unda*
alligat et noviens Styx interfusa coercet,

ma *il sacrificium novendiale* usato anticamente dai Romani, e più che probabilmente da tutti gli altri Italici dimostra come siano applicabili anche in questo caso le osservazioni precedenti. La più antica iscrizione latina che finora possediamo è quella trovata nel 1880 nei pressi del Quirinale. Molto si è discusso intorno a questa iscrizione, ma la sua indole funebre a me pare certa, e una linea, cioè la seguente, si riferisce al sacrificio novendiale:

Dvenos med feced en manom, einom die noine med mano statod,

cioè Dvenos mi fece pel defunto, e il nono giorno al defunto ponimi.

Questa prima traduzione proposta dal Dressel a me pare doversi ammettere. I Mani sono i morti, i buoni, e Mano il morto, il buono; *bonum antiqui dicebant Manum;* Varro, de lingua latina VI, 4. Si è voluto negare da taluno il carattere sacrale, e funebre della iscrizione, ma la parola *mano* non può significare che defunto, *noine* suppone le forme *noueno-*, *nouino-* e corrisponde al latino seriore *nono*, e *statod* ha un senso sacrale e solenne, come nella iscrizione sacrale di Velletri *Deve Declune statom.*

Ma quello che più importa è il culto dei *Novensides.* Incerta era presso gli antichi l'origine di questo nome, e di questo culto; per alcuni derivava dai Sabini, e i Novensides doveano essere per Roma Dei nuovi. Questa derivazione etimologica ricorda quella pur menzionata da Sāyaṇācārya nel commento ad un' inno dei Návagvāḥ dove si spiega *nava* per *nūtana.* Ma il nome dei Návagvāḥ deriva da *návan* nove, come pure quello dei Novensidi, e questa etimologia, che si conserva nella maggior parte dei passi che abbiamo citati di Sāyaṇācārya, ci è stata pure conservata da Varrone: *novenarium numerum tradit Varro,* e secondo la citazione di Arnobio, *Novensiles Piso deos esse credit novem in Sabinis apud Trebiam constitutos.*

Non è pure esatto l'attribuire esclusivamente ai Sabini l'origine di questo culto. Esso era commune a tutti gli Italici, e ciò è provato dalla iscrizione arcaica di Pesaro

DEIV. [nov] E. ϟEDE
T. ΓΟΓΑΙΟ. Γ,,,,,,

e da quella trovata a S. Benedetto, cioè l'antico Marruvio sulla sponda orientale del lago Fucino, preziosa reliquia del dialetto Italico dei Marsi.

IIϟOϟ
NOVIIϟIIDII
PEϟCO PACRE

Non è forse fuori di luogo il notare, come nelle forme delle iscrizioni di Pesaro, e S. Benedetto manchi la nasale, e quindi *novesede* coincida con *návagva* mentre nel latino abbiamo *novemsides*, oppure *novemsiles*. I Novensili, e i Návagvāḥ sono adunque gli Dei Mani, e quindi cadono tutte le combinazioni degli antichi, i quali cercavano nei novensili un sistema di nove divinità, come p. e. le Muse. Novensile e Návagva non vuol dire altro, che nato di nove mesi, come daṣagva nato di dieci mesi, il che ci è confermato dal *Ṣatapathabrāhmaṅa* dove si dice: *taṃ te garbhaṃ dadhāmahe daṣame māsi sūtave* aggiungendo il commentario la seguente spiegazione *taṃ tathābhūtaṃ garbhaṃ te tava jaṭhare dhārayāmahe daṣame māsi prasotum.* Quindi il *návagva* corrisponde al *garbho navamāsyaḥ* e il *dáṣagvaḥ* al *garbho daṣamāsyaḥ* le quali due parole occorrono pure nello stesso senso al Cap. V. del Vendidad cioè *navamāhya* e *daṣamāhya.*

Sembrerebbe, che agli Itali come agli Ariani dell'India non sarebbero dovuti mancare i decensili. La opinione manifestata da alcuni scrittori antichi, che i Romani non contassero primitivamente che dieci mesi, il che parve confermato dalla parola dicembre, può essere contradetta, come egualmente quella che ne segue, cioè che ai primi dieci mesi siano poi stati aggiunti altri due, cioè gennaio, e febbraio da Numa o da Tarquinio Prisco. Il passo di Plutarco nella vita di Numa non è certo una valida prova di questa opinione:

τὰ πένθη καθ' ἡλικίας καὶ χρόνους ἔταξεν, οἷον παῖδα μὴ πενθεῖν νεώτερον τριετοῦς, μηδὲ πρεσβύτερον πλείονας μῆνας ὧν ἐβίωσεν ἐνιαυτῶν μέχρι τῶν δέκα, καὶ περαιτέρω μηδεμίαν ἡλικίαν. — ἐφ' ὅσον (χρόνον καὶ χηρεύουσιν αἱ τῶν ἀποθανόντων γυναῖκες·

Ma se in questo passo di Plutarco non è contenuta la prova che i Romani nei primi tempi contassero solamente dieci mesi, evidente è la connessione del lutto vedovile col presunto periodo dei dieci mesi di gravidanza. Non dovrebbero adunque mancare i *decensili,* e di fatti ci sono menzionati nel *deve declune* dei Volschi.

I *Návagvāḥ*, i *Dáṣagvāḥ*, i *Novemsides* non sono altro, che quelli nati di nove, o dieci mesi, cioè gli uomini che nella loro evoluzione dalla vita terrestre a quella oltremondana diventano.

Dei *αἰσοί*, e il numero che è contenuto nel loro nome si riferisce al mese del nascimento, e non già alla consociazione di nove o dieci esseri. Il numero dei *Návagvāḥ*, dei *Daṣagvāḥ dei Novensidi* è indefinito, come indefinito è quello di coloro che sono morti dopo aver fatto il bene.

Die Geschichte der classisch-armenischen Schriftsprache.

Von

Dr. **Johann Thumajan,**
Mitglied der Wiener Mechitharisten-Congregation.

Die Geschichte der classischen Sprachen bezeugt uns eine Thatsache, welche vielleicht am meisten im Armenischen sichtbar ist, dass nämlich der Blüthezeit dieser Sprachen ein Verfall gefolgt ist. Obwohl das Zeitalter der Arsaciden (Arschakunier) in der armenischen Literatursprache oder die mesropianische Sprache (mit dem Zeitalter des Augustus der Römer oder mit der ciceronianischen Sprache vergleichbar), eine sehr kurze Zeit wegen unglückseliger Vorfälle dauerte, so ist es doch ziemlich reich an gediegenen ausgezeichneten Werken. Diese mesropianische Sprache ist in Folge der in späteren Jahrhunderten erlittenen Entstellungen und Alterationen so begraben und verborgen, so unbekannt und in totaler Vergessenheit geblieben, dass sie selbst dann, als man sie in unserem Jahrhundert durch mühsame Ausgrabung zum Vorschein brachte, wie bemerkt wird, ein Gegenstand der Disputation und Opposition geworden ist.

Von Seite der Urheber dieser Entdeckung wurden dann und wann allgemeine Phrasen betreffs dieser Sprache publicirt; ein praktischer Führer war jedoch nicht vorhanden. Mit der Absicht dieser wesentlichen Lücke abzuhelfen gab der hochwürdigste Herr Dr. Arsenius Aïdyn, gegenwärtig General-Abt der hiesigen Mechitharisten-Congregation, eine ziemlich ausführliche Grammatik der mesropianischen (classisch alt-armenischen)

Sprache heraus, in welcher der hochgeschätzte Autor verschiedene sprachliche Fragen und Observationen durch geeignete Excurse behandelt. Aus diesen oberwähnten Observationen ist meine Abhandlung entnommen, welche, wie wir wohl hoffen, jedem einzelnen Armenisten, besonders aber sich mit dem Classisch-Armenischen befassenden Orientalisten als ein interessanter und genauer Fingerzeig zum Verständniss der von Jahrhundert zu Jahrhundert erlittenen Umwandlung dieser Sprache und zur Beseitigung vieler Anachronismen in der orientalischen Literatur dient.

Ich erachte es nicht für überflüssig, meine Leser im Vorhinein darauf aufmerksam zu machen, dass diese meine Abhandlung sich mit der classischen armenischen Schriftsprache allein befasst, nicht auch zugleich mit der Geschichte der armenischen Literatur.

Anfangs des V. Jahrhunderts (etwa im Jahre 405), nahm die classische armenische Literatur zu gleicher Zeit mit der Erfindung des vollständigen armenischen Alphabets ihren Anfang; nämlich: es wurde die bis zur Zeit ungeschrieben gebliebene, elegante und mustergiltige Sprache niedergeschrieben. Mesrop der Grosse, der Erfinder dieses Alphabets, und seine zahlreichen Mitarbeiter hinterliessen der Nation durch ihre unermüdliche Thätigkeit einen Reichthum der gediegensten Werke, deren eines erhabener als das andere ist, sammt einer Gradation des schönen Styls vom einfachen bis zum eleganten. Obwohl die Mehrzahl dieser Meister-Werke Uebersetzungen sind (ohne von denen zu reden, welche verloren gegangen, wie es die Geschichte uns überliefert), sind sie dennoch für uns von ungemein grosser Wichtigkeit und von unvergleichlichem Vortheile; insofern der Vergleich dieser Uebersetzungen mit den Urtexten uns genau kennen lehrt den exacten Sinn der armenischen Wörter, die Eigenthümlichkeiten der nationalen Ausdrücke, welche gewöhnlich in den Abweichungen vom Urtexte bemerkbar werden, dann den Geist und den Wortschatz des Armenischen in verschiedenen kleinen Zusätzen und das angeborene Talent des geschickten Uebersetzers und Aehnliches. Unter diesen classischen Werken und Uebersetzungen sind unter andern zu erwähnen: Die vortreffliche Uebersetzung der Schriften des Alten und Neuen Testamentes; Esnik's Schriften; die Uebersetzungen des heiligen Chrysostomus; die Homilien von Severinus (nach dem Armenischen Seberianos, eigentlich Eusebius Emessenus); Chronikon Euseb's von Cäsarea und anderes. Ferner sind noch zu erwähnen die in einfacher und ruhiger Schreibart aus den syrischen Autoren übersetzten Werke, namentlich die vielbändigen echten Schriften Ephrem's des Syrers — nur bei den Armeniern jetzt echt erhalten — nebstdem die in verziertem, üppigem Styl geschriebenen Werke, in welchen die sprachliche Licenz am meisten hervortritt, nämlich: die drei Bücher der Makkabäer, Koriun, Faustus von Byzanz, Agathangelus, einige Theile aus dem Leben der Väter u. s. w.

In diesen ausschliesslich classischen Werken findet man die ausgesuchtesten Wörter, die regelrechte Bildung und den wahren Sinn derselben, grammatische Regeln, die Erhabenheit und den Wortschatz der Sprache in vielen Synonymen und in unzähligen ausschliesslich nationalen Redensarten. Ferner findet man die von den fremden Sprachen ganz und gar unabhängigen Eigenthümlichkeiten des Armenischen und insbesondere einen feinen Geschmack des Styls, welchen ausser dieser Periode ausfindig machen zu wollen eine vergebliche Mühe ist. Es gibt natürlicherweise eine Abstufung unter diesen Schriften, doch sind sie alle im Wesentlichen gleichartig. Dies ist eben das Kennzeichen des goldenen Zeitalters der classisch alt-armenischen Literatursprache.

Hier schliesst sich vor uns das glückliche mesropianische Zeitalter. In den folgenden unglückseligen Jahren wird die armenische Literatur von anderen Schriftstellern fortgesetzt, aber in zwei Richtungen:

1. Eine Gruppe der Neulinge, welche von Mesrop in ihrer Jugend allein unterrichtet, später aber in allen griechischen Wissenschaften bewandert und unter den Griechen aufgewachsen waren, unternahmen gleich nach dem Tode ihres grossen Lehrers, indem sie nicht alle Genauigkeiten des Griechischen im Arme-

nischen zu finden glaubten, die Mittel zu ersinnen, um das Fehlende mit armenischen Elementen zu vervollständigen. So wurden unermesslich zahlreiche, dem Griechischen nachgemachte, absurde Neuerungen einerseits selbst in den wesentlichen Theilen der Sprache eingeführt, andererseits sehr viel Einheimisches auf die Seite geschoben. Es wurde die Scheidung zwischen den classischen Wörtern und den unclassischen gänzlich beseitigt; man ersetzte echt nationale Redewendungen durch neue, eigenmächtig erfundene; es wurden mit den hellenisch gebildeten Wörtern auch hellenische Formen, sowohl grammatische als sonstige eingeführt. Auf diese Umwandlung nun gestützt, begannen jene Neuerer schriftstellerisch thätig zu sein und somit sind sie Begründer einer sozusagen neuerfundenen Sprache. Diese Transformation ist eben die erste Revolution in der Geschichte der armenischen Sprache. Unter den Schriftstellern sind uns nur der berühmte Moses Chorenensis und David der Philosoph namentlich bekannt, welche ihre Werke in dieser Diction verfassten.

2. Eine zweite Gruppe von Schriftstellern setzte zu gleicher Zeit mit den vorigen die mesropianische Literatur fort. Obwohl diese von den Folgen der ersten Revolution nicht verschont blieben und die Erhabenheit der früheren Classiker nicht erreichten, war ihre Sprache doch ziemlich rein und auch classisch, aber nicht überall. Die berühmtesten dieser Gruppe sind: Elisäus, Lazar von Parb, Mambré, Küd und Johann von Montaguni, welche das fünfte Jahrhundert, den ersten Schauplatz unserer Literatur beschliessen. Bei diesen genannten Schriftstellergruppen bemerkt man noch mehrere Spuren der alten classischen Sprache, besonders betreffs der richtigen Anwendung der Wörter, welche in den nächstfolgenden Jahrhunderten corrumpiert vorkommen.

Nunmehr trat beinahe Stille in der Literatur ein, und die wenigen Schriftsteller dieses Zeitraumes bieten uns die ziemlich gleiche Sprache mit den Vorgängern in ihren einzelnen kleinen Werken. Erst gegen Anfang des VIII. Jahrhunderts fing man wieder an fleissig zu schreiben; in einer Zeit aber, wo sich die vulgär-armenische Sprache aus der classischen allmählich herausbildete und die alte Schriftsprache nicht mehr eingebornes Eigenthum jedes Einzelnen war, mussten die Schriftsteller entweder auf schwachen Füssen vorwärtsschreiten oder je nach ihrem Talent eine durch eigenmächtig selbsterfundene, ja sogar absurde Redensarten colorirte, dem Griechischen nachgeahmte Sprache benützen, was wirklich in den meisten Werken der damaligen Autoren vorkommt: z. B. bei Johann dem Mamigonier, wahrscheinlich auch in den Stromaten, auf armenisch Յաճախապատում, welche von Mehreren Gregor dem Erleuchter zugeschrieben sind, einerseits, andererseits in den schwülstigen Schriften Johannes des Philosophen und seines Zeitgenossen Theodorus und in dem Buche *ton Cräon*.

Diesen Zeiten folgten einige noch erbärmlichere Jahrhunderte (vom Ende des IX. bis zum XIV. Jahrhundert), in welchen die erhabene Schriftsprache so herabgesunken und je nach Verlauf der Zeit von dem Vulgär-Armenischen so überwältigt wurde, dass sogar manche Werke ganz und gar im Vulgär-Armenischen geschrieben sind. Trotzdem bemerkt man, dass einige Schriftsteller manche Versuche mit mehr oder weniger Erfolg gemacht haben, dem mesropianischen Jahrhundert nachzuahmen. Erwähnenswerth sind unter Anderen Chosrov der Grosse, Ananias und Gregor von Nareg, die Historiker Johann Katholikos und Aristakes von Lastiwert, die Doctoren Ignatius und Sergius, und die beiden Nerses Klajensis und Lampronensis. Aus diesem Zeitraum stammen auch die in der eigenthümlich nationalen Sprachform und Metrik verfassten Kirchenlieder und Hymnen und viele andere originelle Werke und Uebersetzungen.

Während sich die armenische Schriftsprache in diesem Verfalle befand, machte eine zweite Revolution im XIV. Jahrhundert Epoche in der Geschichte derselben. Die Wissenschaften des Occidents fassten in diesem Jahrhundert in Armenien Wurzel; die Folge aber war eine nochmalige Transformation in der Sprache; man wollte die Mängel durch Nachahmung einer fremden Sprache wieder ersetzen, wie dies ein mal im V. Jahrhundert geschah; nur mit dem Unterschiede, dass sie diessmal nicht mittelst des Griechischen, sondern mittelst des Lateinischen in Ausführung kam. Wahrlich, diese Umwälzung beseitigte das vulgäre Element aus der Schriftsprache, doch gab sie damit derselben den letzten Gnadenstoss, nämlich die Sprache bekam eine abscheulich unnatürliche Form in der Grammatik und Wortbildung. Zahlreiche Werke, zum grössten Theil Uebersetzungen, wurden in dieser absurden Sprache verbreitet, und haben das Land drei bis vier Jahrhunderte lang so mächtig beherrscht, dass diese allein unter dem Namen Գրաբար (das heisst Schriftsprache) zu verstehen war. Es dürfte auch bemerkt werden, dass sich eine kleine Anzahl von Schriftstellern bestrebte, diese Barbarei zu vermeiden.

Das ist also die Geschichte des äussersten Verfalls der Schriftsprache. Wie aus dem bisher Gesagten ersichtlich, waren es drei Factoren, welche die literarische Sprache zum Verfall brachten; ein natürlicher Factor, und zwei künstliche, nämlich: Das natürliche Hervorkommen und die allmählige Verbreitung einer Vulgär-Sprache aus der literarischen im Verlauf der Jahrhunderte, und die beiden künstlich hervorgebrachten obenerwähnten Umwälzungen. Das vulgäre Element, sagten wir, wurde bereits durch den Latinismus beseitigt; es blieben nun die zwei anderen zu beseitigen, damit wir die primitive Reinheit und Eleganz der mesropianischen Sprache erreichen könnten.

Den ersten Schritt in dieser wünschenswerthen Reform machte die eine Schule des grossen Mechithar, des Gründers der beiden Mechitharisten-Congregationen, in der Mitte des verflossenen Jahrhunderts, welche mit Fleiss und Mühe anstrebte, die bei der zweiten Umwälzung hervorgebrachten Entstellungen auszurotten. Es gelang ihr in der That sehr leicht durch vereinte Mitwirkung, indem man die Schriftsprache der vom V. bis zum XIII. Jahrhundert geschriebenen Literatur zum Führer nahm, in der Meinung, durch die einfache Beseitigung der groben, bei der letzten Umwälzung eingeführten Entstellungen die echt classische Sprache erreichen zu können; denn man erkannte die bis zum XIII. Jahrhundert eingeführten Fehler und Barbarismen noch nicht. Diese grosse und sehr nützliche Reform war die erste Reaction, welche den Grund zu einer neuen, reichen Literatur bei allmähligem Fortschritt legte und sich in einem, aus mit einander fast unvereinbaren Elementen zusammengesetzten Zustande, bisweilen nur den Spuren der wahren mesropianischen Sprache nachahmend, beinahe bis zur Hälfte unseres Jahrhunderts fortpflanzte.

Es war wirklich in dieser Zeit, wo ausser der Uebersetzung der Bibel fast alle anderen ausgezeichneten Werke des goldenen Jahrhunderts noch unbekannt waren, und diejenigen Schriftsteller, welche den sogenannten Erhabenheiten der in den späteren Jahrhunderten geschriebenen Sprache nahe kamen, schon als eminente Armenisten galten, diese Annahme zu entschuldigen. So spurlos war die classische Sprache in dem grossen Strome der eintausendjährigen Alteration verschwunden! Es darf uns daher nicht in Verwunderung setzen, wenn die Nachwelt einige pseudonyme Schriften als echte Werke des Patriarchen Isaak oder des grossen Mesrop oder der Mitarbeiter derselben annahm. Es ist aber jene Unachtsamkeit nicht so leicht zu entschuldigen, nachdem die wunderschönen zahlreichen Werke dieser Classiker in dem ersten Viertel unseres Jahrhunderts allmählich gefunden worden und an das Licht der gelehrten Welt gekommen waren. Also diejenigen, welche nicht nur den einer scharfsichtigen Beobachtung sich selbst augenscheinlich zeigenden Unterschied zwischen einer echt classischen Sprache und einer unclassischen, nicht nur den die erste Hälfte des V. Jahrhunderts von der zweiten desselben und insbesondere von den folgenden Jahrhunderten scheidenden Abgrund nicht erkannten, sondern auch nicht einmal anerkennen wollten, sind wahrhaftig nicht zu entschuldigen.

Es war eben diese Beobachtung der anderen Schule des grossen Mechithar, zu der auch meine Wenigkeit gehört, gewissermassen vorbehalten, welche gegen Ende der ersten Hälfte unseres Jahrhunderts durch scharfsinnige, haarkleine Erforschung und beständige besondere Studien dieselbe zu Tage brachte; sie verbreitete ein neues Licht auf das zur Zeit noch begraben gebliebene Alterthum im Zeitraume einiger Jahre; sie zeigte auch den obenerwähnten tiefen Abgrund und führte die zweite

Reaction der armenischen Schriftsprache glücklich aus: nämlich sie erkannte die reine noch unbekannt gebliebene mesropianische Sprache und wies gründlich die von Jahrhundert zu Jahrhundert stattgefundene Veränderung dieser Sprache nach. Nachdem diese Reform in's Werk gesetzt worden und die Theorie schon vervollständigt war, trat man nun in den practischen Schauplatz ein. Es wurde eine ziemlich grosse Literatur in genauer Nachahmung dieser goldenen Sprache herausgegeben.

Selbstverständlich erfuhr diese Neuerung eine namhafte Opposition von Seite der damaligen im Bereiche des Armenischen vorhandenen Capacitäten, welche sie als aus blossem Neuerungstrieb erfundenes grundloses System ansahen, und auch dagegen als gegen eine unerreichbare und unausführbare Theorie protestirten. Sie meinten, es sei dies nach allgemeiner Auffassung eine vergebliche Anstrengung und eine unnütze, sogar gefährliche Auswählerei, welche einer tausendjährigen ehrwürdigen Literatur Unehre bringe, und den unermesslichen Wortschatz nicht unbedeutend verminderc. Doch erkannte man nach und nach das reale Resultat. Heutzutage, obwohl dieses Unterscheiden eine ziemlich allgemein bekannte, den Eingeweihten leicht zugängliche und einzig beliebte nationale Schönheit ist, ist sie doch kein allgemeines, alleiniges Eigenthum des Armenischen; desswegen ist diese Schriftsprache noch in zwei Richtungen getheilt geblieben; eine ist die genaue Nachahmung der mesropianischen Sprache, und die andere die Zusammenmischung der bis zum XII. Jahrhundert aufgeschriebenen Schriftsprachen; mit anderen Worten, eine eigene Schriftsprache des XIX. Jahrhunderts, aber keineswegs die des Alterthums. Schliesslich ist hier noch als charakteristisch zu bemerken, dass die in späteren Jahrhunderten eingeführten Abweichungen von der Sprache des goldenen Zeitalters so gross und in die innersten Theile der Sprache so tief eingedrungen sind, dass man kaum einige gleichlautende Zeilen in diesen beiden Schriftsprachen hören kann.

Hochgeehrte Zuhörer, ich bin schon zu Ende meines Vortrags. Bevor ich aber schliesse, möchte ich meinerseits einige

Bemerkungen sehr gerne hinzufügen. Man bemerkt wirklich in Europa besonders in diesen letzten Jahren reges Interesse für die armenische Sprache unter den hochgeehrten Linguisten, dessen lebendiger Zeuge diese hohe Versammlung selbst ist, in welcher sich mehrere sehr berühmte Armenisten befinden. Es erscheinen untereinander kleine, wie auch ausführliche Sprachlehren und Lesebücher. In diesen meisten Werken und selbst bei manchen Armenisten bemerkt man einen sprachlichen oder stylistischen Indifferentismus, indem man keinen Unterschied zwischen den Schriftsprachen verschiedener Jahrhunderte macht, und selbst solche Elemente unter dem Namen ‚Sprachlehre der classisch alt-armenischen Schriftsprache‘ und anderes, zusammenstellt, welche wahrlich nicht zusammenstehen dürfen und können, und mit einander thatsächlich disharmoniren. Es schmerzt einen Freund des Classicismus sehr, solches zu hören und zu lesen. Desswegen möchte ich die hochgelehrte Welt Europa's bitten, ihre hochgeschätzte Aufmerksamkeit auf die classisch-armenische Schriftsprache in dieser Richtung zu wenden, und durch ihre erprobte Erfahrung und hohes Wissen diese classische Sprache in jene Höhe emporzuheben, in welcher sich die alten classischen heute befinden.

Ueber die Entwickelung der philosophischen Ideen bei den Indern und Chinesen.

Von

Dr. M. Straszewski,

Professor der Philosophie an der Universität in Krakau.

Ich muss mir vor Allem Verzeihung erbitten und um gütige Nachsicht ersuchen, dass ich es überhaupt wage das soeben genannte Thema zu berühren. Es sind doppelte Ursachen, die mich eigentlich abhalten sollten hier in Ihrer Mitte das Wort zu ergreifen. Als Philosoph sollte ich eigentlich schweigen dort, wo so viele bedeutende Gelehrte über die Ergebnisse und die weiteren Ziele eines grossen Forschungsgebietes vom fachmännischen Standpunkte berathen, zweitens ist die Antwort auf die Fragen, die ich in meinem Vortrage zu berühren beabsichtige, noch so wenig vorbereitet, dass dem, der sich hereinwagt, vielleicht eine starke Dosis philosophischer Waghalsigkeit zugemuthet werden könnte. Allein es ist schon einmal so, die Philosophen sind ein Volk, das bei jeder Gelegenheit mitreden will. Es ist schon gut, wenn sie sich hiebei anstatt auf eigene Speculationen zu berufen, wissenschaftliche Thatsachen zum Ausgangspunkte wählen. Trotz alledem glaube ich jedoch von Ihrer Seite, hochgeehrte Herren, auf grössere Nachsicht rechnen zu dürfen, als dies von Seite mancher Philosophen und Philosophie-Historiker geschehen würde. Die meisten unter denselben haben ja schon längst entschieden, dass die Geschichte der Philosophie eigentlich erst in Griechenland beginne, sie haben sich ihr Urtheil über den Orient bereits gebildet! Sie behaupten, dass von einer Geschichte der Philosophie nur dort die Rede sein kann, wo sich der menschliche Geist wenigstens theilweise vom Einflusse religiöser Ideen emancipirte und selbstständig zu denken begann. Es kann nun bei den Orientalen keine Philosophie geben, da ihr ganzes Sinnen und Denken unter dem Einflusse der Religion steht. Infolge dessen haben die Philosophie-Historiker dem Vater Thales ein Patent auf die Erfindung einer echt religionsfreien Philosophie ausgestellt, und schreiben mit behaglicher Ruhe ihre dickbändigen Werke über Geschichte der Philosophie ‚von Thales bis zur Gegenwart‘. Wohl wird manchmal zugestanden, dass gewisse Ansätze zum philosophischen Denken auch im Oriente zu finden sind, allein die Möglichkeit einer geschichtlichen Entwickelung wird mit einem blossen Hinweis auf ‚die bekannte Stabilität orientalischer Culturzustände‘ abgefertigt. Solchen Anschauungen brauche ich hier gar nicht entgegenzutreten, es stellen sich mir aber dafür andere Schwierigkeiten in den Weg. Wer mit indischen Sachen so vertraut ist, wie Sie, hochgeehrte Herren, der weiss es am besten wie lückenhaft noch unser Wissen sei, dort wo es sich um Entwickelungsgeschichte indischer Culturzustände handelt. Es bleibt hier noch sehr viel zu thun übrig, es müssen noch gewaltige Anstrengungen von Seite bedeutendster Fachgelehrten gemacht werden, bevor wir einen klaren Ueberblick, sowohl über einzelne Entwickelungsstadien, wie über das Ganze werden gewinnen können. Wenn ich trotzdem den Versuch wage eine Entwickelungsgeschichte philosophischer Ideen bei den Indern zu skizziren, so fühle ich mich dazu durch die grosse Wichtigkeit der Frage, so wie auch durch die Erwägung angespornt, dass, soll eine wissenschaftliche Frage gelöst werden, so muss doch einmal ein Anfang mit ihr gemacht werden. Es ist für die Kenntniss indischer Kultur von höchster Wichtigkeit zu erfahren, wie sich hier die denkende Betrachtung des Weltganzen allmählig entwickelte, es ist aber auch für die Kenntniss der geistigen Geschichte der Menschheit überhaupt nicht gleichgiltig, ob eine Entwickelung philosophischer Bestrebungen, das ist jener Bestrebungen, welche das Ganze der Welt in einheitlichen Gedankenbildern zu umfassen trachten, erst in Griechenland begonnen und in Europa weiter fortgeführt werde, oder ob es auch einzelnen orientalischen Culturgebieten an solcher Ideenentwickelung nicht gefehlt hat. Und wenn es sich zeigen würde, dass die in Griechenland entstandene europäische Philosophie nur einen einzelnen geschichtlichen Typus repräsentirt, dem andere gegenübergestellt werden können, und wenn sich dann weiter aus der Vergleichung dieser einzelnen Entwickelungsreihen, wichtige allgemeine Gesetze ergeben würden, welche die Welt menschlicher Gedanken beherrschen, würde das nicht einen grossen Fortschritt in der Wissenschaft vom Menschen bedeuten — einen Fortschritt, den wir in dem Falle der Erforschung des Orientes zu danken hätten? Das sind jene Gesichtspunkte, die mich endgiltig bewogen haben, hier jene Ergebnisse ganz kurz und flüchtig zu skizziren, die ich durch langjährige Studien hauptsächlich der indischen Philosophie gewonnen zu haben glaube.

Wer über die Entwickelungsgeschichte indischer Philosophie reden will, der muss vor Allem die Frage nach dem Ursprunge und den Ursachen, welche den Geist der Inder zur denkenden Betrachtung des Weltganzen hinführten, berühren. Aristoteles hat gesagt, dass die Verwunderung den eigentlichen Anfang aller Philosophie bilde. Wenn wir nun die hohe Begabung der arischen Race und hauptsächlich ihre ungemein rege Phantasie in Erwägung ziehen, so wird es uns klar, welchen Grad von Verwunderung in den Geistern arischer Eindringlinge die Grossartigkeit indischer Naturumgebung hervorrufen musste. Wir könnten aus den Hymnen der Rig-veda eine Fülle von Stellen nennen, welche deutlich beweisen mit welcher Innigkeit, mit welcher Lebhaftigkeit und Tiefe die alten Arier alles Schöne und Grosse in der Natur erfassten. Was sie aber vor Allem in Staunen versetzte, das war jene wunderbar schöne Weltordnung, welche ihr lebhafter Geist überall aufzufinden und zu entdecken verstand. Die Bewunderung dieser Weltordnung, des in der Welt sich manifestirenden *ṛtám*, bildete unzweifelhaft den ersten Ansatz zur denkenden Betrachtung der Welt als eines geordneten Ganzen. Dieses rein theoretische Bedürfniss wäre jedoch nie im Stande gewesen eine Philosophie ins Leben zu rufen, hätten sich nicht andere echt praktische Bedürfnisse zugesellt. Es ist allgemein bekannt, welche Rolle in der Vedareligion die Opfer und Gebete spielten. Durch Opfer und Gebete werden die Götter im Kampfe wider die bösen Geister gekräftigt, Opfer und Gebete bedingen ihren Sieg, also auch die Erhaltung der ganzen Weltordnung.

Das Opfern und Beten wurde hiedurch zum Range einer kosmischen Thätigkeit erhoben, und es musste als eine Aufgabe von höchster Wichtigkeit erscheinen, das Verhältniss zwischen den Opfern und Gebeten einerseits und der Weltordnung andererseits so genau als möglich zu bestimmen. Dies führte nun von selbst zur Betrachtung dieser Weltordnung, das ist zur Philosophie. Der religiöse Glaube braucht ergänzt zu werden, infolge dessen beginnt die Arbeit der Vernunft, und die Philosophie entsteht als ein natürliches Product praktischer religiöser Bedürfnisse und des eine gesetzmässige Ordnung in der Welt ahnenden Denkens.

Die Art und Weise, wie die Philosophie in Indien entstand, drückt sich mit grosser Deutlichkeit in ihrer ganzen Entwickelung aus. Es handelte sich dort um Opfer und Gebete im Verhältnisse zur Weltordnung. Die Hauptrolle spielt hier also das menschliche Wort, die Handlung und der als Quelle beider geltende menschliche Gedanke. Auf diese Weise wird das Wort des Gebetes Brahman zur Hauptgottheit in der Religion, wird der Gedanke zum Hauptprincipe in der Philosophie. Ist in der christlichen Religion das göttliche Wort Fleisch geworden, so ist in der indischen das menschliche Gott geworden. Ihres Gleichen fand diese Denkrichtung erst in der deutschen idealistischen Philosophie des XIX. Jahrhunderts, welche ebenfalls den Gedanken zum Range eines Weltgrundes erhob.

Hätten jedoch die ersten indischen Denker aus der Kaste der Brahmanen nur über das Verhältniss der Opfer und Gebete zur Weltordnung nachgedacht, so würde daraus eine sehr complicirte Liturgik neben einer theologischen Dogmatik entstanden sein, allein eine Entwickelung philosophischer Ideen wäre unmöglich gewesen. Wo eine Entwickelung stattfinden soll, dort muss ein Ferment vorhanden sein; etwas, was zur Entwickelung anspornt. Solch ein Ferment bildete in Indien der Doppelgegensatz, 1. zwischen der Priester- und Kriegerkaste, 2. zwischen der arischen und nichtarischen Bevölkerung.

Den Königen und Kriegern war die Bürde priesterlicher Ueberlegenheit unbequem, sie trachteten dieselbe abzuschütteln. Aeltere Sanskrittexte liefern uns manchen Beweis, dass um eine solche Emancipation, sowohl auf dem politischen, wie auf dem geistigen Gebiete gekämpft wurde. Die Höfe der Könige waren Schauplätze mancher Wortkämpfe, sie wurden zu Pflanzstätten freier Gedanken. Sogar Brahmanen wurden manchmal von Denkern in fürstlicher Krone belehrt und stellten sich auf die Seite einer mehr hetorodoxen Richtung. Der Unterschied lag nicht im Principe, sondern in dessen Deutung: heilige Handlungen und Gebete sind Hauptstützen der Weltordnung, sie wurzeln in menschlichen Gedanken, ja noch tiefer in dem Ich, welches als die Quelle aller Gedanken erscheint. In seinem eigenen ‚Ich' also in dem *âtman* findet der Mensch das Urprincip aller Weltordnung. Der Mensch erkennt es, indem er sich von der Welt abwendet und in sich selber vertieft. Durch Opfer und Gebete erreicht man nur eine niedrigere Stufe der Vollkommenheit, zur höheren führt das Erkennen des *âtman* Der Liturgik und Dogmatik der Brahmanen tritt hier eine kühne Metaphysik entgegen, eine Art rationalistischer Theosophie. Das waren die ersten zur Entwickelung treibenden Motive, als zweites tritt der Glaube an die Seelenwanderung auf. Er ist, meiner Ueberzeugung nach, auf den Einfluss der eingeborenen Race Indiens auf die arische Cultur zurückzuführen. Ich kann mich hier darüber nicht verbreiten, und werde vielleicht wo anders Gelegenheit finden, die Ergebnisse meiner Forschungen über den Seelenwanderungsglauben anzugeben. Hier kann ich nur andeuten, dass dieser Glaube die Frage nach der Emancipation von der ewigen Wiederholung des Lebens in den Vordergrund stellte und zum Nachdenken über Leben und Tod im Verhältnisse zur Weltordnung nöthigte. Zum rationalistischen kam auf diese Weise noch ein pessimistischer Anstrich, von dem in den früheren vedischen Zeiten keine Spur zu finden ist. Der Pessimismus der indischen Philosophie und späterer indischer Religionen ist nicht, wie dies oft behauptet wird, eine Folge allgemeiner Erschlaffung, er ist eine natürliche Frucht des Seelenwanderungsglaubens in Verbindung mit der metaphysischen Speculation. Wird einmal das *âtman* für das Urprincip der Welt erklärt, und in den Tiefen des menschlichen Bewusstseins dessen reinste Manifestation gefunden, so wird hiedurch die ganze übrige Wirklichkeit zu einem unerklärlichen Räthsel, sie erscheint als etwas Irrationales, Nichtseinsollendes, als eine Entfremdung des *âtman* von sich selber. Eine transcendentale Metaphysik kommt mit logischer Consequenz zum Pessimismus. So war es in Indien, so ist es in der europäischen Philosophie der Gegenwart!

Ueberblicken wir nun die Ergebnisse, zu denen diese ganze geistige Bewegung geführt, so können wir mit grosser Wahrscheinlichkeit behaupten, dass infolge all dieser Kämpfe und Controversen eine Fülle neuer philosophischer Standpunkte gewonnen wurde. Immerwährend wurden neue und abermals neue Wege gesucht und gefunden, welche zur Emancipation von der Herrschaft des Todes führen sollten. Der Geister bemächtigte sich eine gewaltige Unruhe, welche zum rastlosen Forschen und Denken anspornte. Die transcendentale Âtman-Theorie mit ihrer Welt, als einem blossen Schein, konnte unmöglich Allen einleuchten. Wir finden daher auch Anhänger anderer Schulen: dem auf die Spitze getriebenen idealistischen Monismus, stellen sich realistische Denkrichtungen entgegen. Der Realismus kann materialistisch oder dualistisch sein. Materialistisch ist die Schule des Tscharwâka, der uns an Demokrit und Epikur erinnert, dualistisch dagegen ist die Sâṁkhya, deren Anfänge wahrscheinlich auch bis in jene Zeiten reichen. Ueber das Alter des Sâmkhya wird viel gestritten. Manche hervorragende Gelehrte behaupten, sie sei älter als der Buddhismus und glauben sogar Spuren eines Einflusses des Sâmkhya auf den Buddhismus gefunden zu haben. Meiner Meinung nach kann man das mit Sicherheit nicht behaupten; mir erscheint die Sâmkhya-Schule als gleichzeitig mit dem Buddhismus oder sogar als nachbuddhistisch; wiewohl nicht geläugnet werden kann, dass sich gewisse Anklänge an diese Richtung schon in den älteren Upanischaden und sogar in dem ältesten Denkmal indischer Speculation, in dem Nasadya-Súkta nachweisen lassen. Die Sâmkhya-Philosophie ist, so gut wie der Buddhismus, als eine Reaction gegen die allzu radicale Âtman-Theorie aufzufassen. Der Behauptung, dass die Welt ein blosser Schein sei, stellt das Sâmkhya die These von der wirklichen, selbständigen und ewigen Existenz der Materie neben dem geistigen Principe entgegen, und begründet auf diese Weise eine mehr realistische Richtung der indischen Philosophie. Die Materie ist hier nicht nur etwas wirkliches, sie ist sogar ein schaffendes und gebärendes Princip. Ihre Existenz ist auch für den Geist unumgänglich nothwendig, der Geist gelangt nämlich zur Emancipation, indem er sich als etwas von der Materie verschiedenes erkennt. Der Realismus ist jedoch nicht blos in der Sâmkhya-Schule vertreten, wir finden ihn auch in der Nyaya und Waiseschika-Philosophie verbunden mit einer atomistischen Weltanschauung. Diese beiden Schulen sind wahrscheinlich jünger als das Sâmkhya, jedoch als allzu jung kann man sie nicht auffassen. Man kann nämlich mit grosser Wahrscheinlichkeit die Behauptung aufstellen, dass, je schroffer irgend eine Richtung den orthodoxen Theorien sich entgegensetzt, desto älter sie sei, desto näher reihet sie sich den buddhistischen Zeiten an. Vermittelnde Richtungen gehören unzweifelhaft späteren Zeiten an.

Als Hauptfrucht dieser grossen und gedankenreichen Epoche gilt die Entstehung neuer Religionsformen, die sich aus philosophischen Schulen herausgebildet haben. Es waren religiöse Bedürfnisse, welche im Anfang die Philosophie in's Leben rufen, diese trägt nun das ihrige zur Ausbildung einer Theologie bei, entfremdet sich ihr dann aber allmälig, geräth mit dem alten Glauben in Kampf und trachtet den alten durch einen neuen Glauben zu ersetzen. So entwickelten sich die Dinge und zwar nicht blos in Indien sondern überall, denn dies ist ein grosses Culturgesetz. Zu den bedeutendsten unter diesen neuen Religionsformen gehören der Buddhismus und die Dschaina-Religion. Dass sich dieselben selbständig aus den brahmanischen Philosophen-Schulen entwickelt hatten, darauf brauche ich, nach dem gediegenen und so lehrreichen Vortrage des Herrn Professors Dr. Jacobi hier nicht weiter einzugehen. Ueber den philosophischen Inhalt der Dschaina-Religion werden wir erst dann reden können, nachdem wir über die heiligen Bücher derselben genauere Aufschlüsse als dies bis jetzt geschehen werden erhalten haben.

Der Buddhismus ist nach seiner philosophischen Seite, ebenfalls eine Reaction gegen die brahmanische Weltanschauung und die auf die Spitze getriebene Âtman-Theorie. Er wurde zur Religion, indem er eine philosophische Dogmatik mit einer volksthümlichen, hauptsächlich den eingeborenen Racen Indiens angehörigen Mythologie, verband und zugleich eine sociale Reform unternahm. Philosophisch bildet die Karma-Theorie des Buddhismus einen directen Gegensatz zu der Âtman-Theorie der Upanischaden, wiewohl beide wiederum in ihren pessimistischen Consequenzen zusammentreffen.

Der Buddhismus bildet den Hauptwendepunkt in der Geschichte des indischen Denkens. Im Kampfe mit ihm erstarkt die brahmanische Reaction und es erfolgt ein Zurückgehen auf alte Standpunkte, jedoch verbunden mit einer Assimilirung aller jener Elemente, die sich überhaupt assimiliren liessen. Spuren eines Kampfes und der Reaction manifestiren sich vor Allem im Zustandekommen der ganzen Šutra-Literatur, man sieht hier ganz deutlich das Streben nach genauer Formulirung alter Satzungen gegenüber dem Andrange neuer Ideen. Die Brahmanen haben jedoch rechtzeitig erkannt, dass ein geistiger Kampf nur dann von Erfolg gekrönt sein könne, wenn er nicht blosse Vernichtung, sondern auch Assimilirung und Vermittlung anstrebe. Wir sehen nun in nachbuddhistischen Zeiten, sowohl auf religiösem wie auch auf philosophischem Gebiete, Vermittlungs- und Assimilirungsversuche auftreten. Zu solchen gehört die Yoga des Patandschali, welcher eine Art Eklekticismus predigt; ähnliche Spuren trägt auch das berühmte Gedicht Bagawátgita. Allmälig wird die Reaction immer stärker und der Buddhismus verliert in Indien ganz den Boden unter den Füssen. Auf philosophischem Gebiete manifestirt sich der Sieg der Reaction in dem sogenannten Vedanta-System des Badaráyaṇa.

Die Zeit, in welcher Badaráyana wirkte, lässt sich nicht genau bestimmen, wahrscheinlich zwischen 400 und 500 n. Chr. Die ihm zugeschriebenen Brahmaśutra sind ohne Zweifel das Werk einer ganzen Schule. Man braucht das System nur oberflächlich kennen zu lernen, um zur Ueberzeugung zu gelangen, dass dasselbe eine Frucht der Reaction sei, die womöglich alle Gegensätze in sich aufzunehmen trachtet. Was Hegel von seinem System behauptet hat, dass in ihm nämlich die ganze Geschichte der Philosophie enthalten sei, dasselbe könnten wir dem Vedanta-System nachsagen. Es bildet eine Art von Synkretismus, in welchem alle wichtigsten Denkrichtungen Indiens als aufgehobene Momente erscheinen. Der Vedanta vermittelt so gut zwischen dem Brahman- und Âtman-Begriffe, wie auch zwischen der Werke- und Wissenstheorie, nimmt einiges aus dem Sâmkhya, dem Nyaya, dem Yoga auf, und steht sogar augenscheinlich in einigen Punkten unter dem Einflusse des Buddhismus, nur gegen den Materialismus ist er unbedingt feindlich gesinnt. Das ist jenes System, welches endgiltig den Sieg davontrug, mit ihm hört eigentlich jede weitere Entwickelung indischer Philosophie auf. Trotzdem war das philosophische Leben auch später noch in Indien sehr rege. Der chinesische Pilger Huen-Tsang erzählt, dass zu seiner Zeit eine Menge philosophischer Schulen und Systeme in Indien bestand, die heftig einander bekämpften. Im VIII. und IX. Jahrhunderte tritt noch Samkara auf. Die Schriften desselben beweisen jedoch am besten, dass es damals mit eigentlicher Entwickelung schon vorbei war. Samkara's Ziel war ein dreifaches, wie dies Paul Regnaud in seinen Studien über die Vedanta-Philosophie gezeigt hat: 1. die Doktrin des Vedanta zu popularisiren, 2. dieselbe genauer zusammenzufassen, und 3. womöglich mit ältesten philosophischen

Denkmälern in Einklang zu bringen. Seit den Zeiten Samkara's behielt die Vedanta-Philosophie die Herrschaft über die aufgeklärten Geister Indiens. Dies schloss aber nicht aus, dass daneben eine Menge früher entstandener Richtungen existirte und Anhänger fand. Manche unter ihnen wurden von den Anhängern des Vedanta geduldet, andere heftig bekämpft. Der im XIV. Jahrhunderte lebende Mâdhava-Âtschârya hinterliess uns in seiner Sarwa-Darsana-Samgraha einen Ueberblick über die wichtigsten Systeme Indiens. Er beschreibt und kritisirt 16 derselben, beginnt mit denjenigen, denen er sich am schroffsten entgegenstellt, d. i. mit dem Tschârwaka und Buddhasystem und kommt bis zur Vedanta-Philosophie. Ein neuer Ideenaufschwung beginnt in Indien erst unter dem Einflusse europäischer Cultur.

Wenden wir uns nun jetzt der chinesischen Philosophie zu, so können wir hier ein sehr ähnliches Entwickelungsgesetz constatiren. Ihren Ursprung verdankt die denkende Betrachtung des Weltganzen in China ebenfalls gewissen religiösen Bedürfnissen. Die Urreligion des chinesischen Volkes beruhte auf dem Geisterglauben, den wir mit Herrn Taylor ‚Animismus‘ nennen können, die Hauptrolle spielte hier die Wahrsagerkunst, welche bis zum heutigen Tage in China in höchster Verehrung steht, und auf der Beobachtung gewisser Zeichen und Vorgänge in der Aussenwelt begründet ist. Den chinesischen Wahrsagern musste nun viel daran gelegen sein, die in der Welt der Dinge und Vorgänge herrschende Ordnung so genau wie möglich zu erfassen, um auf diesem Wege die Zukunft kennen zu lernen. Dies führte von selbst zur Betrachtung der Welt als eines geordneten Ganzen, also zur Philosophie. Dass diese unsere Behauptung keine philosophische Formel sei, sondern auf Thatsachen beruhe, hiefür liefert uns den besten Beweis das berühmte Buch I-king. Die Grundlage desselben bilden kabbalistische Zeichen, welche der mythische König Fo-hi auf dem Rücken einer Riesenschildkröte gefunden haben soll. Der I-king ist nun in China das Hauptbuch der Wahrsagerkunst, zugleich aber die Grundlage aller Philosophie. Wie in Europa aus der Astrologie die Astronomie, aus der Alchemie die Chemie, so entwickelte sich in China aus der Wahrsagerei die denkende Betrachtung des Weltganzen, die Philosophie. Wie das zu Stande kam ist nicht schwer zu errathen. Man begann kabbalistische Zeichen auf verschiedene Art zu deuten und zu commentiren. Da die Wahrsagerei mit der Regierungspraxis im innigsten Zusammenhange stand, so knüpfte man daran auch politische und ethische Bemerkungen.

Sind kabbalistische Zeichen als der älteste Bestandtheil des I-king zu betrachten, so bilden dagegen die Combinationen dieser Zeichen und die ersten Commentare, welche dem Kaiser Wuwang zugeschrieben werden, die zweite Schichte des Buches. Wäre dies in der That so, dann könnten wir den Anfang chinesischer Philosophie in jene Zeiten versetzen, in welchen die zweite Dynastie Schang gestürzt und die dritte Tscheu zur Herrschaft gelangte. Es ist sehr möglich, dass der spätere Begründer der Tscheu-Dynastie Wu-wang im Gefängnisse die Zeichen des I-king zu combiniren und dieselben mit politischen und philosophischen Reflexionen zu bereichern begann. Sollte nun dieser Anfang zu einer Entwickelung führen, so wären auch hier gewisse zu einer solchen Entwickelung treibende Motive unbedingt nothwendig. Wir finden dieselben in einem Gegensatz zwischen der herrschenden Klasse und gewissen volksthümlichen Elementen. Dieser Gegensatz ist schon in den Mythen Chinas ausgeprägt. Fo-hi gilt für den Begründer chinesischer Staats- und Gesellschaftsordnung, dagegen der zweite mythische Kaiser Hwang-tï gilt für den Wohlthäter des Volkes und wird in den Traditionen der herrschenden Klasse für einen Usurpator gehalten. Auf dem Gebiete des religiösen und des speculativen Lebens manifestirt sich derselbe Gegensatz in der Rivalität, einer auf das reale und nächste gerichteten Denkrichtung mit dem mystischen Schamanismus. Die erste dieser Richtungen bleibt bei dem thatsächlichen Dualismus (der himmlischen und irdischen Kräfte) stehen, während die zweite zur mystischen Erfassung des Alleinheitsbegriffes vorzudringen trachtet. In den Zeiten vor Konfucius ist die erste Richtung durch den Kaiser Wu-wang den Begründer der Tscheu-Dynastie und dessen

Lehrer Iuh-tse repräsentirt, die zweite durch Hui-kung (um 720), welcher einen volksthümlichen Communismus gepredigt haben sollte. Den besten Beweis für die Existenz eines philosophisch-religiösen Gegensatzes, und zwar schon in der vorkonfucianischen Epoche, liefert uns das Buch ‚Yin-fu-king': ‚Der Weg zur mystischen Einheit', dessen Uebersetzung und Commentar wir dem Herrn Philastre verdanken (Annales du Musée Guimet I, 255—318). Die Anhänger der Religion Tao bezeichnen den Kaiser Hwang-ti als den Verfasser dieses Buches. Diese ganze geistige Bewegung erreicht ihren Höhepunkt in der ersten klassischen Epoche chinesischer Philosophie, welche wiederum in der Thätigkeit des Kong-fu-tse einerseits, des Lao-tse andererseits gipfelt. Kong-fu-tse repräsentirt eine auf den Traditionen der herrschenden Race aufgebaute Weltanschauung, dagegen ist Lao-tse Repräsentant einer mystischen auf dem Schamanismus begründeten Richtung, welche dem Realen abgewendet in mystischer Contemplation zur Alleinheit vordringt. Man hatte früher einen Einfluss des Buddhismus auf Lao-tse angenommen, dies ist aber durchaus unwahrscheinlich, da Buddha gewiss jünger ist als Lao-tse, seine Lehre wird ganz verständlich, wenn man sie als eine Philosophie des Schamanismus auffasst. Kein Wunder, dass sie zur Grundlage einer sehr verbreiteten Volksreligion — der Tao-Religion — wurde, welche, wie sich ganz treffend Herr Philastre ausgedrückt hat, der echte und directe Abkömmling der ersten Glaubenssatzungen der chinesischen Race sei. Haben in Indien philosophische Controversen zur Ausbildung neuer Religionen geführt, so geschah dasselbe auch in China. Konfucianismus wird zur Staatsphilosophie und Staatsreligion, die Tao-Lehre zur Volksreligion. (In Indien Brahmanismus — Buddhismus.)

Sowohl Kong-fu-tse wie Lao-tse haben Schüler zurückgelassen, welche die Lehren ihrer Meister zu systematisiren und weiter zu entwickeln begannen. Nun kommt es zwischen den Anhängern beider Denkrichtungen zu erbitterten Kämpfen. Es sind das Zeiten in China, welche stark an die unmittelbar nachbuddhistische Epoche erinnern. Neben diesen zwei Hauptrichtungen sehen wir eine Menge anderer, welche ebenfalls durch hervorragende Denker vertreten sind. So z. B. predigt Mih-thi einen auf allgemeiner Liebe beruhenden Communismus und Socialismus, er verbreitete demokratische Ideen und war ein gewaltiger Gegner chinesischer Orthodoxie. China hat auch seinen Tscharwaka, den Iang-tschu nämlich, welcher einen crassen Materialismus und Egoismus lehrte. Hauptsächlich war jedoch der Zeitraum nach Kong-fu-tse und vor dem Sturze der dritten Dynastie mit Controversen zwischen den Anhängern der beiden grossen Meister ausgefüllt. Meng-tseu vertrat mit grossem Erfolge die Lehre des Kong-fu-tse, Tschwang-tseu die seines Gegners. Nach dem Sturze der dritten Dynastie gerieth die Philosophie in Verfall, es kommt nun zu einer Annäherung zwischen der Tao-Richtung und dem Konfucianismus, und damit beginnt eine Epoche eklektischer Vermischung. Im ersten Jahrhunderte n. Ch. dringt der Buddhismus nach China ein, der mit der Tao-Religion sehr nahe verwandt ist. Im Kampfe mit ihm erstarkt allmälig die Reaction, ganz ähnlich wie in Indien, wo der Brahmanismus durch den Kampf mit dem Buddhismus zur neuen Blüthe kam. Der Buddhismus scheint nicht nur zur Universal-Religion Asiens bestimmt zu sein, er spielte in den beiden grossen ostasiatischen Culturgebieten noch eine andere Rolle: im Kampfe mit ihm erstarkten auch ältere Denk- und Glaubensrichtungen, und wurden zum neuen Leben geweckt. Wohl gilt dies nur in China vom Konfucianismus, da die Taolehre sich mit dem Buddhismus beinahe gänzlich vermengte. Die Wiedergeburt chinesischer Philosophie beginnt unter der Tang-Dynastie mit Han-jü, einem heftigen Gegner des Buddhismus und erreicht ihren Höhepunkt mit Tschu-hi (1130 bis 1200), welcher neben Kong-fu-tse und Meng-tseu gewiss als der bedeutendste Philosoph Chinas zu betrachten ist. Seine Stellung in der Geschichte der chinesischen Philosophie ist sehr ähnlich der des Badarayana in Indien. Da Tschu-hi ursprünglich ein Anhänger des Buddhismus war, so nimmt er auch manche buddhistische und taoistische Ideen in sein System mit, und trachtet dieselben mit chinesischer Grundansicht zu assimiliren.

Herr Dr. Eitel in seinem vortrefflichen Ueberblicke der philosophischen Literatur Chinas (Travaux de la IIIe session du congr. int. des Orientalistes II, pag. 13) sagt sehr treffend, Tschu-hi's kosmogonische Theorien vom Universum, seine Speculationen über das grosse Absolute, über das männliche und weibliche Princip, über die beiden Zweige der Natur, wurden zum nationalen Glauben Chinas als willkommene Grundlage statt vieler schlechter Vorurtheile. Mit Tschu-hi endet die eigentliche Entwickelung chinesischer Philosophie, in späteren Zeiten ist uns kein selbständiger Denker mehr bekannt, bis zum heutigen Tage betrachten sich alle für Schüler Tschu-hi's.

Ueberblicken wir nun das Ganze so sehen wir, dass so gut in Indien wie in China gewisse religiöse Bedürfnisse die Philosophie (d. i. die denkende Betrachtung des Weltganzen) in's Leben riefen. Hier und dort prägt dieser Ursprung seinen Stempel auf der ganzen weiteren Entwickelung, welche durch gewisse ursprüngliche Gegensätze ermöglicht wird. Der Kampf zwischen Gegensätzen führt der Philosophie neue Kräfte zu. Die Philosophie trägt wiederum das Ihrige bei zur Ausbildung neuer Religionsformen: die Entstehung derselben, das sind Zeiten heftigster Controversen! Im Kampfe mit neuen erstarken nun alte Denkrichtungen, es kommt zu einer eklektischen Annäherung, dann zu einer Reaction und das Zurückgehen auf alte Standpunkte ist mit einer Assimilirung aller Ideen, die nur assimilationsfähig waren, verbunden. Ein philosophischer und religiöser Synkretismus bildet so gut in Indien wie in China das Ende des ganzen Entwickelungsprocesses. Und jetzt, bevor ich zu Ende komme, erlaube ich mir nur noch eine Frage. Hat sich die Philosophie derart nur in Indien und China entwickelt? War es in Europa anders? Ja, wer die europäische Philosophie ohne Vorurtheile betrachtet, der wird in ihr dasselbe Entwickelungsgesetz entdecken. Aus religiösen Bedürfnissen und in Anlehnung auf die Religion entstand sie in Griechenland, entwickelte sich auf Grund gewisser ursprünglicher Gegensätze, trug dann weiter das Ihrige zur Entstehung neuer höherer Religionsformen bei, trachtete die herrschende Religion entweder zu begründen und zu ergänzen, oder zu verdrängen und durch etwas anderes zu ersetzen, und beschloss jede ihrer grossen Entwickelungsepochen bis an den heutigen Tag mit einer Art Synkretismus, in welchem alle früheren Standpunkte als aufgehobene Momente erscheinen. Wir können hier den Gedanken nicht weiter verfolgen, er ist zu gross und zu umfangreich, um ihn in einigen dürftigen Zeilen zu erschöpfen. Wir constatiren hier nur die Möglichkeit, die Entwickelungsgesetze der Philosophie durch entsprechende Vergleichung indischer, chinesischer und europäischer Entwickelungsreihen auffinden und bestimmen zu können. Wir müssen nur einmal zu glauben aufhören, dass wir Europäer die Einzigen sind, welche eine Philosophie besitzen.

[illegible]

Ueber Jasna XXIX, 1—2.

Von

Friedrich Müller.

Der Text lautet nach Geldner's Ausgabe:

I.

[illegible]

II.

[illegible]

Statt *āhišhājā* hat Spiegel in seinen Text *ahišhahjā* aufgenommen, wogegen er im Commentar *āhišhāhjā* für die richtige Leseart hält, Westergaard liest *āhušhujā,* Geldner meint, man müsse nach dem Metrum *hišhājā* herstellen.

Statt *tęwišča* haben Spiegel und Westergaard *tawiščā*, die Leseart von I_2 und K_5 (die beiden werthvollsten Jasna-Handschriften).

wāstā liest auch Westergaard, ‚corrected from *wāstrā*, found in all copies‘. — *wāstā* haben aber I_2, Pt_4 (wo *r* von später Hand hinzugefügt ist), $Mf_{1.2}$, Pd., wodurch die Richtigkeit von Westergaard's Emendation bestätigt wird. Spiegel liest mit seinen Handschriften *wāstrā*.

Westergaard schreibt *uštā-ahurem* als Compositum.

Die Uebersetzung der beiden Strophen lautet nach Spiegel:

I.

Gegen euch klagte die Seele des Stieres: Für wen habt ihr mich geschaffen, wer hat mich geschaffen,
Mich verunreinigt Aeshma (Zorn), Haza (Räuber), Remo (Argwohn), Dere (Leiden) und Tawi (Dieb),
Nicht habe ich Futter ausser von euch, also lehrt mich die Güter, die Futterkräuter kennen.

II.

Darauf fragte der Bildner der Kuh den Asha: Wo hast du einen Herrn für die Kuh?
Damit er mächtig mache, mit Futter versehen die, welche sich der Viehzucht befleissen,
Wen, heil sei dir, (hast du gemacht) zum Herrn der den Aeshma zu den Bösen zurückschlägt?

Die Huzvaresch-Uebersetzung, an welche man sich zunächst zu wenden hätte, um den richtigen Sinn der Stelle zu ermitteln, hilft uns nicht viel; man erfährt blos das, was man in Betreff des allgemeinen Sinnes aus dem Grundtexte selbst herauszubringen im Stande ist, während man in Betreff der einzelnen Worte meistens im Stiche gelassen wird. Blos das wollen wir bemerken, dass der Paraphrast die Anrede, welche in der ersten Strophe enthalten ist, an die Amschaspands gerichtet sein lässt ([illegible]).

Obwohl nun die Huzvaresch-Uebersetzung in *gęręždā* die dritte Person erblickt (Justi 3. Pers. Imperf. Med.; Spiegel ein Participialperfectum), so zweifle ich dennoch an der Richtigkeit dieser Auffassung und möchte lieber in demselben die erste Person Singul. von *gęręžd-*, einer Weiterbildung von *gęręz-* erblicken.

Die eigentliche Schwierigkeit, um derentwillen ich die Stelle hier behandle, liegt in der zweiten Zeile der ersten Strophe. Dieselbe enthält nämlich, ohne mit dem Vorhergehenden verbunden zu sein, kein deutlich erkennbares Verbum finitum. Spiegel glaubt auch in der That ohne dieses auskommen zu können, indem er aus *ā* ein solches in dem Sinne ‚heran(kommt)' supplirt. Er fasst daher *ā mā aēshęmo hazas-čā ręmo āhišhahjā daręščā tawiščā* als: ‚gegen mich (kommt) Zorn, Räuber, Argwohn um mich zu verunreinigen (Genitiv von *āhišha-*, von *ā-hiš* = *ā-hi*, im Sinne eines Infinitivs), Leiden und Dieb.' Justi, welcher Westergaard's Lesung adoptirt, sucht in *āhušhujā* einen Locativ des Stammes *ā-hušh-u-* ‚Austrockung' und supplirt die Copula, indem er übersetzt: ‚gegen mich (ist) Aēshma in Austrocknung' u. s. w.

Dem gegenüber scheint Geldner, welcher aus metrischen Gründen die Lesart *hišhājā* herstellen will, darin ein Verbum finitum, etwa ein Perfectum von *hi-* zu erkennen.

Auffallend ist in zweiter Linie an unserer Stelle die unverhältnissmässig grosse Anzahl der ein- oder blos zweimal vorkommenden Wörter. *daręš* oder wie Justi liest *dęręš*, kommt blos hier vor, es wird von Justi auf *darš-*, von Spiegel auf *dęrę-*, von Geiger auf *daręz-* bezogen; ebenso *tawiš* (Geldner *tęwiš*), das Justi mit altindisch. *tāju-* zusammenstellt, Geldner wohl mit *tęwīšhi-* in Zusammenhang bringen wird. *ręmo* kommt ausser an unserer Stelle noch vor in Jasna XLVIII, 7 (Spiegel XLVII, Justi *paiti-ręmo*) an einer Stelle, aus der sich für die Bedeutung des Wortes wenig gewinnen lässt.[1])

---

[1]) Diese Stelle lautet:

ni aēšhęmo ni djātām paiti ręmęm paiti sjodūm
joi ā wańhęuš manańho dīdrayžodujē.

‚abgelegt werde der Zorn, vernichtet den Argwohn (?) die ihr an dem guten Geiste festhalten wollt'

Wie man sieht, ist mit unserer Stelle, wenn man conservativ vorgehen will, wie es Spiegel und Justi gethan haben, nichts anzufangen, weil nur eine sehr gewaltsame Erklärung herauskommt und — was die Hauptsache ist — die Zeile um zwei Silben zu viel enthält, als sie aus metrischen Gründen haben sollte.

Man wird daher zu dem leidlichen letzten Mittel, der Conjectur seine Zuflucht nehmen müssen. Diesen Weg hat bereits Geldner eingeschlagen, indem er, um die zwei überschüssigen Silben zu eliminiren, die eine an *āhišhājā*, die andere an *tawišćā* einbringt und demgemäss *hišhājā, tęwišćā* liest, wodurch den Anforderungen der Metrik entsprochen wird.

Es möge mir nun hier gestattet sein mich derselben Freiheit, der Conjectur, zu bedienen, um unserer kranken Stelle auf die Beine zu helfen.

Ich suche das Verbum des Satzes nicht in *āhišhājā*, sondern in dem folgenden [illegible], welches ich einfach in [illegible] emendire und mit dem vorangehenden [illegible] verbinde. Die Form *ā-daręštā* ist 3. Pers. Sing. Aor. Med. und stellt sich zum altindischen *ā-dhṛṣ-* ‚angreifen‘. Auf der Verwechslung von [illegible] und [illegible] beruhen in unseren Texten manche Varianten, so z. B.:

Jasna XXXXIII (Spiegel XXXXII), 16:

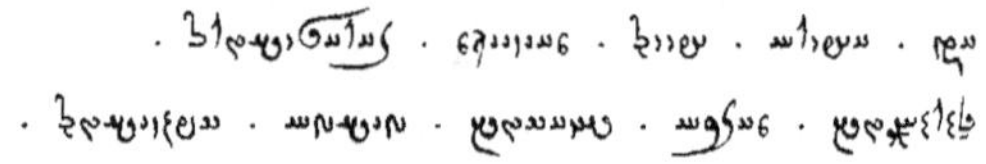

Für *ćišćā* bieten S_1, K_{11}, C_1 und $L_{1,2,3}$ die Leseart *ćištā* und $I_{4,6,7}$, H_1, L_{13}, B_2, S_2, Bb_1 die Leseart *ćistā*, welche nach meiner Ansicht die richtige ist. Ich übersetze:

‚Darauf Ahura Mazda wählt sich (*węręntē* = altind. *wṛṇītē*) Zarathuštra selbst den Geist, der in deiner Weisheit (*ćistā* Local von *ćisti-*) der heiligste ist.‘

---

dīdrayžodujē (für *dīdrayžoduē*), 2. Pers. Plur., Med. des Desiderativums von *daręz-* oder *draž-*. Man kann *paiti-ręmęm* lesen wie Westergaard und Justi oder, wie in *nī aęšhęmo nī-djātām*, auch hier *paiti ręmęm paiti-sjodūm* construiren.

Ist nun *darę̄štā* als Verbum anerkannt, dann gehören die beiden vorangehenden Ausdrücke zusammen, da sie durch kein *ćā* verbunden sind. In einem von beiden, in *āhišhājā* oder in *rę̄mo*, muss ein Genitiv stecken. So sehr nun *āhišhahjā* einem Genitiv gleichsieht, so sehe ich dennoch einen solchen lieber in *rę̄mo*, indem ich 𐬭𐬆𐬨𐬋 in 𐬭𐬇𐬨𐬋 verändere, welches bekanntlich einsilbig gesprochen werden muss. *āhišhājā* verändere ich mit Anlehnung an Westergaard's Leseart in *ā hušhjā*. Die beiden *ā* gehören zu *darę̄štā*; statt das Verbum zu wiederholen, ist an der ersten Stelle blos die es begleitende Präposition gesetzt.

Meine Lesung und Uebersetzung der beiden Strophen stellt sich daher folgendermassen dar:

I.

χšhmaibjā gę̄uš urwā gę̄rę̄ždā | kahmāi mā ϑwaroždūm kę̄ mā tašhaṭ
ā mā aēšhę̄mo hazasćā | zę̄mo ā hušhjā darę̄štā tawišćā
noiṭ moi wāstā χšhmaṭ anjo | aϑā moi sāstā wohū wāstrjā.

II.

adā tašhā gę̄uš pę̄rę̄saṭ | ašhę̄m kaϑā toi gawoi ratuš
hjaṭ hīm dātā χšhajanto | hadā wāstrā gaōdājo ϑwaχšho
kę̄m hoi uštā ahurę̄m | ję̄ drę̄gwodę̄bīš aēšhę̄mę̄m wādājoiṭ.

Uebersetzung.

I.

Zu euch klage ich Seele des Rindes: ,Wozu habt ihr mich geschaffen, wer hat mich gebildet?
Angegriffen haben mich Zorn, Gewalt, der Erde Trockenheit und Misshandlung[1])
Nicht ist mir ein anderer Beschützer ausser euch; daher weiset mir gute Weidekräuter an.'

[1]) *tawiš* = altind. *tavas*.

II.

Da fragte des Rindes Bildner Ašha: ,Wie soll dem Rinde ein Ratu werden,
Damit ihr ihm o Mächtige! zugleich mit der Weide beim Viehzüchter Kraft gebet?
Wen wünscht ihr[1]) für ihn als Herrn, der den Bösen den Zorn austriebe?'

---

[1]) *uštā*, 2. Pers. Plur. Präs. von *was-*.

The Râmânujîya and the Bhâgavata or Pâñcharâtra systems.

By

R. G. Bhandarkar.

A work entitled Arthapañchaka that has recently fallen under my observation gives a summary, of the doctrines, of the school of Râmânuja. The whole subject is treated of under five heads viz (I) Jîva, *i. e.*, animal spirit or dependent spirit; (II) Îśvara, *i. e.*, God; (III) Upâya, *i. e.*, the way to God; (IV) Phala or Purushârtha, *i. e.*, the end of life; and (V) Virodhinaḥ, *i. e.*, obstructions to the attainment of God.

(I.) — Jîvas are of five kinds, viz. (1) Nitya, *i. e.*, those who never entered on Saṁsâra or the succession of lives and deaths at all, such as Garuḍa, Vishvaksena, and others; (2) Mukta, *i. e.*, those who have shaken off the fetters of life and whose sole purpose and joy is attendance (Kaiṁkarya) on God; (3) Kevala, *i. e.*, those whose hearts being purified are fixed on the highest truth and who are thus free from the succession of births and deaths; (4) Mumukshu, *i. e.*, those who having experienced the misery of life are averse to its enjoyments and have fixed their desire only on the highest end, *viz.*, the attainment of the condition of an attendant on God; and (5) Baddha, *i. e.*, those who devoting themselves to the life whether of a god, man, or brute that their previous merits or demerits (Karman) have assigned to them, seek only the enjoyments of such a life and are averse to the joys of Brahman.

II. The manifestations of Îśvara or God are five; viz., (1) Para, *i. e.*, he who lives in Vaikuṇṭha and whose presence is enjoyed by the Nitya and Mukta spirits who dwell near him, who is unbeginning and endless, who wears celestial ornaments, celestial garments, and celestial weapons, who possesses celestial beauty and an endless number of holy attributes, and who is accompanied by Śrî, Bhû, and Lîlâ; (2) Vyûha, *i. e.*, the forms of Saṁkarshaṇa, Pradyumna, and Aniruddha assumed for the creation, protection, and dissolution of the world; (3) Vibhava, *i. e.*, incarnations such as Râma and Kṛishṇa for the establishment of Truth, the protection of the good and the destruction of the wicked; (4) Antaryâmin, who has two forms in one of which he dwells in every thing and rules over all, is bodiless, all-pervading, and the store of all good attributes and is called Vishṇu, Nârâyaṇa, Vâsudeva, &c., and in the other he possesses a body bearing celestial weapons such as a conch-shell and a discus, and celestial ornaments, dwells in the heart of man, is the store of all good attributes, and is known by the names of Hṛishîkeśa, Purushottama, Vâsudeva, &c.; and (5) Archâ, *i. e.*, idols of stone, metal, &c., in which he dwells and allows himself to be worshipped by his devotees. In the Yatîndramatadîpikâ to be noticed below and in other places the Vyûhas are given as four, Vâsudeva possessed of the six great attributes being the first, Saṁkarshaṇa possessed of two viz., Jñâna and Bala being the second, Pradyumna having Aiśvarya and Vîrya, the third, and Aniruddha possessed of Śakti and Tejas, the fourth. The first Vyûha is assumed in order that it may serve as an object of devotion, and the other three for the creation &c., of the world. In the present work the Vâsudeva Vyûha is put down as the second form of the Antaryâmin.

III. The Upâyas or ways to God are five, viz. (1) Karmayoga, (2) Jñânayoga, (3) Bhaktiyoga, (4) Prapattiyoga, and (5) Âchâryâbhimânayoga. Under the first comes the whole Vedic sacrificial ritual and the Smârta or domestic ceremonies along with the fasts and observances, by going through which the person is purified. Then by means of Yama, Niyama, &c., mentioned in the Yoga Śâstra, one should concentrate his mind upon himself. This concentration leads to Jñânayoga which consists in fixing the mind on Nârâyaṇa or Vâsudeva described in the Vâsudeva Vyûha, as the person on whom one's own self on which the mental powers have already been concentrated depends. Thus the devotee arrives at God through himself. The Jñânayoga leads to Bhaktiyoga which consists in continuously seeing nothing but God. Prapatti is resorted to by those who cannot avail themselves of or are not equal to the first three methods. It consists in throwing one's self entirely on the mercy of God. There are many details given which need not be reproduced here. The last method, Achâryâbhimânayoga, is for one who is unable to follow any of the others, and consists in surrendering oneself to an Âchârya or preceptor and being guided by him in everything. The preceptor goes through all that is necessary to effect his pupil's deliverance, as a mother takes medicine herself to cure an infant.

IV. The Purushârthas are five, viz., (1) Dharma, (2) Artha, (3) Kâma, (4) Kaivalya, and (5) Moksha. The first three do not differ from those ordinarily called by those names, and the last two are the conditions attained by the Kevala and Mukta spirit (I, 3 and 2 above.)

V. The Virodhins are five, viz., (1) Svasvarûpavirodhin, *i. e.*, that which prevents ones own real or spiritual nature from being seen, such as the belief that the body, is the soul; (2) Parasvarûpavirodhin or that which prevents one's approach to the true God, such as devotion to another or false deity or belief in God's incarnation being but human being &c. (3) Upâyavirodhin or that which prevents the true ways from being resorted to, as the belief in ways other than those mentioned above being more efficacious or in the latter being inadequate; (4) Purushârthavirodhin or attachment to other than the true or highest object of life; (5) Prâptivirodhin, *i. e.*, the being connected with a body that one's own Karman has entailed or with other spirits who are so embodied.

At the end of another work the Yatîndramatadîpikâ, the author gives a variety of views entertained by different classes of writers belonging to this school. The Sûris admit only one entity (Tattva); the Ṛishis divide it into two, Âtman and Anâtman; and the Âchâryas professing to follow the Śruti propound three Tattvas or entities, viz., (1) Bhogya or what is to be enjoyed or suffered; (2) Bhokṭri, the enjoyer or sufferer; (3) Niyantṛi or the ruler and controller. Some Âchâryas teach the system under the four heads of (1) Heya or what is to be shunned, (2) the means of keeping it off, (3) Upâdeya or what is to be sought and secured, and (4) its means. Other teachers (Deśikas) divide the subject into five parts, *viz.* (1) what is to be attained or got at (Prâpya), (2) he who attains it (Prâpṭri), (3) the means of attainment (Upâya), (4) the fruits or objects of life (Phala), and (5) obstructions or impediments. These are the five topics or Arthapañchaka described above. Some teachers add one more topic which is called Saṁbandha (relation), and thus expound six. There is no real difference according to our author between these several views, since the variety is due to the adoption of a different principle of division by each teacher. The true substance of the Vedântas or Upanishads is that there is only one Brahman with the animal spirits and the dead world as its attributes (Chidachidviśishṭâdvaitam).

The doctrines of Ramanuja's school here given are the same as the doctrines of an older school, that of the Pâñcharâtras or Bhâgavatas, reduced to a systematic form. In the Nârayaṇîya section of the Mokshadharmaparvan which forms part of the twelfth or Śântiparvan of the Mahâbhârata, there occurs a text in which the Sâṁkhyayoga, Pâñcharâtra, Vedas or Âraṇyakas, and Pâśupata are mentioned as five distinct systems of religious truth.[1]) The Vedas or Âraṇyakas here spoken of are the system afterwards known by the names of Aupanishada and Vedânta. The doctrines of the Pañcharâtra system are explained in Chapter 339 of the same book. Vâsudeva is the supreme, unborn, eternal and all-pervading soul, the cause of all. From him sprang Saṁkarshaṇa or the soul that animates all bodies, regarded as one, from him Pradyumna, the sum total of all in-

[1]) Chap. 349, First Bombay Edition.

telligence (Manas), and from him Aniruddha who represents Ahaṁkâra or egoism, and who created all objects. Narasiṁha, Râma, Kṛishna and others are represented as subsequent incarnations of the supreme Vâsudeva. Bhakti or love and faith is the way of reaching God. The Nârayaṇîya section is older than Râmânuja, since he refers to it in the passage in his Vedântabhâshya, to be noticed below, and older also than Śaṁkarâchârya who quotes in his Bhâshya under II, 1, 1. from Chapters 334 and 339,[1]) and 350 and 351.[2]) In his Vedântasûtrabhâshya Śaṁkarâchârya gives under II, 2, 42 these same doctrines as maintained by the Bhâgavatas and refutes them on the ground that if Jîva or the animating soul is to be considered as created by Vâsudeva, it must be capable of destruction, and hence there can be no such thing as eternal happiness. Then under Sûtra 44 he gives the same doctrines in a modified form. Saṁkarshaṇa and others are not the animating soul, intelligence, and egoism, independent of Vâsudeva, but they are different Vyûhas or forms of the same Vâsudeva regarded as possessing, certain attributes viz. Jñâna and Aiśvarya, Śakti and Bala, and Vîrya and Tejas, respectively. This too is refuted by Śaṁkarâchârya. In connection with this modified doctrine, the name Pâñcharâtra is used as of those who advocated it. Râmânuja in his Vedântasûtrabhâshya introduces his comments on these Sûtras by the observation ‚Raising an objection against the authoritativeness or truth of the Pañcharâtra dispensation which was revealed by Bhagavat and which shows the way to the highest bliss, from its being a (separate) system like those of Kapila and others (which have been refuted), he refutes it‘. The objection that is raised is this. The Bhâgavatas maintain that Saṁkarshaṇa the animating soul and others were created; but the Śrutis lay down that souls are not created. Then under Sûtra 44 which, however, is 41 in his Bhâshya, Râmânuja says that this objection is based on a misconception of the doctrine of the Bhâgavatas. The correct doctrine is that Vâsudeva the supreme soul assumes these four forms

[1]) p. 409, vol. I, Bibl. Ind. Ed.

[2]) p. 413, ibid.

cut of love for those who depend upon him, in order that they may resort to him under those forms. In support of this he quotes a text from the Paushkarasaṁhitâ; and another from the Sâtvatasaṁhitâ is quoted to show that the worship of these four forms is really the worship of the supreme Vâsudeva. The supreme Vâsudeva is attained by his devotees when they worship him according to their abilities in his Vibhava and Vyûha manifestations or in his original subtle form. By worshipping the Vibhavas, they reach the Vyûhas, and through the Vyûhas they reach the subtle form. The incarnations Râma, Kṛishṇa and others are Vibhavas, the Vyûhas are those mentioned above, and the subtle form is the supreme Brahma(n) called Vâsudeva possessed only of the six attributes, Jñâna, Aiśvarya etc.

According to Râmânuja therefore the Bhâgavata doctrine when properly understood is not opposed to the Śruti and it is therefore not refuted by the author of the Vedântasûtras but pronounced as correct. It will thus appear that the system was known by two names, Pâñcharâtra and Bhâgavata, though Bâṇa in his Harshacharita speaks of these as two different schools. If they were different, the distinction between them was probably due to one having adopted one form of the doctrine explained above and the other, the other. Under Sûtra 45, Śaṁkarâchârya accuses the Pâñcharâtras of treating the Vedas with contempt since it is stated in one of their books that Śâṇḍilya not having found the way to the highest good in the four Vedas had recourse to this Śâstra. Râmânuja answers this accusation by saying that a similar statement occurs in the Bhûmavidyâ (Chhândogya Up vii. i.). Nârada is represented there as saying that he has studied all the Vedas and other branches of learning and still he only knows the Mantras and not the Âtman. This does not involve the contempt of the Vedas, but the object of the statement is simply to extol the Bhûmavidyâ or the philosophy of he highest object that is explained further on. Or the sense ist that Nârada studied all the Vedas but was not keen enough to comprehend the nature of the Âtman though set forth in those works. Precisely the same interpretation should be laid on this statement of Śâṇḍilyâś not having found the way to the highest good in the four Vedas, and it should not be construed as involving contempt for the Vedas.

Râmânuja's system is thus the same as the Pâñcharâtra or Bhâgavata. The sacred books of this latter are the Pâñcharâtra-saṁhitâs three of which, the Paushkara, Sâtvata, and Parama are quoted by Râmânuja in the passage referred to above. The following exist in the library of Jasvantrâo Gopâlrâo of Pâṭaṇ:

a) Lakshmî Saṁhitâ, Gr. s. 3,350.
b) Jñânâmṛitasâra Saṁhitâ, Gr. s. 1,450.
c) Paramâgamachûḍâmaṇi Saṁhitâ, Gr. s. 12,500.
d) Paushkara Saṁhita, Gr. s. 6,350.
e) Padma Saṁhitâ, Gr. s. 9,000.
f) Vṛiddhabrahma Saṁhitâ, Gr. s. 4,533.

The book printed as Nâradapañcharâtra in the Bibliotheca Indica is only one of these that marked *b)*. A copy of *c)* was purchased by me for the government of Bombay two years ago. Whatever may be the time when these and other Saṁhitâs were written and the religion received a definite shape, the root of the Bhâgavata or Pañcharâtra system is to be traced to very remote times. Its distinguishing features are as we have seen, the worship of Vâsudeva as the supreme Brahma and the doctrine of Bhakti or faith and Love as the way to salvation. It does not trace all our finite thought and feeling to a principle alien to the soul such as Prakṛiti or Mâyâ as the Sâṁkhya or Advaita Vedânta does; and look upon freedom from that sort of thought and feeling as Moksha or deliverance. It is a system of popular religion and has not such a metaphysical basis as either of those two has. Vâsudeva was recognised as the supreme deity even in the time of Patañjali, for under Pâṇini iv, 3, 98, the author of the Mahâbhâshya states that the Vâsudeva occurring in the Sûtra is not the name of a Kshattriya, but of Tatrabhagavat, which term is explained by Kaiyaṭa as signifying a certain [form of the] Supreme deity. And since Pâṇini himself directs us in that Sûtra to append the termination *aka* to Vâsudeva in the sense of ,one whose

Bhakti or object of devotion is Vâsudeva', the worship of Vâsudeva is older than that grammarian also. In forming some conception of the origin of this cultus other circumstances than those hither to mentioned must be taken into consideration. In the Nârâyaṇîya section of the Mahâbhârata, the Pâñcharâtra is represented as an independent religion professed by the Sâtvatas and is also called the Sâtvata religion;[1]) and Vasu Uparichara who was follower of that religion is spoken of as worshipping the Supreme God according to the Sâtvata manner (vidhi) which was revealed in the beginning by the Sun.[2]) The religion is stated to be the same as that taught to Arjuna by Bhagavat himself when the armies of the Pâṇḍavas and the Kurus were drawn up in battle-array and Arjuna's heart misgave him.[3]) Thus the Bhagavadgîtâ belongs to the literature of Vâsudeva worship. In the Bhâgavata the Sâtvatas are represented as calling the highest Brahma(n), Bhagavat and Vâsudeva, and as worshipping and adoring Kṛishṇa in a peculiar way.[4]) Râmânuja too refers, as we have seen, to the Sâtvatasaṁhitâ. Satvat was the name of a descendent of Yadu as we learn from the Purâṇic genealogies, and his race was the race or clan of the Sâtvatas. The Sâtvatas are mentioned in the Bhâgavata along with the Andhakas and Vṛishṇis which were two of the Yâdava tribes.[5]) Vâsudeva himself was a prince of that race, being called Sâtvatarshabha and Sâtvatapuṁgava.[6]) About the time when Pâṇini flourished or when the Upanishads were written, and even later when Buddhism and Jainism arose, the energies of the Indian mind were directed to religious speculation, and we find a variety of systems coming into vogue. In this intellectual race the Kshattriyas took a much more active part than the Brahmans. In the Chhândogya Upanishad, a prince of the name

---

1) Chap. 348, vv. 55, 34, 84.
2) Chap. 335, vv. 19, 24.
3) Chap. 348, v. 8; Chap. 346, v. 11.
4) X. 9, 49; XI. 21, 1.
5) I. 14, 25; III. 1, 29.
6) Bh. XI. 21, 1; I. 9, 32

of Pravâhaṇa, the son of Jaibala[1]) and Aśvapati, king of the Kekaya country,[2]) appear as teachers of religious truth and Brahmans as learners; and in the former passage it is even stated that the Kshattriyas were the original possessors of that knowledge. Similarly, in the Kaushîtakibrâhmanopanishad, we find Ajâtaśatru, king of Kâśî, explaining the true Brahma (n.) to Bâlâki the Gârgya, who had only pretended to teach it to the king, but did not know it really. The same story is told in the Bṛihadâraṇyaka. Buddha was a Kshattriya and belonged to the Śâkya clan; so was Mahâvîra who belonged to the race of the Jñâtṛikas. Since then the Kshattriyas were so active at the time in propounding religious doctrines and founding sects and schools, we may very well suppose that a Kshattriya of the name of Vâsudeva belonging to the Yâdava, Vṛishṇi, or Sâtvata race founded a theistic system as Siddhârtha of the Śâkya race and Mahâvîra of the Jñâtṛika race founded atheistic systems. And just as Buddha under the title of ‚Bhagavat‘ is introduced as the teacher in Buddhistic works, so is Vâsudeva as Bhagavat introduced in the Bhagavadgîtâ and some other parts of the Mahâbhârata. That must have been one of his most prominent names, since his followers were in later times called Bhâgavatas. Or perhaps, it is possible that Vâsudeva was a famous prince of the Sâtvata race and on his death was deified and worshipped by his clan; and a body of doctrines grew up in connection with that worship, and the religion spread from that clan to other classes of the Indian people. In the course of time other elements got mixed with it. We have seen that Râmânuja considers Râma, Kṛishṇa and others to be only Vibhavas or incarnations of Vâsudeva and they are so represented in the Nârâyaṇîya also. This means that the legends and worship of those deified heroes became identified with Vâsudeva; and the traditions about the Vedic Vishṇu and the Purâṇic Nârayaṇa who drew out the submerged earth were also in

---

[1]) v. 3.
[2]) v. 11.

subsequent times referred to him, and thus the various forms of modern Vaishṇavism arose.

It is therefore clear that the Pâñcharâtra was a distinct system independent of the Vedas and Upanishads. But during the early centuries of the Christian era, while the country was under the domination of foreigners of the Śaka, Palhava, and Yavana races, the Buddhists had grown powerful. With the restoration of the native dynasties in the fourth century, the influence of Brahmans increased and they then began a fierce conflict with all heretics. These were cried down as scoffers, atheists, nihilists (Vainâśikas), &c. The great Mîmâṁsakas, Śabarasvâmin, Maṇḍanamiśra, Kumârila and others, flourished during this period of conflict. They ran down even the Aupanishadas or the holders of the Jñânamârga, *i. e.*, the religion of the Upanishads, as against the Karmamârga or the sacrificial religion. The Bauddhas and Jainas who had no regard for the Vedas whatever met them on independent or rationalistic grounds. But the Aupanishadas fought them on the field of Vedic orthodoxy and succeeded in maintaining their position. There were unquestionably in ancient times several Aupanishada systems; but it was the doctrine of the unreality of the world and the unity of spirit with which the name of Śaṁkarâchârya is connected and which has been characterized by the Mâdhvas as but Buddhistic nihilism in disguise, that succeeded on the present occasion. And that doctrine was by others considered as subversive of religion and certainty. Śaṁkarâchârya and his followers did not treat tenderly the religious systems that had become popular such as that of the Bhâgavatas or Pâñcharâtras and of the Pâśupatas. It was, therefore, Râmânuja's endeavour to put down the pernicious doctrine of Mâyâ or unreality, and seek a Vedântic and philosophic basis for the religion of Bhakti or Love and Faith that had existed from times immemorial; and thus the Pâñcharâtra system which was independent of the Vedas before, became in his hands a system of the Vedânta or an Aupanishada system.

On a newly discovered form of Indian character.

By

Cecil Bendall.

(With an alphabetic table traced by the author from the MS., in his possession and a photo-lithograph of a portion of the text.)

The MS. forming the chief groundwork of the present essay was purchased by me at Kathmandu, Nepal in November 1884. It has some literary interest as containing a portion of a somewhat rare work, the Cāndra-vyākaraṇa.

[See Note at the end of this paper, on the Candrālaṃkāra.]

Its chief interest, however, is its peculiar writing, which, as far as I can find, has never been noticed in any inscription or book. Its remarkable archaism can of course only be fully shown by an examination of details; but at the first glance, one may single out a predominant feature distinguishing it from the various North Indian alphabets to which in other respects it may be nearest akin.

This is the small triangle with apex uppermost placed at the top of each letter. The use of a wedge-like top with point downwards, in early Indian writing, has often been commented on.[1]) Here however the exact reverse is seen; so that, instead of 'nail-headed' or the like, we might call the character 'point-headed' or 'arrow-headed'.

The discovery of a new literary character was in itself of sufficient interest, but it was most curiously illustrated and confirmed during the same journey. For a few weeks later, on

[1]) See, for example, Bühler, Remarks on the Horiuzi MSS. (Appendix to *Anecdota Oxoniensia.* Aryan Series. Vol. I. Pt. III. p. 69).

visiting the Calcutta Museum, I observed a figure of Buddha (Bihar. 68), the history of which was unknown, except that it was brought from Bihar, with an inscription of two lines beneath. The inscription was very badly and unevenly carved, insomuch that I failed to make any satisfactory copies, whether by heelball or estampage. I subsequent wrote for photographs; but Calcutta is hopelessly behindhand in matters like photography and I only received some imperfect attempts. [These were exhibited to the Congress.] I have not succeeded in making out all that remains of the inscription; but the Buddhist confession (ये धर्मा०), in a form slightly varying from its usual text, can be read at the end. This however suffices to show that the character is substantially the same as that of the MS., with just the variations that one usually finds between writing on stone and on leaf. The difference is indeed far less than might have been expected, when we see from the Gurjara plates how considerable was the divergence between the written and engraved forms of letters in the early middle ages.[1]) I was at first disposed to consider this as a mere variety of medieval North Indian character; yet there are some remarkable archaisms, and above all several peculiar forms not easy to parallel amongst the alphabets descended from the Southern Açoka, which lead one to regard them as survivals of some very early form of writing. At all events, as the two specimens have been found in districts of specially Buddhistic associations, and since both documents are more or less identified with this religion,[2]) it is not too much to conjecture that this alphabet is one of those given in the well-known list of the Lalita-vistara (ed. Bibl. Ind., p. 143). For corresponding passages in Jain writings see Weber, Indische Studien XVI, 400 sqq.

Before entering into more minute palæographical details I will call attention to a few points that tend to place this al-

---

[1]) See *Indian Antiquary* V. 113 and the other places cited by Bühler, Remarks on the Horiuzi MS., p. 65, note 7.

[2]) One of the chapters of our MS. begins with नमो बुद्धाय, as is generally the case in MSS. of Candragomin.

phabet, in my opinion, in the position of a very remarkable archaic survival.

Dr Bühler in his account of the Horiuzi palm-leaves which share with the two earliest of the Cambridge collection and Dr Hörnle's Bakshālī MS. described in the present volume the honour of being ranked as the earliest written Indian documents, lays some stress on the use of wedge-formed tops in early written characters (*Anecdota Oxon.* [Aryan.] III, p. 68, Appendix). The wedges to which he refers correspond in place and general use to the pointed or triangular heads of strokes already noticed, which however are turned in just the opposite direction, viz. apex uppermost. But besides these may be noticed in the alphabetical table a second and distinct set of marks still more like wedges in form, and slanting downwards towards the right-hand side of several letters: viz., *ga, ṅa, ṭa, ṭha, ṇa, tha, dha, la* and *ça*.

A third point is the absence of what may be considered as the two distinguishing features of modern North Indian hand, the top-line and — what is of still earlier date — the vertical side-line forming a kind of prop in the letters **घ च त न ध प म य ल व ष** and **स**. This latter feature is to be observed in quite early Mss. of North Indian origin, as may be seen from the Tables of Letters in my Cambridge Catalogue, or in Dr Bühler's work already cited.

We may now pass to a detailed consideration of the alphabet, in which the forms of *e* initial, *ṭa* and *ça* may be noted as amongst the most remarkable and unique forms. The absence of distinction between *ṛi* medial and *ra* conjunct is archaic and noteworthy, especially in a treatise on grammar where it might be expected that the identity of words like *vṛita* and *vrata* would lead to serious confusions. The double forms of *u* medial and of *pa* are likewise of importance.

The works chiefly referred to in the following essay are:
Burnell (A. C.) Elements of South Indian Palaeography. Ed. 2. London, 1878.
Bühler (J. G.) Appendix on the Horiuzi Palm-leaves (*Anecdota Oxoniensia.* Aryan Series. Vol. I. Pt. III).

Burgess (James) Archæological Survey of Western India. Vol. IV. (With table of letters forming Plate V.)
Also my own
Catalogue of Buddhist Sanskrit MSS. at Cambridge. Cambridge, 1883
and
Journey . . in Nepal and Northern India. *Ibid.* 1886.

Letters.

I. Initial vowels.

a The sweeping stroke, similar to the sign for medial *u* in this MS., attached to the bottom of main downstroke, cannot be exactly matched in any alphabet known to me, though several of the alphabets in Burgess's table have an analogous ornamental curve in the corresponding part of the letter.[1])

ā The length is here marked by the addition of a loop as well as the curve. A similar expedient is adopted in the IVth century Vengi (Burnell, S. Indian Palæography, Pl. I).

i ī The use of small semicircles for the usual dots or circles is a slight peculiarity, though in general form the letters correspond to the forms cited by Burgess and by Bühler (Arch. Surv. W. I. Vol. IV., p. 81 and Horiuzi Palm-leaves, p. 74). The form of the long vowel especially is strikingly similar to that of the Gurjara plates.

u is of the ordinary medieval form without the archaic curve to the right.

[ū] I have not succeeded in finding an example of this letter.

ṛi, ṛī These letters are of course not to be illustrated from the earliest inscriptions. But the archaism of the present MS. is well illustrated by the extreme simplicity of their formation which comes nearest to the Çārada, where however the curve distinguishing *ṛi* from *ra* is turned in the opposite direction. It may however be observed from the

[1]) Burgess, Archæological Survey W. India. Vol. IV. Plate V. nos 10, 12, 14 etc.

Table of Letters in my Catalogue of the Buddhist Sanskrit MSS. at Cambridge that an analogous form survived in Nepal as late as A. D. 1179. All these forms illustrate of course our introductory remarks on the similarity of *ra* and *ṛi* throughout in this alphabet, and separate it from the group of alphabets which, begining with the Horiuzi example, have developed a much more elaborate symbol for this initial sound.

e This is a very curious form, which I have not exactly paralleled in any inscription. The nearest is the Cera of the Vth century (Burnell, Pl. II), which taken with some the specimens to Burgess's Table (N°s 18, 19, 21, 29) partly illustrates its development from the original triangular form.

II. Simple consonants.

ka This letter has the modern appendage at the right hand; which, however, as Bühler shows, begins tolerably early. The flourish in the opposite direction from the bottom of the vertical stroke resembles that already noticed in a initial and may be compared with the Cālukya forms.

kha This letter takes a simple form, resembling that of the Kshatrapa and Gupta alphabets (Burgess Table N°s 10, 13, 19 etc.), but distinguished from them and from the modern form by the top of the letter, which is neither rounded nor flat, but pointed.

ga is curiously analogous to *kha* in likewise showing a pointed top in contrast to the rounded form of the middle period and the flat form of the later. Here however it may be noted that the angular top occurs in the earliest forms, from which indeed our letter is distinguished by little else than by the addition of determinative side-wedge, already noticed, and the thickenings at the bottoms of each of the component strokes.

gha is at first sight somewhat modern in form; but the middle of the three upright strokes of which this letter ordinarily consists is found quite early of much smaller size than the others, as in the Ajanta inscriptions (Burgess, Table N° 5). The curious twist in the right-hand stroke is always found, throughout the MS. and resembles a similar feature in the *sha* noticed below.

ṅa The main portion of this letter is of a form common to most of the older alphabets that give specimens of it at all: but the characteristic feature of this form is that, instead of the single pendant or downward wedge on the left-hand side to which I called attention in the earliest Nepalese MSS. (*Cambr. Catal.,* p. XLVI; cp. Bühler, *Horiuzi,* p. 78), we find a combination of two wedges, forming a down-turned angle.

ca This is the form of the Cave and Gupta inscriptions, plus the surmounting arrow-head. The absence of the modern vertical side-line has been noted above.

cha The body of the letter is of the form usual in all the earlier North Indian alphabets: the difference between the two forms given in the table simply consisting in the occasional use of a determinative wedge added to the side of the small vertical top-line instead of the normal arrow-head.

ja This letter has been very curiously altered as to the position of its component parts, so that though not essentially different from several of the early forms, it is at first one of the hardest to identify of the letters of this alphabet. All the three originally horizontal members have been turned aslant, and not merely two as in the Horiuzi *ja*. Besides this we get two 'arrow-heads' above, and a hooked end added to the right-hand stroke.

jha This curious form apparently arises from the expansion of the wedge, which marks in the Horiuzi and early Nepalese the bottom of the main vertical stroke into a flourish similar to that noted above in a initial and *ka*. A hook has been added to the right as in the Çārada though differently placed, and the termination of the hook is marked by a wedge as in *pa* below.

ña This letter is practically the same as the VI—VIIth century forms. The right-hand appendage however is enlarged and surmounted by an arrow-head and the curve at bottom of the main vertical stroke becomes the long flourish already noticed. This last feature is preserved in the modern Bengali form of *ña*.

ṭa This form seems to be quite unique. It may be noted however that the original semicircle like a Roman C was replaced in several of the Southern alphabets by a fanciful wrinkled stroke. But this stroke represents the lower and not the upper segment of the circle. If our letter were turned just upside down, we should get a form not unlike that of the Cera or Western Cālukya, as given by Burnell. This however is of course a mere analogy. The form probably arose from shapes like the Horiuzi and early Nepalese; the determinative wedge having first given rise to the curling form, and then having been replaced in its turn by another wedge.

ṭha, ḍha These are the usual early N. Indian shapes, with the addition in the case of *ṭha* of the determinative wedge at the side, and of the arrow head to the *ḍha*.

ṇa affords another good instance of the double determinative wedge. Just as *ṅ* (guttural) was distinguished by this addition from *ha* or the not very dissimilar *da*, so this letter is parted from the dental nasal. There is a considerable resemblance between these two nasals from the Açoka downwards, as may be seen from Dr Burgess's Table, where also we observe that the distinction is made as a rule by the lengthening or twisting of the top of the cerebral letter.

In the dental group:

ta, *na* have a resemblance which from Gupta times is as troublesome as it is common. *Ta* is in fact nearly identical in form with the modern Nāgarī न, though the left-hand member generally preserves something of the characteristic downward slope.

tha This is the ordinary Gupta form, replacing the earlier dotted circle, together with a determinative side-wedge.

da is of the ordinary shape, with arrow-head.

dha differs from *ṭha* only by its smaller size and less fully circular shape. It is in fact a slight modification of the Açoka semicircle that occurs tolerably early.

pa The double form of this letter is, as already observed, remarkable. Just as in ordinary Nāgarī, क and ग assume more simple and archaic forms when compounded with certain other letters, so here in the forms for *pā* and *pi*, we find a distinct survival of the simple 'pot-hook' of the Açoka symbol, while the normal form of the character (that used with other vowels) reproduces the next stage of the letter, still archaic, and without the modern top stroke or rounded base. The absence of the supporting vertical line has been noted above (p. 113).

pha The aspirate as in the Horiuzi MS. is marked by an added curve, the exact position of which seems unique, though the general form of the letter is not remarkable, and can be traced in modern Bengali.

ba is more clearly distinguished from *va* and comes nearer the square form of the Açoka and early alphabets, than in any of the ancient MSS. hitherto discovered.

bha The general shape agrees with the Nepalese and Horiuzi MSS.; although the open loop, like that in the Nāgarī न, seems to be a peculiarity. The nearest form that I have found is that of the Samangaḍh plate (VII, 50 in Bühler's Table).

ma Dr Bühler (*Horiuzi* MSS., p. 82) notes that 'in the literary alphabets the lower half of the ancient *ma* has always been turned sideways'. Here, then, we find for the first time in MSS.[1]) at all events, a transitional form, in which the loop is on its way, as it were, from the position immediately below, as seen in all early inscriptions, to that alongside the body of the letter, as hitherto found in MSS.,

---

[1]) The Nandi-nāgarī constitutes, indeed, a slight exception to this. But the loop is very diminutive, and the remainder of the letter square as in ordinary Nagari.

in which indeed this loop has always diminished in size and generally passed into a mere round dot. The form with *Virāma,* which I also give in the Table, is still nearer the archaic type.

ya As Dr Bühler observes, this a 'test-letter'. From the table in Burgess it will be seen that down to Gupta times, the straight perpendicular line forming the stem of the letter divided the curves tolerably equally. About the beginning of Gupta era however the left-hand curve became much diminished and finally disappeared. The present form is thus not only more archa icthan any known MSS., but represents a stage slightly earlier than the Gupta or early Cālukya inscriptions (Burnell, Pl. III—V).

ra The left-hand member commented on at length by Dr Bühler is here developed, perhaps as a kind of penman's flourish, so much further than in other known alphabets, as to constitute this a unique form.

la This letter shows the archaic form of the Gupta Indo-Khera plate (Bühler, p. 83 and Table IV. b. 44) plus the double-wedged top already commented on.

va Except that the characteristic arrow-head takes the place of the vertical top-line of the Açoka, this letter preserves the form of the very earliest alphabets. The rounded loop, without side-line, distinguishes it from MSS. hitherto known.

ça This form is, I think, quite unique, at all events as regards the dot in the middle. This feature may be compared with the early dotted form of *tha,* where the dot develops in Gupta times into a line. As the occurrence of this letter is rare or doubtful before Gupta times, it may be not too much to suppose a complete parallelism, which would lead us to see in this form a survival of an early form of *ça* coeval with the early *tha.* It may be observed that the dot is distinctly visible in our inscription, where the use of a line would have been equally easy to the engraver and perhaps somewhat clearer to the reader.

sha is separated from the ordinary Nagari and kindred forms by the absence of the vertical side-line, while the small nick or twist on the right-hand side distinguishes it from the earliest forms, which, before the introduction of the modern cross-stroke, show a somewhat similar circle on the left.

sa This letter nearly agrees with the curious and somewhat isolated form of the Gupta Kuhaon inscription given in the tables of Burgess and of Bühler. To preserve, however, the distinction from *ma* the loop is always level with the body of the letter.

ha calls for no special comment, being of simple form commonly occurring in early alphabets of both Northern and Southern India.

III. Medial vowels.

ā is denoted by the half down-stroke commonly seen in early alphabets. It may be observed that this half down-stroke does not always commence from a point level with the top of the letter that, in pronunciation, it is immediately to follow, but in the case of conjunct groups it often occurs above the line. See especially the group of *r*-conjuncts in the third division of the table *(rthā, ryā).*

i The expression of this letter is one of the most ingenious and peculiar features of the alphabet. Instead of adding a curve above the consonant, as was done in most of the early writings, we find simply the characteristic arrow-head or triangle left open, and forming thus a triangle properly so called, the three sides being distinct and clear. In the case of letters such as *ṭa* and *ṇa* that have no arrow-head, the open triangle is formed by adding two lines to the determinative side-wedge. I may add that in my photograph of the inscription the *i* in the word *nirodha,* occurring in the Buddhist confession, is extremely clear: and shows that we are here dealing with no mere penman's device, but an established mode of expressing the vowel.

ĭ This sign amounts almost to a doubling of the last, there being an approach as it were to the superposition of a second triangle. In the Maurya we likewise find a doubling of the sign for *ĭ* to express *ī*.

u This vowel occurs in two quite distinct forms. 1. A small curve turned not to the left, but to the right, and thus resembling the sign for *ṛi* in Nagari. This form is restricted, as far as I have been able to find, to use with the consonants *ga, ta* and *ra* (compound). 2. The flourish turning to the left and attached to the bottom of the letter by a small vertical. This particular form of flourish seems characteristic of the alphabet and has been already noted in *a* and *i* medial, and in *ka*. With regard to the use of form 1 for *gu* and *tu*, it will be seen from Burnell's Tables, Pl. III—VI that in the Cālukya a right-hand curve is generally used for these, while nearly all the remaining consonants, just as in the present alphabet, use a curve turning to the left. The form of *ru* (as an uncompounded syllable) is peculiar.

ū This letter is denoted by the addition of a small stroke (horizontal except for *rū*) to the *ŭ* symbol.

ṛi, ṛī I have noted above in my preliminary observations the very remarkable and archaic feature of the identity of *ṛi* medial with the sign for *ra* suffixed to consonants. For the long vowel, it will be seen that the sign is simply doubled.

e, ai, o and *au* are expressed in the manner usual in N. Indian alphabets of the middle ages. For *e* and *ai* the marks are angular instead of rounded, preserving herein the general character of the writing.

IV. Conjunct consonants.

Specimens of these are given in the third division of the table. In groups like *stha, shka* we may note that the modern practice of placing the letters alongside of one another, instead of the first above the second, has not come into use.

R-prefixed is always denoted by an additional arrow-head: generally immediately above; but sometimes slightly to the right of the main consonant.

The above detailed examination will have shown that almost every letter has some peculiarity, while some, as *e* initial, *ja*, *jha*, *ṭa*, *ra*, *ça* and *i* medial present forms that may be ranked as unique.

I could have wished that it had been possible to me to publish facsimiles of both MS. and inscription. The former is represented only by the short passage reproduced in the photolithograph given below my table of letters; for the latter my copies are hardly adequate, even if I were allowed more than the lithograph that I publish herewith. The foregoing essay may serve as a preliminary study of this new form of Indian writing until more specimens are discovered: and may stimulate search for what is most needed, dated inscriptions and MSS.

My own impression is that the present documents are of about the same period. Even the Horiuzi MSS. are now thought by some Chinese scholars to be of a less early date than was at first stated, and thus we are not bound to assume after all that in the period between the sixth and twelfth centuries A. D., in which, I take it, this writing falls, the difference between the written and the incised character was generally very considerable. And this, if we put aside for a moment the now[1]) disputed pedigree of the Horiuzi MSS., is just the conclusion to which we are led by the study of most early MSS. and contemporary inscriptions, especially those from Nepal. In that country this holds good not only for the group of documents of both kinds of the VIII—IXth cent. previously compared by the present writer and re-examined by Dr Bühler in his account of the Horiuzi MSS.,

---

1) See the *Athenæum* for July and August 1885, pp. 17, 82, 176.

but also for XI—XIIth century writing, as may be seen from my recently discovered Nepalese inscriptions of this period[1]) which are not more archaic than contemporary MSS.

Further remarks on this subject would be premature. We must await fresh discoveries and fit our theories to facts.

Note on the Candrālaṃkāra.

The work of which our MS. is a fragment is the *Candrālaṃkāra,* a brief commentary or *ṭippaṇaka* on the grammatical *sūtras* of Candragomin. At leaf 17^{b} where[2]) a section of the work ends we get the following description:

Cāndre vyākaraṇe Candrālaṅkāra-nāmni ṭippitake shashṭhasyādhyāyasya tritīyaḥ pādaḥ samāptaḥ ‖

Ṭippitaka is a slip of the pen, of course, for *ṭippinaka. Ṭipinī* is a form for the more usual *ṭippanī* that I have met with elsewhere in colophons. It would seem then that the work is a 'small commentary' or collection of adversaria on the *Cāndra-vyākaraṇa.* Professor Kielhorn, who looked through the MS. when I brought it to Vienna expressed an opinion that it was in fact a super-commentary, and this view is borne out by the expression *ṭīkā-kṛit* at f. 24^{b} 10.

Not being a specialist in grammatical literature I hardly feel qualified to give a full account of the contents of the MS. But I have compared it with texts and commentaries of the *Cāndra vyākaraṇa* in the Wright collection at Cambridge, and I now subjoin a list of the authors quoted by our commentator and a few other passages of interest that I have noted.

fol. 7^{b} 5. *Bhagavān Pāṇiniḥ.*

---

1) See my 'Journey . . in Nepal and Northern India', pp. 8, 81.

2) The numeration of the leaves is all lost with the exception of a few pieces of figures, sufficient only to enable me to see that the system of letter-numerals, or *aksharas* was employed. The above numbering simply records, until the MS. has been throughly read, the order of the leaves in the MS. at the time of purchase.

10[a] 3. *'Kālāpāḥ'*, i. e. the followers of the Kalāpa grammar (cf. 33[b] 8 quoted below).

10[a] 7. *Iti Dhātupradīpaḥ.* This is the commentary on the *Dhatupāṭha* by *Maitreyarakshita* used by Colebrooke (*Essays*, II, 9, 36 etc.).

10[a] 8. *Tathā ca Çabdasāgaraḥ.*

13[b] fin. *Vṛihaspatir Indram pratipadam çabdapārāyaṇam provāca.*

18[b] 3. *Iti Pūrṇacandraḥ.* I purchased in Nepal a portion of the *Dhātupārāyaṇa,* a rare work, of this author. I have lent it to Professor Aufrecht at present.

19[b] 5. *Catushkaṇ ṭakam iti siddham avyutpannāny auṇadikānīti Rakshitaḥ.*[1])

22*[b] 5—6. *Hariçcandreti rājarshir āsīd iti cānukaraṇam iti Purushottamaḥ.*

24[a] 4. *Ata eva çnānnaḥ çnāsor lopa ity atra çitkaraṇasya viçeshaṇārthatvād iti çnama vidhau Jayādityaḥ.*

33[b] 3. *YUSHMA*[2]) ‖ *pūrvva prasiddha çlokānurodhād vakshyamāṇam ihaiva darçitaṃ ekavishayatvāt* | *yuvayor āvayor iti jñeyaṃ* | *tavātra mamātreti ca* | *ekavacanasya te me ity atrāsambhavād iti valāditvasya* | *yadvā na hi yatra yad vihitaṃ tatra tad atidiçyata iti caturthī dvivacane pi aprasaṅgaḥ dvitīyā caturthīshashṭhyantayor ity athavā yugavibhaktitvād āsāṃ yugantayor iti Kātyāyana-sūtravat karttavye vibhaktinirdeço jñāpakam. Geye kena vinītau vām iti Raghuḥ*[3]) | *yuvām ity arthe ca prathamāyāṃ* | *tathātra tritīyāyām* | *yadvarṇair havarṇāt sa* (?) *purā nandena bhashitāḥ* | *çrutaṃ te vacas tasyeti* | *mayā tvaya ity arthe mānto 'yam ādeçaḥ mama tāvan matam adaḥ çrūyatām aṅga vām asi* [sic] *jñātasāro 'pi khalv ekaḥ* | *çandigdhe* [sic] *kāryavastunīti Maghaḥ*[4]) | *vām nau dvitva iti Kālāpāḥ* ‖

34[b] 5. *Vakshyamāṇa-vā-çabdānuvṛittyā jātī yatrāna vā dhā(?) iti Rājaçrīḥ.*

---

[1]) Compare Colebrooke's *Essays* II, 38, note.
[2]) Cf. *Pāṇini* VIII. 1, 20.
[3]) *Raghu-vaṃça,* XV. 69.
[4]) *Çiçupālab*° II. 12.

Cf. 16ᵇ 2. *PHULLA*[1]) ‖ *phullavān iti bhavati kta kta vatvor (?) ādeçatvād iti Rājaçrīḥ.*

Also of the same authority in the plural (honorific?):

33ᵃ 6. *ANYA* ‖ *sūtram idam akṛitraivābhivyaktigrahaṇam. pūrvasūtre Rājaçrībhiḥ kṛitam.*

PARASYA ‖ *parapadasya vibhakter āmā guṇo vidhīyate Rājaçrībhiḥ.*

34ᵇ 8. *iti Jitāriḥ.*

Durgasiṃha and the *Durga-ṭīkā* are thrice mentioned 12ᵃ 10, 33ᵃ 10, and 34ᵇ 10.

Lastly, we have an *udāharaṇa* taken doubtless from the extensive lost literature of the sūtras of Northern Buddhism (34ᵇ 2—3):

Ata eva vyavadhāne pi viparyaye ca pravarttate evaṃ etat Subhūte evaṃ etat | sādhu khalu punas tu Subhūte sādhu | . . [sā]dhu sādhu Subhūte sādhu evaṃ etat Bhagavann evaṃ etat Sugateti Haribhadrapādāḥ ‖

This is doubtless the Haribhadra of the Madhyamaka school mentioned by *Tāranātha* (Wassiliew, p. 324 [355]).

---

[1]) Cf. *Pāṇini* VIII. ɪɪ. 55.

ARROW-HEADED OR POINT-HEADED CHARACTER.

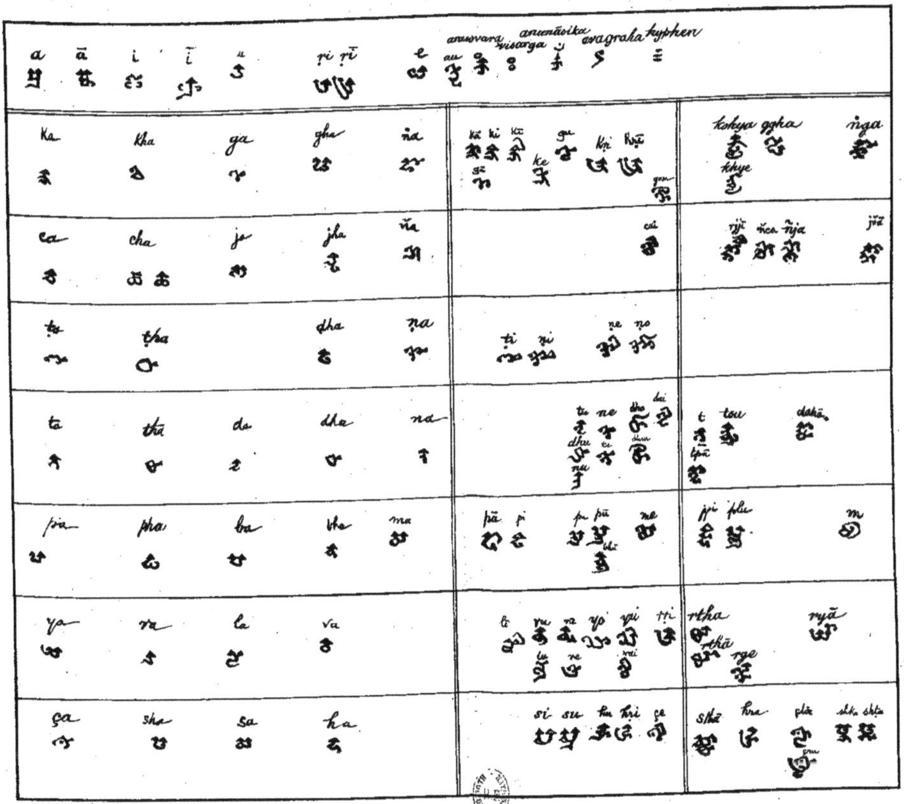

Lithographed from Drawings by the Author, by W. [illegible], 36 Basinghall St. London.

Photo-Lithograph of a portion of Text, showing title of 5th Adhyāya

On the Bakhshālī Manuscript.

By

Dr. R. Hoernle.

With three photozincographs.

The manuscript which I have the honour, this morning, of placing before you, was found, as you will recollect, in May 1881, near a village called Bakhshālī, lying in the Yusufzāī district of the Peshawer division, at the extreme Northwestern frontier of India. It was dug out by a peasant in a ruined enclosure, where it lay between stones. After the find it was at once forwarded to the Lieutenant Governor of the Panjab who transmitted it to me for examination and eventual publication.

The manuscript is written in Shārada character of a rather ancient type, and on leaves of birch-bark which from age have become dry like tinder and extremely fragile. Unfortunately, probably through the careless handling of the finder, it is now in an excessively mutilated condition, both with regard to the size and the number of the leaves. Their present size, as you observe (see Plate I), is about 6 by $3^1/_2$ inches; their original size, however, must have been about 7 by $8^1/_4$ inches. This might have been presumed from the well-known fact that the old birck-bark manuscripts were always written on leaves of a squarish size. But I was enabled to determine the point by a curious fact. The mutilated leaf which contains a portion of the $27^1/_2$ sūtra, shows at top and bottom the remainders of two large square figures, such as are used in writing arithmetical notations. These when completed prove that the leaf in its original state must have measured approximately 7 by $8^1/_4$ inches. The number of the existing leaves is seventy. This can only be a small portion of the whole manuscript. ,For neither beginning nor end is preserved; nor are some leaves forthcoming which are specifically referred to in the existing fragments.[1]) From all appearances, it must have been a large work, perhaps divided in chapters or sections. The existing leaves include only the middle portion of the work or of a division of it. The earliest sūtra that I have found is the 9th; the latest is the 57th. The lateral margins which usually exhibit the numbering of the leaves are broken off. It is thus impossible even to guess what the original number of the leaves may have been.

The leaves of the manuscript, when received by me, were found to be in great confusion. Considering that of each leaf the top and bottom (nearly two thirds of the whole leaf) are lost, thus destroying their connection with one another, it may be imagined that it was no easy task to read and arrange in order the fragments. After much trouble I have read and transcribed the whole, and have even succeeded in arranging in consecutive order a not inconsiderable portion of the leaves containing eighteen sūtras. The latter portion I have also translated in English.

The beginning and end of the manuscript being lost, both the name of the work and of its author are unknown. The subject of the work, however, is arithmetic. It contains a great variety of problems relating to daily life. The following are examples. ,In a carriage, instead of 10 horses, there are yoked 5; the distance traversed by the former was one hundred, how much will the other horses be able to accomplish?‘ Te following is more complicated: ,A certain person travels 5 yojanas on the

[1]) Thus at the end of the 10th sūtra, instead of the usual explanation, there is the following note: *evaṁ sūtraṁ | dvitīya patre vivaritāsti.* The leaf referred to is not preserved.

first day, and 3 more on each succeeding day; another who travels 7 yojanas on each day, has a start of 5 days; in what time will they meet?' The following is still more complicated: 'Of 3 merchants the first possesses 7 horses, the second 9 ponies, the third 10 camels; each of them gives away 3 animals to be equally distributed among themselves; the result is that the value of their respective properties becomes equal; how much was the value of each merchant's original property, and what was the value of each animal?' The method prescribed in the rules for the solution of these problems is extremely mechanical, and reduces the labour of thinking to a minimum. For example, the last mentioned problem is solved thus: 'Subtract the gift (3) severally from the original quantities (7, 9, 10). Multiply the remainders (4, 6, 7) among themselves (168, 168, 168). Divide each of these products by the corresponding remainder ($\frac{168}{4}$, $\frac{168}{6}$, $\frac{168}{7}$). The results (42, 28, 24) are the values of the 3 classes of animals. Being multiplied with the numbers of the animals originally possessed by the merchants (42 . 7, 28 . 9, 24 . 10), we obtain the values of their original properties (294, 252, 240). The value of the properts of each merchant after the gift is equal (262, 262, 262).' The rules are expressed in very concise language, but are fully explained by means of examples. Generally there are two examples to each rule (or sûtra), but sometimes there are many; the 25th sûtra has no less than 15 examples. The rules and examples are written in verse; the explanations, solutions and all the rest are in prose. The metre used is the *shloka*.

The subject-matter is divided in *sûtras*. In each sûtra the matter is arranged as follows. First comes the rule, and then the example, introduced by the word *tadâ*. Next, the example is repeated in the form of a notation in figures, which is called *sthâpana*. This is followed by the solution which is called *karaṇa*. Finally comes the proof, called *pratyaya*. This arrangement and terminology differ somewhat from those used in the arithmetic of Brahmagupta and Bhâskara. Instead of simply *sûtra*, the latter use the term *karaṇa-sûtra*. The example they call *uddeshaka* or *udâharaṇa*. For *sthâpana* they say *nyâsa*. As a rule they give no full solution or proof, but the mere answer to the problem. Occasionally a solution is given, but it is not called *karaṇa.*

The system of notation used in the Bakhshālī arithmetic is much the same as that employed in the arithmetical works of Brahmagupta and Bhāskara. There is, however, a very important exception. The sign for the negative quantity is a cross (+). It looks exactly like our modern sign for the positive quantity, but is placed after the number which it qualifies. Thus $\begin{smallmatrix}12\\1\end{smallmatrix}\ \begin{smallmatrix}7\\1\end{smallmatrix}+$ means 12—7 (i. e. 5). This is a sign which I have not met with in any other Indian arithmetic; nor so far as I have been able to ascertain, is it known in India at all. The sign now used is a dot placed over the number to which it refers. Here, therefore, there appears to be a mark of great antiquity. As to its origin I am unable to suggest any satisfactory explanation. I have been informed by Dr. Thibaut of Benares, that Diophantus in his Greek arithmetic uses the letter ψ (short for λείψις) reversed (thus ψ), to indicate the negative quantity. There is undoubtedly a slight resemblance between the two signs; but considering that the Hindūs did not get their elements of the arithmetical science from the Greeks, a native origin of the negative sign seems more probable. It is not uncommon in Indian arithmetic to indicate a particular factum by the initial syllable of a word of that import subjoined to the terms which compose it. Thus addition may be indicated by *yu* (short for *yuta*), e. q. $\begin{smallmatrix}5\\1\end{smallmatrix}\ \begin{smallmatrix}7\\1\end{smallmatrix}\ yu$ means 5 + 7 (e. e. 12). In the case of substraction or the negative quantity *ṛiṇa* would be the indicatory word and *ṛi* the indicatory syllable. The difficulty is to explain the connection between the letter *ṛi* (ऋ) and the symbol +. The latter very closely resembles the letter *k* (क) in its ancient shape (+) as used in the Ashoka alphabet. The word *kaṇa* or *kaṇīyas* which had once occurred to me, is hardly satisfactory.

A whole number, when it occurs in an arithmetical operation, as may be seen from the above given examples, is indicated by placing the number 1 under it. This, however, is a practice which is still occasionally observed in India. It may be worth noting that the number one is always designated by the word *rūpa*;[1]) thus *sarūpa* or *rūpādhika* 'adding one', *rūpoṇa* 'deducting one'. The only other instance of the use of a symbolic numeral word is the word *rasa* for six which occurs once in an example in sūtra 53.

The following statement, from the first example of the 25th Sūtra, affords a good example of the system of notation employed in the Bakhshālī arithmetic:

$$\left|\begin{array}{cccc} & 1 & 1 & 1 \\ \bullet & 1 & 1 & 1 \\ 1 & 3+ & 3+ & 3+ \end{array}\ \textit{bhā}\ 32\ \right| \ \textit{phalaṁ}\ 108$$

Here the initial dot is used very much in the same way as we use the letter x to denote the unknown quantity the value of which is sought. The number 1 under the dot is the sign of the whole (in this case, unknown) number. A fraction is denoted by placing one number under the other without any line of separation; thus $\begin{smallmatrix}1\\3\end{smallmatrix}$ is $\frac{1}{3}$, i. e. one-third. A mixed number is shown by placing the three numbers under one another; thus $\begin{smallmatrix}1\\1\\3\end{smallmatrix}$ is $1 + \frac{1}{3}$ or $1\frac{1}{3}$, i. e. one and one-third. Hence $\begin{smallmatrix}1\\1\\3+\end{smallmatrix}$ means $1 - \frac{1}{3}$ (i. e. $\frac{2}{3}$). Multiplication is usually indicated by placing the numbers side by side; thus $\left|\begin{smallmatrix}5 & 32\\8 & 1\end{smallmatrix}\right|$ *phalaṁ* 20 means $\frac{5}{8} \times 32 = 20$. Similarly $\begin{smallmatrix}1\\1\\3+\end{smallmatrix}\ \begin{smallmatrix}1\\1\\3+\end{smallmatrix}\ \begin{smallmatrix}1\\1\\3+\end{smallmatrix}$ means $\frac{2}{3} \times \frac{2}{3} \times \frac{2}{3}$ or $(\frac{2}{3})^3$, i. e. $\frac{8}{27}$. *Bhā* is an abbreviation of *bhāga* 'part' and means that the number preceding it is to be divided. Hence $\begin{smallmatrix}1\\1\\3+\end{smallmatrix}\ \begin{smallmatrix}1\\1\\3+\end{smallmatrix}\ \begin{smallmatrix}1\\1\\3+\end{smallmatrix}$ *bhā* means $\begin{smallmatrix}27\\8\end{smallmatrix}$. The whole statement, therefore,

$$\left|\begin{array}{cccc} & 1 & 1 & 1 \\ \bullet & 1 & 1 & 1 \\ 1 & 3+ & 3+ & 3+ \end{array}\ \textit{bhā}\ 32\ \right| \ \textit{phalaṁ}\ 108$$

means $\frac{27}{8} \times 32 = 108$, and may be thus explained: 'a certain number is found by dividing with $\frac{8}{27}$ and multiplying with 32; that number is 108'.

The dot is also used for another purpose, namely as one of the ten fundamental figures of the decimal system of notation

[1]) This word was at first read by me *ūpa*. The reading *rūpa* was suggested to me by Professor A. Weber, and though not so well agreeing with the manuscript characters, is probably the correct one.

or the zero (0 1 2 3 4 5 6 7 8 9). It is still so used in India for both purposes, to indicate the unknown quantity as well as the naught. With us the dot, or rather its substitute the circle (◦), has only retained the latter of its two intents, being simply the zero figure, or the 'mark of position' in the decimal system. The Indian usage, however, seems to show, how the zero arose and that it arose in India. The Indian dot, unlike our modern zero, is not properly a numerical figure at all. It is simply a sign to indicate an empty place or a hiatus. This is clearly shown by its name *shūnya* 'empty'. The empty place in an arithmetical statement might or might not be capable of being filled up, according to circumstances. Occurring in a row of figures arranged decimally or according to the 'value of position', the empty place could not be filled up, and the dot therefore signified 'naught', or stood in the place of the zero. Thus the two figures 3 and 7, placed in juxtaposition (37) mean 'thirty seven', but with an 'empty space' interposed between them (3 7), they mean 'three hundred and seven'. To prevent misunderstanding the presence of the 'empty space' was indicated by a dot (3·7), or by what in now the zero (307). On the other hand, occurring in the statement of a problem, the 'empty place' could be filled up, and here the dot which marked its presence, signified a 'something' which was to be discovered and to be put in the empty place. In the course of time, and out of India, the latter signification of the dot was discarded; and the dot thus became simply the sign for 'naught' or the zero, and assumed the value of a proper figure of the decimal system of notation, being the 'mark of position'. In its double signification which still survives in India, we can still discern an indication of that country as its birth place.

Regarding the age of the manuscript am unable to offer a very definite opinion. The composition of a Hindū work on arithmetic, such as that contained in the Bakhshālī MS. seems necessarily to presuppose a country and a period in which Hindū civilisation and Brahmanical learning flourished. Now the country in which Bakhshālī lies and which formed part of the Hindū kingdom of Kabul, was early lost to Hindū civilisation through the conquests of the Muhammedan rulers of Ghazni, and especially through the celebrated expeditions of Mahmūd, towards the end of the 10th and the beginning of the 11th centuries A. D. In those troublous times it was a common practice for the learned Hindūs to bury their manuscript treasures. Possibly the Bakhshālī MS. may be one of these. In any case it cannot well be placed much later than the 10th century A. D. It is quite possible that it may be somewhat older. The Shārada characters used in it, exhibit in several respects a rather archaic type, and afford some ground for thinking that the manuscript may perhaps go back to the 8th or 9th century. But in the present state of our epigraphical knowledge, arguments of this kind are always somewhat hazardous. The usual form, in which the numeral figures occur in the manuscript are the following:

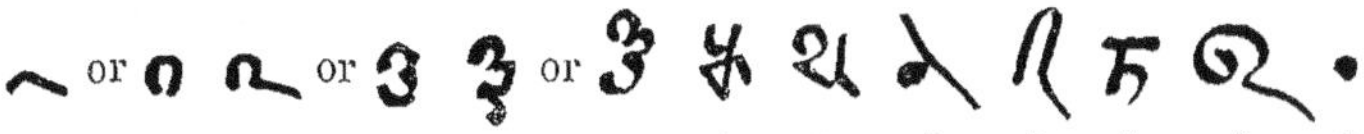

1 2 3 4 5 6 7 8 9 0

Quite distinct from the question of the age of the manuscript is that of the age of the work contained in it. There is every reason to believe that the Bakhshālī arithmetic is of a very considerably earlier date than the manuscript in which it has come down to us. I am disposed to believe that the composition of the former must be referred to the earliest centuries of our era, and that it may date from the 3d or 4th century A. D. The arguments making for this conclusion are briefly the following.

In the first place, it appears that the earliest mathematical works of the Hindūs were written in the *Shloka* measure;[1] but from about the end of the 5th century A. D. it became the fashion to use the Ārya measure. Āryabhaṭṭa c. 500 A. D., Varāha Mihira c. 550, Brahmagupta c. 630, all wrote in the latter measure. Not only were new works written in it, but also Shloka works were revised and recast in it. Now the Bakhshālī arith-

[1]) See Professor Kern's Introduction to Varāha Mihira.

metic is written in the Shloka measure; and this circumstance carries its composition back to a time anterior to that change of literary fashion in the 5th century A. D.

In the second place, the Bakhshālī arithmetic is written in that peculiar language which used to be called the 'Gāthā dialect', but which is rather the literary form of the ancient Northwestern Prākrit (or Pāli). It exhibits a strange mixture of what we should now call Sanskrit and Prākrit forms. As shown by the inscription (e. g., of the Indoscythian kings in Mathurā) of that period, it appears to have been in general use, in Northwestern India, for literary purposes till about the end of the 3d century A. D., when the proper Sanskrit, hitherto the language of the Brahmanic schools, gradually came into general use also for secular compositions. The older literary language may have lingered on some time longer among the Buddhists and Jains, but this would only have been so in the case of religious, not of secular compositions. Its use, therefore, in the Bakhshālī arithmetic points to a date not later than the 3d or 4th century A. D. for the composition of that work.

In the third place, in several examples, the two words *dīnāra* and *dramma* occur as denominations of money. These words are the Indian forms of the latin *denarius* and the greek *drachme.* The former, as current in India, was a gold coin, the latter a silver coin. Golden *denarii* were first coined at Rome in 207 B. C. The Indian gold pieces, corresponding in weight to the Roman gold *denarius,* were those coined by the Indoscythian kings, whose line beginning with Kadphises, about the middle of the 1st century B. C., probably extended to about the end of the 3d century A. D. Roman gold *denarii* themselves, as shown by the numerous finds, were by no means uncommon in India, in the earliest centuries of our era. The gold dīnārs most numerously found are those of the Indoscythian kings Kanishka and Huvishka, and of the Roman emperors Trajan, Hadrian and Antonius Pius, all of whom reigned in the 2nd century A. D. The way in which the two terms are used in the Bakhshālī arithmetic seems to indicate that the gold *dīnāra* and the silver *dramma* formed the ordinary currency of the day. This circumstance again points to some time within the three first centuries of the Christian era as the date of its composition.

A fourth point, also indicative of antiquity which I have already adverted to, is the peculiar use of the cross (+) as the sign of the negative quantity.

There is another point which may be worth mentioning though I do not know whether it may help in determining the probable date of the work. The year is reckoned in the Bakhshālī arithmetic as consisting of 360 days. Thus in one place the following calculation is given: 'If in $\frac{800}{727}$ of a year 2982 $\frac{480}{727}$ is spent, how much is spent in one day?' Here it is explained that the lower denomination *(adha-ch-chheda)* is 360 days, and the result *(phala)* is given as $\frac{1807}{240}$ (i. e. $\frac{2168400 \cdot 727}{727 \cdot 800 \cdot 360}$).

In connection with this question of the age of the Bakhshālī work, I may note a circumstance which appears to point to a peculiar connection of it with the Brahmasiddhānta of Brahmagupta. There is a curious resemblance between the 50th sūtra of the Bakhshālī arithmetic, or rather with the algebraical example occurring in that sūtra, and the 49th sūtra of the chapter on algebra in the Brahmasiddhānta. In that sūtra, Brahmagupta first quotes a rule in prose, and then adds another version of it in the Āryā measure. Unfortunately the rule is not preserved in the Bakhshālī MS., but as in the case of all other rules, it would have been in the form of a shloka and in the North-western Prākrit (or 'Gāthā dialect'). Brahmagupta in quoting it, would naturally put it in what he considered correct Sanskrit prose, and would then give his own version of it in his favourite Āryā measure. I believe it is generally admitted that Indian arithmetic and algebra, at least, is of entirely native origin. While siddhānta writers, like Brahmagupta and his predecessor Aryabhaṭṭa, might have borrowed their astronomical elements from the Greeks or from books founded themselves on Greek science, they took their arithmetic from native Indian sources. Of the Jains it is well known that they possess astronomical books of a very ancient type, showing no traces of western or Greek influence. In India arithmetic and algebra are usually treated as portions of works on astronomy. In any case it is impossible that the Jains should not have possessed their own treatises on arithmetic when they possessed such on astronomy. The early Buddhists, too, are known to have been proficients in mathematics. The prevalence of Buddhism in Northwestern India, in the early centuries of our era, is a well known fact. That in those early times there were also large Jain communities in those regions is testified by the remnants of Jain sculpture found near Mathurā and elsewhere. From the fact of the general use of the Northwestern Prākrit (or the 'Gāthā dialect') for literary purposes among the early Buddhists it may reasonably be concluded that its use prevailed also among the Jains between whom and the Buddhists there was so much similarity of manners and customs. There is also a diffusedness in the mode of composition of the Bakhshālī work which reminds one of the similar characteristic observed in Buddhist and Jain literature. All these circumstances put together seem to render it probable that in the Bakhshālī MS. we have preserved to us a fragment of an early Buddhist or Jain work on arithmetic (perhaps a portion of a larger work on astronomy) which may have been one of the sources from which the later Indian astronomers took their arithmetical information. These earlier sources, as we know, were written in the shloka measure, and when they belonged to the Buddhist or Jain literature, must have been composed in the ancient Northwestern Prākrit. Both these points are characteristics of the Bakhshālī work. I may add that one of the reasons why the earlier works were, as we are told by tradition, revised and rewritten in the Āryā measure by later writers such as Brahmagupta, may have been that in their time the literary form (Gāthā dialect) of the Northwestern Prākrit had come to be looked upon as a barbarous and ungrammatical jargon as compared with their own classical Sanskrit. In any case the Buddhist or Jain character of the Bakhshālī arithmetic would be a further mark of its high antiquity.

Throughout the Bakhshālī arithmetic the decimal system of notation is employed. This system rests on the principle of the 'value of position' of the numbers. It is certain that this principle was known in India as early as 500 A. D. There is no good reason why it should not have been discovered there considerably earlier. In fact, if the antiquity of the Bakhshālī arithmetic be admitted on other grounds, it affords evidence of an earlier date of the discovery of that principle. As regards the *zero,* in its modern sense of a 'mark of position' and one of the ten fundamental figures of the decimal system (0 1 2 3 4 5 6 7 8 9), its discovery is undoubtedly much later than the discovery of the 'value of position'. It is quite certain, however, that the application of the latter principle to numbers in ordinary writing would have been nearly impossible without the employment of some kind of 'mark of position', or some mark to indicate the 'empty place' *(shūnya).* Thus the figure 7 may mean either 'seven' or 'seventy' or 'seven hundred' according as it be or be not supposed to be preceded by one (7 · or 70) or two (7 · · or 700) 'empty places'. Unless the presence of these 'empty places' or the 'position' of the figure 7 be indicated, it would be impossible to read its 'value' correctly. Now what the Indians did, and indeed still do, was simply to use for this purpose the sign which they were in the habit of using for the purpose of indicating *any* empty place or omission whatsoever in a written composition; that is the dot. It seems obvious from the exigencies of writing that the use of the well known dot as the mark of an empty place must have suggested itself to the Indians as soon as they began to employ their discovery of the principle of 'value position' in ordinary writing. In India the use of the dot as a substitute of the zero must have long preceded the discovery of the proper zero, and must have been contemporaneous with the discovery of that principle. There is nothing in the Bakhshālī arithmetic to show that the dot is used as a proper zero, and that it is any thing more than the ordinary 'mark of an empty place'. The employment, therefore, of the decimal system of notation, such as it is, in the Bakhshālī arithmetic is quite consistent with the suggested antiquity of it.

I have already stated that the Bakhshālī arithmetic is written in the so-called 'Gāthā dialect', or in that literary form of the Northwestern Prākrit, which preceded the employment, in secular composition, of the classical Sanskrit. Its literary form consisted in what may be called (from the Sanskrit point of view) an imperfect sanskritisation of the vernacular Prākrit. Hence it exhibits at every turn the peculiar characteristics of the underlying vernacular. The following are some specimens of orthographical peculiarities.

Insertion of euphonic consonants: of *m*, in *eka-m-ekatvaṁ*, *bhṛitako-m-ekapaṇḍitaḥ*; of *r*, in *tṛi-r-āshīti*, *labhate-r-aṣṭau*.

Insertion of *s*: *vibhaktaṁ-s-uttare*, *Kṣiyate-s-traya*. This is a peculiarity not elsewhere known to me, either in Prākrit or in Pāli.

Doubling of consonants: in compounds, *prathama-d-dhānte*, *eka-s-saṁkhyā*; in sentences, *yadi-ṣ-ṣaḍbhi*, *ete-s-samadhanā*.

Peculiar spellings: *tṛiṅshā* or *tṛiṅsha* for *triṁshat*. The spelling with the guttural nasal before *sh* occurs only in this word; c. q., *chatvāliṁsha* 40. Again *ṛi* for *ri* in *tṛidine*, *kṛiyate*, *vimishṛitaṁ*, *kṛiṇāti*; and *ri* for *ṛi* in *riṇaṁ*, *driṣṭaḥ*. Again *katthyatāṁ* for *kathyatāṁ*. Again the *jihvāmūlīyo* and the *upadhmānīya* are always used before gutturals and palatals respectively.

Irregular sandhi: *ko so rā°* for *kaḥ sa rā°*, *dvayo kechi* for *dvayaḥ k°*, *dvayo cha* for *dvayash cha*, *dvibhi kri°* for *dvibhiḥ kri°*, *ādyo vi°* for *ādyor vi°*, *vivaritāsti* for *vivaritam asti*.

Confusion of the sibilants: *sh* for *ṣ*, in *shaṣṭi* 60, *māshako*; *ṣ* for *sh*, in *dashāṃṣha*, *viṣodhayet*, *ṣeṣaṁ*; *sh* for *s*, in *sāshyaṁ*, *sāsyatāṁ*; *s* for *sh*, in *esa* ,this'.

Confusion of *ṇ* and *n*: *utpaṇṇa*.

Elision of a final consonant: *bhājaye*, *kechi* for *bhājayet*, *kechit*.

Interpolation of *r: hrīṇaṁ* for *hīnaṁ*.

The following are specimens of etymological and syntactical peculiarities.

Absence of inflection: nom. sing. masc., *esha sā rāshi* for *rāshiḥ* (s. 50), *gavāṁ visheṣa kartavyaṁ* for *visheṣaḥ* (s. 51). Nom. plur., *sevya santi* for *sevyāḥ* (s. 53). Acc. plur., *dīnāra dattavān* for *dīnārān* (s. 53).

Peculiar inflection: gen. sing., *gatisya* for *gateḥ* (s. 15); ātm. for parasm., *ārjayate* for *arjayati* 'he earns' (s. 53); parasm. for ātm., *vikriṇāti* for *vikrīṇīte* 'he sells' (s. 54).

Change of gender: masc. for neut., *mūlā* for *mūlāni* (s. 55); neut. for masc., *vargaṁ* for *vargaḥ* (s. 50); neut. for fem., *yutiṁ cha kartavyā* for *yutish* (s. 50).

Exchange of numbers: plur. for sing., *(bhavet) lābhāḥ* for *lābhaḥ* (s. 54).

Exchange of cases: acc. for nom., *dvitīyaṁ paṁchadivase rasam ārjayate* for *dvitīyaḥ* (s. 53); acc. for instr., *kṣayaṁ saṁguṇya* for *kṣayeṇa* (s. 27); acc. for loc., *kiṁ kālaṁ* for *kasmin kāle* (s. 52); instr. for loc., *anena kālena* for *asmin kāle* (s. 53); instr. for nom., *prathamena dattavān* for *prathamo* (s. 53), or *ekena yāti* for *eko* (s. 15); loc. for instr., *prathame dattā* for *prathamena* (s. 53), or *mānave gṛihītaṁ* for *mānavena* (s. 57); gen. for dat., *dvitīyasya dattā* for *dvitīyāya* (s. 53).

Abnormal concord: incongruent cases, *ayaṁ praṣṭe* for *asmin* (s. 52); incongruent numbers, *esha lābhāḥ* for *lābhaḥ* (s. 54) *rājaputro kechi* for *rājaputrāḥ* (s. 53); incongruent genders, *sā kālaṁ* for *tat kālaṁ* (s. 52), *visheṣa kartavyaṁ* for *kartavyaḥ* (s. 51), *sā rāshiḥ* for *sa* (s. 50), *kāryaṁ sthitaḥ* for *sthitaṁ* (s. 14).

Peculiar forms: *nivarita* for *nivṛita*, *ārja* for *ārjana*, *divaddha* 'one and one-half', *chatvāliṁsha* 40, *paṁchāshama* 50th, *chaupaṁchāshama* 54th, *chaturāshīti* 84, *tṛi-r-āshīti* 83, etc.

The following extracts may serve as specimens of the text.

Sūtraṁ |

Ādyor visheṣadviguṇaṁ chayashuddhi vibhājitaṁ |
Rūpā*dhikaṁ tathā kā*laṁ gatisāsyaṁ tadā bhavet ||

tadā ||

Dvayāditṛichayash chaiva dvi*chayatryā*dikottaraḥ |
Dvayo cha bhavate paṁthā kena kālena sāsyatāṁ ||

sthāpanaṁ kṛiyate | *eṣāṁ* || ā $\begin{smallmatrix}2\\1\end{smallmatrix}$ || u $\begin{smallmatrix}3\\1\end{smallmatrix}$ || pa $\begin{smallmatrix}\cdot\\1\end{smallmatrix}$ || dvi || ā $\begin{smallmatrix}3\\1\end{smallmatrix}$ || u $\begin{smallmatrix}2\\1\end{smallmatrix}$ || pa $\begin{smallmatrix}\cdot\\1\end{smallmatrix}$ || karaṇaṁ || ādyor visheṣa . . . .
. . . . tā dvi 2 . . . .
. . . .
. . . .

tadā ||

. . . . ||
. . . . ||

ā $\begin{smallmatrix}5\\1\end{smallmatrix}$	u $\begin{smallmatrix}6\\1\end{smallmatrix}$	pa $\begin{smallmatrix}\cdot\\1\end{smallmatrix}$	dha $\begin{smallmatrix}\cdot\\1\end{smallmatrix}$
ā $\begin{smallmatrix}10\\1\end{smallmatrix}$	u $\begin{smallmatrix}3\\1\end{smallmatrix}$	pa $\begin{smallmatrix}\cdot\\1\end{smallmatrix}$	dha $\begin{smallmatrix}\cdot\\1\end{smallmatrix}$

karaṇaṁ | ādyor visheṣaṁ adi 5 | *10 visheṣa* 5 | chayashuddhi chayaṁ 6 | 3 shuddhi 3 ādisheṣa 5 dviguṇaṁ 10 uttaravisheṣa 3 vibhaktaṁ $\begin{smallmatrix}10\\3\end{smallmatrix}$ sarūpaṁ $\begin{smallmatrix}13\\3\end{smallmatrix}$ eṣa padaṁ anena kā*lena* samadhanā bhavanti || pratyayaṁ || rūpoṇakaraṇena phalaṁ || $\begin{smallmatrix}65\\ \text{dvi } 65\end{smallmatrix}$ ||
Aṣṭhādasashamasūtraṁ 18 || ⁜ ||

Idānī*ṁ* suvarṇakṣayaṁ vakṣyā*mi* yasyeda*ṁ* sūtraṁ |

Sūtraṁ |

Kṣayaṁ saṁguṇya kanakās tadyuti-b-bhāja*yet* tataḥ |
Saṁyutair eva kanakair ekaikasya kṣayo hi saḥ ||

tadā ||

*Ekadvitrichatu*ssaṁkhya suvarṇā māṣakai riṇai |
Ekadvitrichatussaṁkh*yai* rahitā samabhāgatāṁ ||

sthāpanaṁ kṛiyate | eṣāṁ || $\begin{smallmatrix}1+\\1\end{smallmatrix}$ || $\begin{smallmatrix}2+\\2\end{smallmatrix}$ || $\begin{smallmatrix}3+\\3\end{smallmatrix}$ || $\begin{smallmatrix}4+\\4\end{smallmatrix}$ || karaṇaṁ || kṣayaṁ saṁguṇya kanakādibhi kṣayena saṁguṇya jātaṁ | 1 | 4 | 9 | 16 | *tadyuti* | eṣa yati 30 kanakā yuti 10 anena bhaktvā labdhaṁ
. . . .
. . . .

. . . .	$\frac{10}{1}$	$\frac{30}{1}$	$\frac{1}{1}$	*pha māse* $\frac{3}{1}$
. . . .	$\frac{10}{1}$	$\frac{30}{1}$	$\frac{2}{1}$	*pha māse* $\frac{6}{1}$
. . . .	$\frac{10}{1}$	$\frac{30}{1}$	$\frac{3}{1}$	*pha māse* $\frac{9}{1}$
. . . .	$\frac{10}{1}$	$\frac{30}{1}$	$\frac{3}{1}$	pha māse $\frac{12}{1}$

tadā ‖

Ekadvitṛ*chatussaṁkhyā* suvarṇa projjhitā ime |
Māsakā dvitṛitāṁ chaiva chatuḥpaṁchakarāṁshakaṁ [1]) kim kṣayaṁ ‖

‖ $\frac{1}{1}$ $\frac{}{2}$ ‖ $\frac{2}{1}$ $\frac{}{3}$ ‖ $\frac{3}{1}$ $\frac{}{4}$ ‖ $\frac{4}{1}$ $\frac{}{5}$ ‖ karaṇaṁ | kṣayaṁ saṁguṇya kanakā esha sthāpyate | | $\frac{1}{2}$ | $\frac{2}{3}$ | $\frac{3}{4}$ | $\frac{4}{5}$ | -s-tadyuti-b-bhājayeta [2]) tataḥ harasāsye kṛite yutaṁ | $\frac{163}{60}$ | saṁyutaiḥ kanakair bhaktvā tadā kanakā 10 anena bhaktaṁ jātaṁ | $\frac{163}{60}$ | esha ekaikasuvarṇasya kṣayaṁ ‖ pra*tyayaṁ trairā*shikena kartavya ‖

$\frac{10}{1}$	$\frac{163}{60}$	$\frac{1}{1}$	*pha* $\frac{163}{600}$	. . . .
$\frac{10}{1}$	$\frac{163}{60}$	$\frac{2}{1}$	*pha* $\frac{163}{600}$	. . . .
$\frac{10}{1}$	$\frac{163}{60}$	$\frac{3}{1}$	*pha* $\frac{163}{600}$	. . . .
$\frac{10}{1}$	$\frac{163}{60}$	$\frac{4}{1}$	pha $\frac{163}{600}$	. . . .

tadā ‖

. . . . |
. . . . shruṇushva me ‖

Krameṇa dvaya māṣādi uttare ekahīnatāṁ |
Suvarṇaṁ me *tu* sammishrya katthyatām gaṇakottama ‖

sthāpanaṁ ‖ $\frac{4+}{5}$ ‖ $\frac{5+}{6}$ ‖ $\frac{6+}{7}$ ‖ $\frac{7+}{8}$ ‖ $\frac{8+}{9}$ ‖ $\frac{9+}{10}$ ‖ $\frac{1+}{2}$ ‖ $\frac{2+}{3}$ ‖ $\frac{3+}{4}$ ‖ kṣayaṁ saṁguṇya jātaṁ 20 | 30 | 42 | 56 | 72 | 90 | 2 | 6 [3]) eṣāṁ yuti 330 kana*kā*naṁ yuti 45 | anena bhaktvā labdhaṁ | $\frac{330}{45}$ | paṁchadash abhāge-sh-chheda kṛiyate phalaṁ | 7 she $\frac{1}{3}$ | esha ekaikamāshakakṣayaṁ | pratyaya trairā*shikena* | $\frac{45}{1}$ | $\frac{330}{1}$ | $\frac{1}{1}$ | phalaṁ $\frac{22}{3}$ | evaṁ sarveṣāṁ pratyaya *kartavya* ‖ . . . .

. . . .

Saptaviṁshatimasūtraṁ 27 ‖ ⁜ ‖

---

[1]) Read *chatuḥpaṁchāṁshaṁ kiṁ kṣayaṁ*, metri causa.
[2]) Read *bhājayet*.
[3]) Here | 12 | is omitted in the text, by mistake.

Sūtraṁ |

Ahadravyaharāshauta[1]) tadvisheṣaṁ vibhājayet |
Yallabdhaṁ dviguṇaṁ kālaṁ dattā samadhanā prati ||
tadā ||

Tṛidine ārjaye paṁcha bhṛitako-m-ekapaṇḍitaḥ |
Dvitīyaṁ paṁchadivase rasam ārjayate budhaḥ ||
Prathamena dvitīyasya sapta dattāni . . taḥ |
Datvā samadhanā jātā kena kālena katthyatāṁ ||

|| $\begin{smallmatrix}5\\3\end{smallmatrix}$ rū || $\begin{smallmatrix}6\\5\end{smallmatrix}$ rū || . . . ṁ . . . . ṁ harāṁshauta *tadvisheṣaṁ* .
. . . .
. . . .
anena kālena samadhanā bhavanti || pratyaya trairāshike kṛiyate

$\begin{smallmatrix}3\\1\end{smallmatrix}$	$\begin{smallmatrix}5\\1\end{smallmatrix}$	$\begin{smallmatrix}30\\1\end{smallmatrix}$	pha 50
$\begin{smallmatrix}5\\1\end{smallmatrix}$	$\begin{smallmatrix}6\\1\end{smallmatrix}$	$\begin{smallmatrix}30\\1\end{smallmatrix}$	pha 36

prathame dvitīyasya-s-sapta dattā | 7 sheṣaṁ 43 || 43 | 43 ete samadhanā jātā ||
tadā ||

*Rā*japutro dvayo kechi nṛipati-s-sevya santi vaiḥ |
M-ekāsyāhne dvaya-ṣ-ṣadbhāgā[2]) dvitīyasya divarddhakaṁ ||
Prathamena dvitīyasya dasha dīnāra dattavān |
Kena kālena samatāṁ gaṇayitvā vadāshu me ||

|| $\begin{smallmatrix}13\\6\end{smallmatrix}$ || $\begin{smallmatrix}3\\2\end{smallmatrix}$ || dattaṁ $\begin{smallmatrix}10\\1\end{smallmatrix}$ || karaṇaṁ || aha dravyavisheṣaṁ cha | tatra
. . . .
. . . .
pratyayaṁ trairāshikena

$\begin{smallmatrix}1\\1\end{smallmatrix}$	$\begin{smallmatrix}13\\6\end{smallmatrix}$	$\begin{smallmatrix}30\\1\end{smallmatrix}$	pha 65
$\begin{smallmatrix}1\\1\end{smallmatrix}$	$\begin{smallmatrix}3\\2\end{smallmatrix}$	$\begin{smallmatrix}30\\1\end{smallmatrix}$	pha 45

prathamena dvitīyasya 10 dattā jātā | 55 | 55 || samadhanā jātā || Sūtraṁ tṛipaṁchāshamaḥ sūtrāṁ 53 || ∻ ||

Translation.

The 18th Sūtra.

Let twice the difference of the two initial terms be divided by the difference of the (two) increments. The result augmented by one shall be the time that determines the progression.

---

1) Read °*harāṁshauta.*

2) Read *ekasyāhne dviṣaḍbhāgā.* The error appears to have been noticed by the scribe of the manuscript.

First Example.

A person has an initial (speed) of two and an increment of three, another has an increment of two and an initial (speed) of three. Let it now be determined in what time the two persons will meet in their journey.

The statement is as follows:

N° I, init. term 2, increment 3, period x
N° II, » » 3, » 2, » x.

Solution: the difference of the two initial terms (2 and 3 is 1; the difference of the two increments 3 and 2 is 1; twice the difference of the initial terms 1 is 2, and this, divided by the difference of the increments 1 is $^2/_1$, and augmented by 1 is $^3/_1$; this is the period. In this time [3] they meet in their journey which is 15).

Second Example.

(The problem in words is wanting; it would be something to this effect: *A* earns 5 on the first and 6 more on every following day; *B* earns 10 on the first and 3 more on every following day; when will both have earned an equal amount?)

Statement:

N° 1, init. term 5, increment 6, period x, possession x
N° 2, » » 10, » 3, » x, » x.

Solution: 'Let twice the difference of the two initial terms', etc.; the initial terms are 5 and 10, their difference is 5. 'By the difference of the (two) increments'; the increments are 6 and 3; their difference is 3. The difference of the initial terms 5, being doubled, is 10, and divided by the difference of the increments 3, is $\frac{10}{3}$, and augmented by one is $\frac{13}{3}$. This (i. e. $\frac{13}{3}$ or $4\frac{1}{3}$) is the period; in that time the two persons become possessed of the some amount of wealth.

Proof: by the '*rūpoṇa*' method the sum of either progression is found to be 65 (i. e., each of the two persons earns 65 in $4^1/_3$ days).

The 27th Sūtra.

Now I shall discuss the wastage (in the working) of gold, the rule about which is the following.

Sūtra.

Multiplying severally the parts of gold with the wastage, let the total wastage be divided by the sum of the parts of gold. The result is the wastage of each part (of the whole mass) of gold.

First Example.

Suvarṇas numbering respectively one, two, three, four are subject to a wastage of *māṣakas* numbering respectively one, two, three, four. Irrespective of such wastage they suffer an equal distribution of wastage. (What is the latter?)

The statement is as follows:

Wastage	— 1,	— 2,	— 3,	— 4 *māṣaka*
Gold	1,	2,	3,	4 *suvarṇa*.

Solution: 'Multiplying severally the parts of gold with the wastage', etc.; by multiplying with the wastage, the product 1, 4, 9, 16 is obtained; 'let the total wastage', its sum is 30; the sum of the parts of gold is 10; dividing with it, we obtain 3. (This is the wastage of each part, or the average wastage, of the whole mass of gold.)

(Proof by the rule of three is the following:) as the sum of gold 10 is to the total wastage of 30 *maṣakas*, so the sum of gold 4 is to the wastage of 12 *maṣakas*, etc.

Second Example.

There are *suvarṇas* numbering one, two, three, four. There are thrown out the following *māṣakas*: one-half, one-third, one-fourth, one-fifth. What is the (average) wastage (in the whole mass of gold)?

Statement:

quantities of gold,	1,	2,	3,	4 *suvarṇas*
wastage	$^1/_2$,	$^1/_3$,	$^1/_4$,	$^1/_5$ *māṣakas*.

Solution: 'Multiplying severally the parts of gold with the wastage', the products may thus be stated: $^1/_2$, $^2/_3$, $^3/_4$, $^4/_5$. 'Let the total wastage be divided'; the division being directed to be made, the total wastage is $\frac{163}{60}$; dividing 'by the sum of the parts of gold'; here the sum of the parts of gold is 10; being divided by this, the result is $\frac{163}{600}$. This is the wastage of each part of the whole mass of gold.

Proof: may be made by the rule of three: as the sum of the parts of gold 10 is to the total wastage of $\frac{163}{60}$ *maṣaka*, so the sum of gold 4 is to the wastage of $\frac{163}{600}$ *maṣaka*, etc.

Third Example.

(The problem in words is only partially preserved, but from its statement in figures and the subsequent explanation, its purport may be thus restored.)

Of gold *māṣakas* numbering respectively five, six, seven, eight, nine, ten, quantities numbering respectively four, five, six, seven, eight, nine, are wasted. Of another metal numbering in order two *māṣaka*, etc. (i. e., two, three, four) also quantities numbering in order one etc. (i. e. one, two, three) are wasted. Mixing the gold with the alloy, O best of arithmeticians, tell me (what is the average wastage of the whole mass of gold)?

Statement:

wastage:	— 4,	— 5,	— 6,	— 7,	— 8,	— 9;	— 1,	— 2,	— 3,
gold:	5,	6,	7,	8,	9,	10;	2,	3,	4.

(Solution:) 'Multiplying severally the parts of gold with the wastage', the product is 20, 30, 42, 56, 72, 90, 2, 6, 12; their sum is 330; the sum of the parts of gold is 45; dividing by this we obtain $\frac{330}{45}$; this is reduced by 15 (i. e. $\frac{22}{3}$); the result is 7 leaving $^1/_3$ (i. e. $7^1/_3$); that is the wastage of each *māṣaka* (of mixed gold).

Proof: by the rule of three: as the total gold 45 is to the total wastage 330, so 1 *māṣaka* of gold is to $\frac{22}{3}$ parts of wastage. In the same way the proof of all (the other) items is to be made (i. e., $45 : 330 = 5 : \frac{110}{3}$; $45 : 330 = 6 : 44$; $45 : 330 = 7 : \frac{154}{3}$; $45 : 330 — 8 : \frac{176}{3}$; $45 : 330 = 9 : 66$; $45 : 330 = 10 : \frac{220}{3}$).

The 53^d sūtra.

Let the portion given from the daily earnings be divided by the difference of the latter. The quotient, being doubled, is the time (in which), through the gift, their possessions become equal.

First Example.

Let one serving pandit earn five in three days; another learned man earns six in five days. The first gives seven to the second from his earnings; having given it, their possessions become equal; say, in what time (this takes place)?

Statement N° 1, $\frac{5}{3}$ earnings of 1 day, N° 2, $\frac{6}{5}$ earnings of 1 day; gift 7.

Solution: 'Let the portion of the daily earnings be divided by the difference of the latter'; (here the daily earnings are $\frac{5}{3}$ and $\frac{6}{5}$; their difference is $^7/_{15}$; the gift is 7; divided by the difference of the daily earnings $^7/_{15}$, the result is 15; being doubled, it is 30; this is the time), in which their possessions become equal.

Proof: may be made by the rule of three: $3 : 5 = 30 : 50$ and $5 : 6 = 30 : 36$; 'the first gives seven to the second' 7, remainder 43; hence 43 and 43 are their equal possessions.

Second Example.

Two Rājpūts are the servants of a king. The wages of one per day are two and one-sixth, of the other one and one-half. The first gives to the second ten *dīnārs*. Calculate and tell me quickly, in what time there will be equality (in their possessions)?

Statement: daily wages $\frac{13}{6}$ and $\frac{3}{2}$; gift 10.

Solution: 'and the daily earnings'; here (the daily earnings are $\frac{13}{6}$ and $\frac{3}{2}$; their difference is $\frac{2}{3}$; the gift is 10; divided by the difference of the daily earnings $\frac{2}{3}$, the result is 15; being doubled, it is 30. This is the time, in which their possessions become equal).

Proof by the rule of three: $1 : \frac{13}{6} = 30 : 65$; and $1 : \frac{3}{2} = 30 : 55$. The first gives 10 to the second; hence 55 and 55 are their equal possessions.

Notes.

1. In the text, the italicised words are conjecturally restored portions. The dots signify the number of syllables *(akṣara)* which are wanting in the manuscript. The serpentine lines indicate the lines lost at the top and bottom of the leaves of the manuscript. In the translation the bracketed portions supply lost portions of the manuscript. The latter can, to a great extent, be restored by a comparison of the several examples. Occasionally words are added in brackets to facilitate the understanding of the passage.

2. Sūtra 18. Problems on progression. Two persons advance from the same point. At starting B has the advantage over A; but afterwards A advances at a quicker rate than B. Question: when will they have made an equal distance? In other words, that period of the two progressions is to be found, where their sums coincide. The first example is taken from the case of two persons travelling. B makes 3 miles on the first day against 2 miles of A; but A makes 3 miles more on each succeeding day against B's 2 miles. The result is that at the end of the 3d day they meet, after each has travelled 15 miles. For A travels $2 + (2 + 3) + (2 + 3 + 3) = 15$ miles, and B $3 + (3 + 2) + (3 + 2 + 2) = 15$ miles. The second example is taken from the case of two traders. At starting B has the advantage of possessing 10 *dīnārs* against the 5 of A; but in the sequel A gains 6 *dīnārs* more on each day against the 3 of B. The result is that after $4^1/_3$ days, they possess an equal amount of *dīnārs*, viz. 65.

3. Sūtra 27. Problems on averages *(samabhāgatā)*. Certain quantities of gold suffer loss at different rates. Question: what is the average loss of the whole? The first problem is very concisely expressed; the question is understood; some words, like *kutogatā*, must be supplied to *samabhāgatām*.

The original Gypsies and their language.

By

Charles Godfrey Leland.

I read before the Oriental Congress which met in Florence in 1878, a paper in which I said, I believed I had discovered the original stock of the Gypsies of India. This I afterwards repeated more in detail in a book called The Gypsies. The statement met with general discredit from the reviews, some of whom said that the evidence given was insufficent, others that I had been hoaxed, while Mr. Mac Ritchie the latest writer on the subject treats it as 'important, if true'.

Having recently re-examined the Hindoo who is my authority, and having more fully studied the subject, I now propose to deal with the objections which have been urged against my assertions.

The facts are briefly these: One day I met in London a very dark man whom I took by the peculiar expression of his eyes to be a gypsy. I spoke to him in Romany and he understood me, but said he was not of the English Roms but a native of Calcutta, and that he made currypowder for a living. I said to him: 'Rakesa tu Romanes?' (canst thou talk the Gypsy tongue) to which he replied, 'I know what you mean. You ask me if I can talk Rom. But that is not Hindustani, it is common Panjabi.' He said this, or something to the effect that it was common or canting, and not correct. Further conversation elicited the story that he himself had been one of the Romani of India. There were, he said, in his country a great many different kinds of gypsies. A friend of mine who occupied a high position in the police of Bombay says there are at least 150 of these wandering tribes such as Banjari, Nauts or Ḍom. But my Hindoo, who calls himself *Jan Nano* declared that the Rom were the gypsies of the gypsies.

Impressed with the importance of his story, I persuaded my late friend E. H. Palmer, Professor of Arabic, Persian, and other Oriental languages at Cambridge University, to examine the man. He did this, I think, three times, in Hindustani. Now I would call special attention to the fact that Professor Palmer was as a cross-examiner a man among thousands. He was as clever at finding facts as he was at learning languages. The English government has at its command thousands of men, born in India, perfectly familiar with all its dialects, and yet to the last Professor Palmer remained *par éminence* the government examiner in Hindustani, simply because no one could do the work so well, although he had never been in India.

On this occasion he was very deeply interested, being himself perfectly familiar with the Gypsy tongue, and took all possible pains to elicit the truth. There were no leading questions, the Hindoo had no motive whatever to deceive us; far from being crafty I thought him rather obtuse or simple. Had he any idea that it would gratify me to know that his Roms were allied to our gypsies he would have answered in a way to please me, and Prof. Palmer would have caught him tripping at once. He was examined almost like a prisoner at the bar, in a very critical way at times, at others gently and with humour. Throughout Prof. Palmer was to the very last degree impartial and honest, and if anything *apparently* rather inclined to discredit the man than to believe him. What he drew from him at great length with many details was as follows:

There is in Northern India a tribe of wanderers who are really Hindoos, but who are called by other people Trablous or Syrians, although they are not natives of Syria. They live by stealing, begging, or selling objects, and their women tell fortunes. Among themselves they are called *Rom*, and their language Romani. He knew what the Ḍoms were. They were also a kind of gypsies but not the same as the Rom. The Roms were the most Gypsy of all. Their language was common on the roads more or less among similar vagabonds. They wandered very extensively, I think he said even to Syria and Persia. He told us that the *Rom* word for bread was *manro*. He knew six Indian languages, but this did not occur in any of them.

I would here remark that this man had never been in any part of Europe except England. Every gypsy on the continent calls bread *manro*, as all the gentlemen present my verify for themselves by going to the Cszarda Café in the Prater, and asking any one of the musicians there what it means. In England the only word for it among the Romany is *māro*. Now if this man had been attempting to deceive us, how was it that he used the non-English gypsy word which he could not have taken from any of his Indian dialects?

Since writing that sentence I have been informed by Mr. G. A. Grierson, who had made special search for this mysterious word; that in Naghi dialect of Bihari which is the native tongue of the purest tribe of Ḍoms or Bihar who are known as Moghiga Ḍoms, the word for wheat is *manda* or *märra*.

'I have not met' he adds, 'this word in any other of the Indian dialects.' This simply confirms and strengthens what Jan Nano told me. I believe I was the first to suggest, in my work on the English gypsies, the connection between the Romany and the Ḍom, which is however, a subject which will still bear a great deal of investigation.

I do not attach much importance to the fact that Jan Nano understood gypsy words which I put to him, because most of these would be intelligible to a man familiar with six Indian languages. The final conviction of Prof. Palmer was that Jan Nano had simply spoken the truth and that there exists in India a tribe of wanderers, born Hindoos, who from some peculiar incident have received the name of Syrians, though they are really nothing of the kind. They speak a language very much in common with that of the Gypsies of Europe whom they resemble in all other respects.

The greatest objection of all to what I have stated, is not from any of my reviewers, but from myself. It is simply this — that the Trablous or Romani are not mentioned in either of two very excellent works giving an account of all the vagabond tribes or castes of India, and that an Indian magistrate, an intimate friend of mine, has, despite many inquiries, failed to find them. Yet this objection is after all not worth much. Three or four years ago there was probably not an educated man in all Great Britain who was aware of the existence in that country of the very singular Celtic language known as *Shelta* which is peculiar to tinkers, but which is extensively understood and spoken by most of the confirmed tramps and vagabonds. It is not mentioned in the Slang Dictionary, the English Dialect Society has ignored it, thus far I believe that I am the only man who has collected or published a word or a vocabulary of it. The negative argument that no other authority has ever mentioned *Shelta* would come in with great effect here. It could be said that I have the extraordinary luck of discovering men and tongues unknown to all the critical world. Yet I doubt if I ever took a walk in London; especially in the slums; without meeting men and women who spoke Shelta, and I know at this instant of two — I really cannot say promising — little boys who sell groundsel at the Marlboro' Station, who chatter in it fluently. If Shelta could exist all unknown in England, surrounded by tens of thousands of scholars who would have been rejoiced to discover it, how much more likely is it that the Trablous of India who are probably really anxious to avoid publicity, have not been discovered by ethnologists?

If there be any who doubt of the existence of Jan Nano or his story, I would say that he is now in London, and may be easily found and re-examined by those desirous of further testing the truth of my assertions. By his aid and at no great expense the English government or any learned and literary

Society might easily enough discover these mysterious wanderers, these *Gipsissimae* or very Gypsies of the Gypsies of India. I do not pretend to say that they are the one stock from which all our European Gypsies came. For in the first place I think it very likely that *Jats* combined with many kinds of Indian wanderers in the great Western migration, and to these came successive waves, one of which may have been, let me say, simply for illustrations sake, of Ḍoms, another of their closely allied Roms, another more or less of Luri or Nuri, another of Banjars, and so forth. Just so in America we see Scandinavians or Sclavonians from widely different places coming with their dialects and all settling down into communities of speech and languages. But that the Rom as the master vagabond, and the most accomplished in the art of living on the roads should have eventually leavened the whole lump is very likely. Jan Nano speaks of them as being even today the typical gypsies or the *Kern Zigeuner*.

As Shelta is somewhat mixed with Gypsy, and as the two languages are often spoken by the same persons especially the half-blood Romanys, I will here give a brief account of my discovery of it. Once at Bath, England, I met a tramp who told me that Romany was being supplanted by a kind of language like old Irish, and which was difficult to learn. A year after, in company with Prof. Palmer I met with another vagabond, who told us that the language was called Shelta. He knew about a hundred words of it, which we wrote off at his dictation. This vagabond was a well educated man. Two years after in America I found an Irish half-blood gypsy tinker who spoke Shelta quite perfectly, and also Irish, Gaelic and Welsh. He was absolutely certain that Shelta, while it was pure Celtic was quite separate from the other tongues. Its pronunciation is strongly Gaelic, its words are however generally unlike it, though it has roots in common. My informant who very much enlarged my vocabulary, himself pointed out differences between the terms in Shelta and old Irish. According to his account, the tinkers had from very ancient times always been a closely allied clan, intermarrying and speaking this peculiar language. Their unity began to break up 'About the time the rail-roads came in'. Since then Shelta has declined. There are very few now living who can speak it perfectly.

It has been very ingeniously suggested that as the tinkers of Great Britain may be the descendants of the old bronze-workers, so their tongue may come down to us from pre-historic times. Discoveries have shown that the early bronze-smiths were nomadic, that they went about from village to village, making and selling new objects, and buying up old and broken ware to melt and re-mould. The bronze-worker's craft was closely connected with that of the jeweller, in most cases both were exercised by nomads. His wares were immensely valuable in those days, out of all proportion to the present worth of such objects. Therefore the bronze-smiths must have travelled in large bands for mutual protection. Nothing is more likely than that they formed in time a community with distinct laws and language. Nor is it improbable that this was transmitted to the tinkers. It takes a long time for men to form a distinct class with a separate tongue. The Celtic tinkers of England are unanimous in claiming for their class or clan a very great antiquity. Now when we find in the same country two nomadic classes of men, pursuing the same calling of working in metal, though separated by a long historical interregnum, we may rationally surmise, that they had a common origin, and a common language.

I have introduced these observations on Shelta in the hope that they will induce some sound Celtic scholar to take up the subject and investigate it thoroughly. Many curious discoveries await the man who will do this. There are still living in Scotland many old families of Tinklers as they are called, who retain many traditions of their ancestors. If these were thoroughly examined much might be learned.

It is a curious fact to which attention has not yet been drawn, that in the language of our English Gypsies there is a great number of Indian, I may say Persian or Sanskrit words in use, which are not common or else are quite unknown to their brethren on the continent. Such are *Koushto* and *koschko* often pronounced *Chusto* meaning *good, nili,* blue, and *pisali* a saddle, to which I could add scores of other terms. This might be an argument that a separate clan, so to speak, of Romanys came to England; but on the other hand it might be alleged with equal truth, that in the most remote and isolated places a language may be preserved, as old Norse is, in Iceland while it grows modern elsewhere. But the reason why I have found so many Hindi words is probably because I have searched closely. Mr. George Borrow asserted that there were only 1200 words in the English Gypsy dialect. I have gathered fully twice as many, and I am sure, that the stock is not yet exhausted. And I am as certain, that as regards every Romany dialect in Europe only the mere surface diggings have as yet been worked. In making my researches I induced an old gypsy who fortunately had always been given to collecting and remembering old words, to aid me as much as he could. To him I read aloud all the Romany words in the vocabulaires of Pott, Richard Liebich, Paspati, Miklosich, Barth-Smart and others, and also quite through two Hindustani dictionaries, with other works. Whenever he recognised a word, or recalled another suggestion by it, I wrote it down. The man was very old and often an expression would flash upon him from the distant past —he would use it inadvertently. The next day it would be quite forgotten. If such a method of eliciting old or half obsolete words could be tried, let us say with half a dozen old Hungarian Roms, it would be possible to obtain remarkable results. If I had simply read an English dictionary to my gypsy I should not have obtained the tenth or twentieth part of what I got by adopting the system of suggestive sounds. I have been assured more than once even by Hungarian gypsies that their language is rapidly decaying and falling into disuse. Now as there is here and there an old Romani chal who is interested in his peculiar tongue and remembers what others have forgotten, so there have been men like him in the past, and from these he has learned something in his youth. Let such men be sought for. What is wanted now is the material. Theorists in philology we shall always have, in the proportion of about one hundred to a single collector, just as there are generally so many soldiers to one pioneer. But what the future will want will not be theorists but the facts or materials with which the theorists may work. But as no one ever heard of a pioneer being mentioned in a general's report, so but little account is made at the present day of collectors, unless they happen to be at the same time brilliant theorists or shrewd critics—a not very common combination.

My chief object in making these remarks is that those who have in India opportunities for such researches, or who know those who can make them, will endeavour to find the Trablous, and that having found them they will spare no pains to ascertain who and what they really are. Thanks to the labours of Miklosich we have made a great advance in ascertaining the true elements of their language; and I learn that His Imperial Highness the Archduke Josef is engaged on an extensive work which as it will consist of a comparative grammar of all the known Gypsy dialects with those of India, ancient and modern, may prove the most important contribution ever made to what some call Tsinganology. In this as in many other branches of learning, and in its zeal for philology, Austria is indeed truly distinguished. It was in Austria that Grellmann who first fully developed the theory of the Indian origin of the Gypsies, made his observations, and no country is at present doing so much to successfully develop it. As it is it seems as if the day were not far distant when we shall be able to determine with accuracy of the Rom:

Who he is and whence he came?
What his origin and name?

The Mediæval vernacular Literature of Hindūstān, with special reference to Tul'sī Dās.

By

G. A. Grierson.

In offering the contents of this paper to the consideration of the many scholars of Aryan languages who are assembled at this Congress, I must ask for some forbearance in dealing, in what I know is an inadequate way, with a matter which has hitherto attracted little attention in Europe. I shall be amply repaid if I can arouse any interest in a class of studies which will, I am certain, well repay the labour of us Occidentals, and I can but regret that a more competent guide has not stepped into the position in which I find myself placed, in order to point out the many beauties which await those who will venture further on the track. I shall be quite content if I am considered as one of those notices which we see posted so thickly on the hills round German health-resorts with the words 'schöne Aussicht' printed on them. I would ask my fellow-students and the masters whom we all revere for their learning, to ascend the mountain point with me, and gaze for a short time upon the view.

Fortunately, apologies for dealing with the Neo-Indian vernaculars are not now so necessary as they would have been twenty years ago. At first Oriental scholars devoted themselves to Sanskrit alone, and then under the guidance of Burnouf attacked Pālī. In later years the classical Prakrits have attracted scholars, and thus the age of the object of our studies has become more and more modern in its character. I now ask my readers to take one more step over the very short gap[1]) which separates the latest Prakrit from the earliest Gaudian literature. Hemachandra flourished about 1150 A. D.[2]) And Chand Bardāī, the first of the Gaudian poets of whom we have at present any certain remains, died in 1193.

It is possible, however, that some Oriental students may still cling to the old love for Sanskrit, and them I must ask to bear with me for the present, promising them rich ore in an appendix to be subsequently published, containing the names of several vernacular commentaries on difficult Sanskrit books,[3]) and of numerous technical works on such subjects as Grammar, Prosody, Vocabulary,[4]) Composition and the like. The student of inscriptions will also find a productive mine in the literature of Hindūstān, owing to the custom which vernacular poets had of dating their works, and of naming their patrons. Besides this the muse of history, so silent in Sanskrit literature, has been assiduously cultivated by these authors, and we have, still extant, historical works founded on materials which were written so far back as the 9th century.

I therefore venture to put forward claims for attention not only from those scholars who have hitherto devoted themselves to Prakrit literature, but also from those who love to wander in the intricacies of the Naiṣadha or amongst the copper plate grants of the Indian Antiquary.

There is another claim which I would mention, and that is the intrinsic merit of the Gaudian literature. After all that is said, the later Sanskrit and the Prakrit poems are but artificial productions, written in the closet by learned men, for

---

1) Much shorter than has been hitherto supposed.

2) He died 1172.

3) For instance, Gumān Jī wrote a commentary of great repute on the Naīṣadha. He lived early in the 18th century.

4) For instance, Dayā Rām wrote a useful *Anēkārtha kōsa*.

learned men. But the Gaudian poets wrote for unsparing critics, — the people. Many of them studied nature and wrote what they saw. They found 'tongues in trees', and as they interpreted what they heard, successfully or not, so was their popularity great or small, and so their works lived after them or not. Many works exist, whose authors' names we do not even know. But they have remained living voices in the people's hearts, because they appeal to the sense of the true and of the beautiful. [1])

The earliest vernacular poet of whom I have found any mention is one Puṣya (? Paṇḍu, ? Puṣpa) Kavi of Ujain, who, according to the Sib Singh Sarōj, flourished in the year 713 A. D. The Sarōj states categorically that he wrote both in Sanskrit and in the vernacular, and that he is mentioned by Col. Tod in his Rājāsthān. If by vernacular we understand a stage of language later than that of the Prakrits, this seems a most improbable statement, nor can I find that it is borne out by Tod. The only allusion apparently bearing on this point in the Rājāsthān, is a reference (I, 229) to a Puṣya the author of an inscription (translated I, 799). I can find no mention in Tod regarding the language in which he wrote.

The next vernacular poem of which I find any notice is the Khumān Rāy'sā. It was written in honour of Rājā Khumān Singh alias Khumān Rāut Guh'laut of Chitaur in Mēwār, who flourished 830 A. D. [2]) According to Tod [3]) this work is the most ancient poetic chronicle of Mēwār, and was written in the 9th century. It gives a history of Khumān Rāut and of his family. It was recast during the reign of Par'tāp Singh (Fl. 1575 A. D.), and, as we now have it, carries the narrative down to the wars of that prince with Ak'bar, devoting a great portion to the siege of Chitaur by Alāu'ddīn Khiljī in the

---

1) There are numbers of folk-epics, Bārā māsas (songs of the seasons), Kaj'rīs and other songs current throughout India, which I have not included in the appendix because I did not know the authors' names.

2) Tod's Rājāsthān, I, 240.

3) Tod, II, 757.

13th century.[1]) We may therefore presume that the copies now extant are in a dialect of Mēwārī, not later than the end of the 16th century.

The Sib Siṅgh Sarōj mentions a Kēdar Kabi who attended the court of Alāu'ddīn Ghōrī. He therefore flourished about 1150 A. D., and if any of his works can be found they will probably be the oldest specimens of vernacular literature obtainable. I have never seen any of his writings, and I fear they are lost, unless they have been preserved in the Tod MSS. He is possibly mentioned by Tod, but I have not been able to find his name. Towards the end of the same century, an anonymous poet of Rāj'putānā wrote a bardic chronicle entitled the Kumār Pāl Charitra,[2]) detailing the line of the descent of the Buddhist Rājā Kumār Pāl of An'hal from Brahmā downwards. The manuscript exists in the Tod collection.

We now come to the time of Prithwī Rāj Chauhān of Dillī, who was born 1159 A. D. and died 1193 A. D. He was not only a valiant hero,[3]) but was a great patron of literature. If we may believe Sib Siṅgh, the works of two at least of the bards who attended his court have come down to us. These were Ananya Dās, and Chand'r or Chand Bar'dāī. The former, who is the less known of the two was author of a work called the Ananya Jōg, of which I have seen extracts. According to Sib Siṅgh,[4]) he belonged to Chaked'wā, in the district of Gōṇḍā, and was born in 1148 A. D. Chand'r Bar'dāī belonged to the family of an ancient bard entitled Bisāl Dēb Chauhān of Raṇ'thambhōr. He came to Prithwī Rājā's court, and was appointed his minister and poet-laureate *(Kavīçwara)*. His poetical works were collected by Amar Siṅgh of Mēwār[5]) in the 17th century. They were not improbably recast and modernized in parts

[1]) Tod, I, 214, 264; II, 757.

[2]) Tod, I, 79, 80 n., 241 n., 256; II, 247 n.

[3]) For a history of his life and times see Tod, I, 95.

[4]) Sib Siṅgh Sarōj, p. 379. The name of Ananya Dās must be received with caution. I strongly suspect that he was contemporary of another Prithwī Rāj (of Bikanēr) who lived in the 16th century.

[5]) Fl. 1597—1621, see Tod, I, XIII.

FACSIMILE OF A LEAF OF THE BAKHSHÂLÎ MANUSCRIPT.

Containing a portion of Sûtra 25. Plate I.

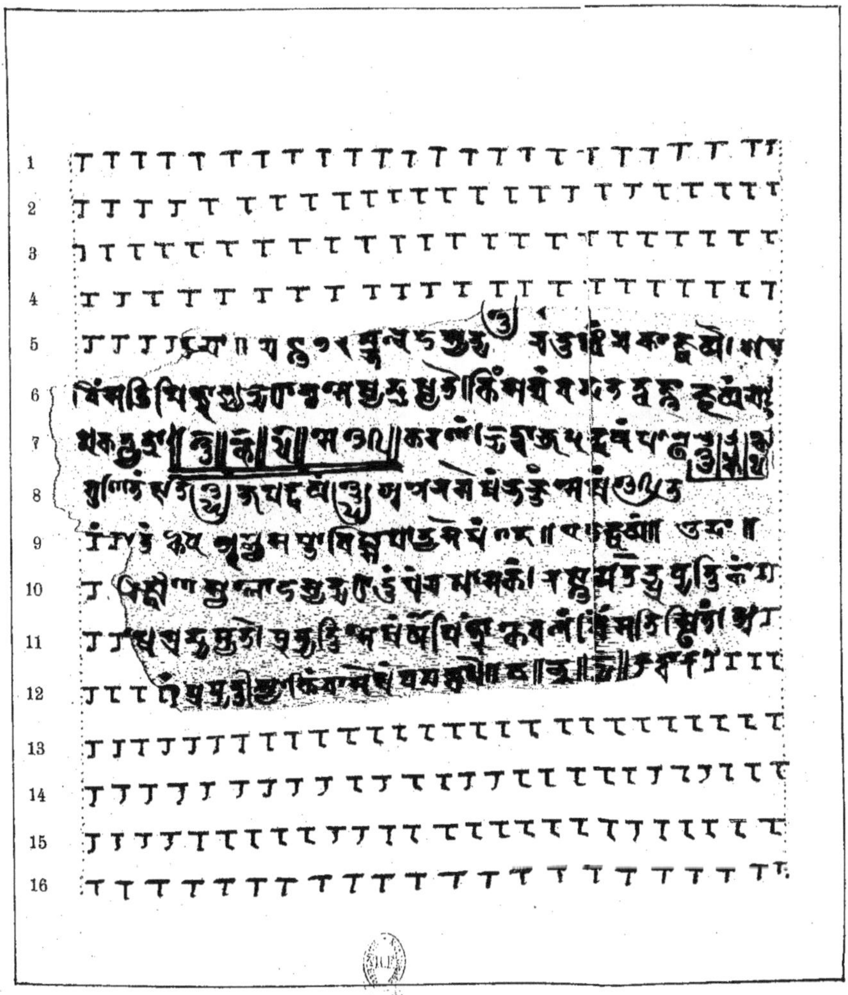

Size 8¼″ by 7″. Obverse restored.

FACSIMILE OF A LEAF OF THE BAKHSHÂLÎ MANUSCRIPT.

Containing a portion of Sûtra 25. Plate II.

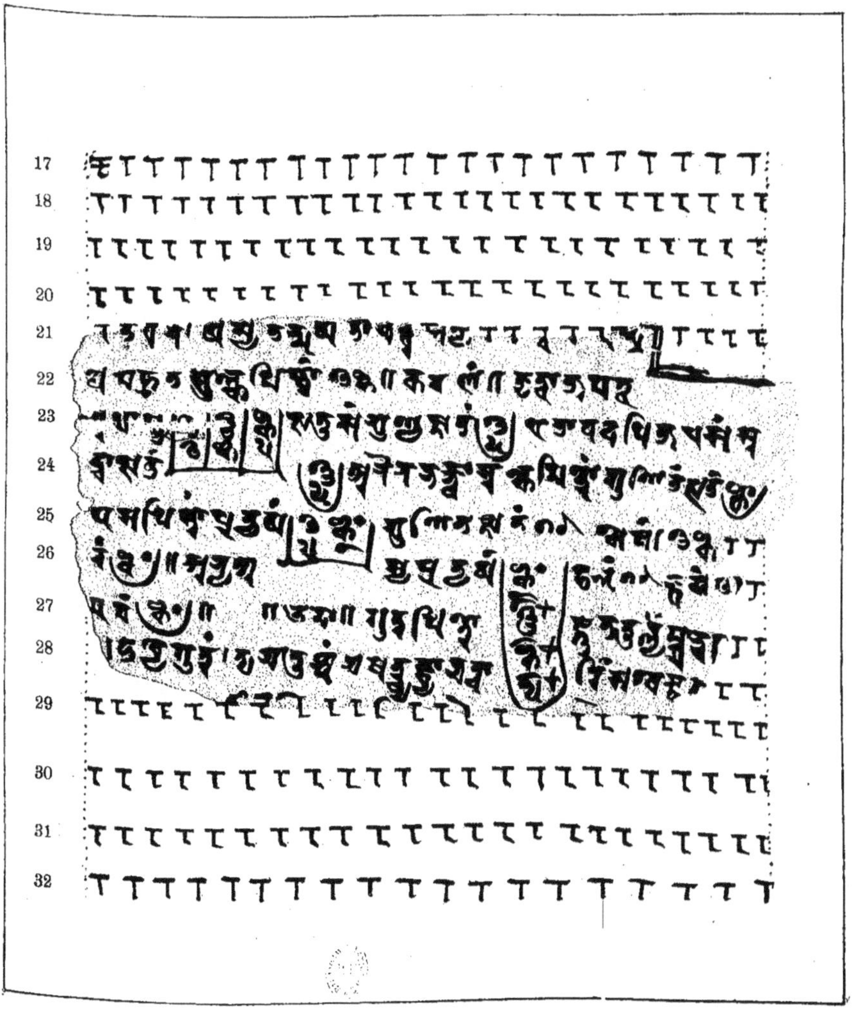

Size 8¼″ by 7″.

Reverse restored.

VII. Or. Congress Ar. Sect.

Jaffé & Albert, Vienna.

FACSIMILES OF LEAVES OF THE BAKHSHÂLÎ MANUSCRIPT.

A. Portions of Sûtras 53—54. Plate III.

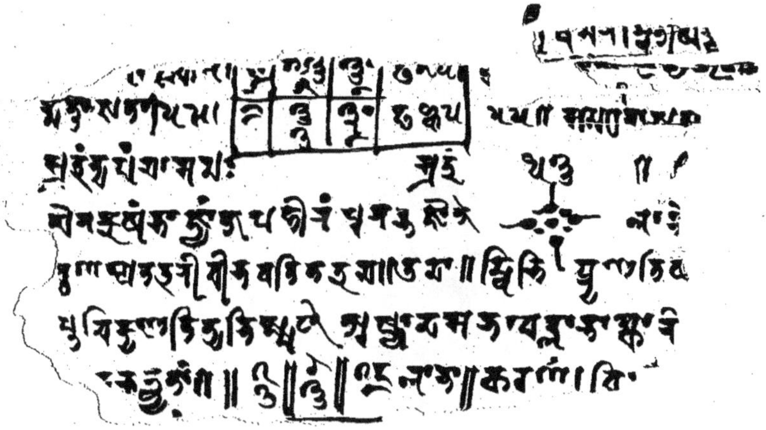

Obverse.

B. A portion of Sûtra 25.

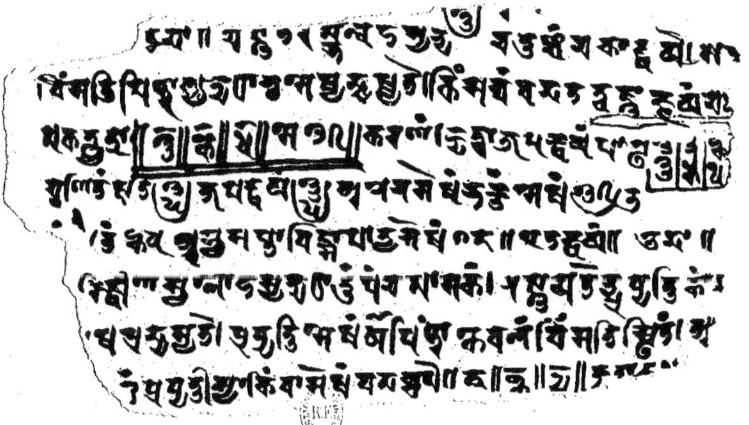

Size 8¼″ by 7″. Obverse.

VII. Or. Congress Ar. Sect. Jaffé & Albert, Vienna.

at the same time, which has given rise to a theory[1]) that the whole is a modern forgery. His principal work is the famous Prithī Rāj Rāy'sā, or life of his patron. According to Tod[2]) it is a universal history of the period in which he wrote, and is in sixty nine books comprising 100,000 stanzas of which Tod has translated 30,000, certainly more than any other European has succeeded in doing. Chand and Prithwī Rāj were both killed in battle fighting against the Muhammadans in the year 1193. Among his descendants were the poets Sūr Das and Sāraṅg Dhar who is said to have written the Hammīr Rāy'sā, and the Hammīr Kābya.[3])

A portion of the text has been edited by Mr. Beames,[4]) and another portion edited and translated by Dr. Hoernle. The excessively difficult character of the text has prevented both scholars from making much progress. My own studies of this poet's work have given me a great admiration for its poetic beauty, but I doubt if anyone not perfectly master of the various Rāj'putānā dialects could ever read it with pleasure. They are however of the greatest value to the student of philology, for they are at present the only stepping stone available to European explorers in the chasm between the latest Prakrit and the earliest Gaudian authors. Though we may not possess the actual text of Chand, we have certainly in his writings some of the oldest known specimens of Gaudian literature, abounding in pure Apabhraṁça Çaurasēnī Prakrit forms.

Contemporary with Chand was the bard Jag'nik (or Jag'nāyak). I am not certain that I have ever seen any of this poet's works. He attended the court of Par'māl (Paramardī) of Mahōbā in Bundēl'khaṇḍ, and chronicled the wars of that prince with Prith'wī Rāj. It is probable that the Ālhā Khaṇḍ, of which

---

1) See J. A. S. B. 1886, p. 5. On the Antiquity, Authenticity, and Genuineness of Chand Bar'dāī's epic, the Prithirāj Rāsau, by Kavirāj Syāmal Dās.

2) Tod, I, 254.

3) Tod, II, 452 n.

4) Cf. Tod, II, 448, 453.

we possess many versions, and which has sometimes been described as a spurious canto of Chand's epic, was originally written by this poet. The Ālhā Khaṇḍ is, so far as I am aware, only current in oral versions sung all over Hindūstān by professional singers. As might be expected these versions differ considerably in language, and each is modernized to suit the dialect of its reciter. For a full account of the Ālhā Khaṇḍ see Indian Antiquary, Vol. III, p. 17—20, 104—108, 174—176.

We have now a gap of a century, and in the year 1300 find flourishing the Sāraṅg Dhar already mentioned as a descendant of Chand. He attended the court of the heroic Rājā Hammīr Dēb the Chauhān of Ran'thambhōr, who belonged to the family of Bisāl Dēb the ancestor of Chand. Hammīr's dogged valour and heroic death has given rise to innumerable proverbs, and has been celebrated in poetical works in many languages of India. None, however, is so popular as Sāraṅg Dhar's three works known as the Sāraṅg Dhar Paddhati, the Hammīr Rāy'sā, and the Hammīr Kābya.[1]) I have only seen detached extracts from this poet's works, and hence am unable to say whether these poems were certainly by him or not. What gives rise to doubt is the existence (in the J. A. S. B., Vol. XLVIII [1879] p. 185) of a translation of a 'Hamīr Rāsā, or History of Hamīr, prince of Ran'thambhōr' by Babu Brajanātha Bandhōpādhyāya of Jaipur. According to the introduction of this work, the original was written by one Jōdh Rāj[2]) of Nīm'rāṇā. He attended the court of a Chauhān prince named Chand'r Bhān, a descendant of Prithwī Rāj, and was by birth a Gauṛ Brāhman, born at Bijāwar.

We now leave the era of the bards, and, emerging from the mists of antiquity, come upon a great revival of literature coincident with the rise of the Vaishṇava religion in the commencement of the 15th century. The first name we meet is Rāmā-

---

[1]) See Tod, II, 452, 447.

[2]) There was a Jōdh Kabi who attended the court of the emperor Ak'bar, who may be the same as this author.

nand[1]) (fl. 1400 A. D.), whose hymns I have collected as far east as Mithilā, followed by his still more famous disciple the wise and witty weaver Kabīr Dās. In this paper I do not propose to deal with them and other famous reformers in the light of their religious teaching, but only consider them with regard to their influence on the literary history of Hindūstān. Kabīr's principal works are the well known Sākhīs and the Sukh Nidhān, which are everywhere known and quoted at the present day. Many of his poems are included in the anthology entitled the Hajārā of Kālidās Tribēdī. According to tradition he was the son of a virgin Brāhman widow. He was exposed by her, and was found on a lotus in Lahar Talāo, a pond near Banāras, by the wife of a Jolāhā, or Musalmān weaver named Nīmā, who, with her husband Nūrī, was there in attendance on a wedding procession. He is said to have lived three hundred years, or from 1149 to 1449 A. D., and, in fact, he flourished about the beginning of the 15th century.[2])

Leaving now, for a time, the central Hindūstān, made famous by Rāmānand and Kabīr, we find flourishing in the year 1400, one of the most famous of the Vaishṇava poets of Eastern India. Bidyāpat'i Ṭhākur was founder of the school of Master-singers which in after years spread over the whole of Bengal, and his name is, to the present day, a household word from the Karm'nāsā to Calcutta. He has been translated into and imitated in most of the dialects falling between these limits. Little is known of his life.

He was the son of Gaṇ'pat'i Ṭhākur who was the son of Jay Datt' Ṭhākur. The founder of the family was Viṣṇu Çarman who lived seven generations before Bidyāpat'i in the village of Bisapī, the modern Bis'phī. This village was given to the poet as a rent free gift by king Sib Siṅgh (then heir apparent) of Sugāonā, in the year 1400 A. D. The deed of endowment is still extant.

---

[1]) See Wilson, Religious sects of the Hindūs, p. 47.
[2]) For further particulars see Wilson, Religious sects of the Hindūs, p. 73.

Bidyāpat'i was author of many Sanskrit works, the principal of which are the wellknown Puruṣa Parīkṣā, the Durgābhakti Taraṅgiṇī, the Dānavākyāvalī, the Vivāda Sāra, and the Gayā Pattana, but his chief glory consists in his matchless sonnets *(pada)* in the Maithilī dialect, dealing allegorically with the relations of the soul to God, under the form of the love which Rādhā bare to Krish'n. These were adopted and recited enthusiastically by the celebrated Hindū reformer Chaitanya, who flourished at the beginning of the 16th century (B. 1484 A. D.), and through him became the house-poetry of the Lower Provinces. Numbers of imitators sprung up, many of whom wrote in Bidyāpat'i's name, so that it is now difficult to separate the genuine from the imitations, especially as the former have been altered in the course of ages to suit the Baṅgālī idiom and metre.

Bidyāpat'i was a contemporary of the Baṅgālī Chaṇḍī Dās, and of Umāpat'i and Jay Dēb, and was, we know, on terms of intimate friendship with the first.

He was, we have seen, a famous poet in A. D. 1400, and a copy of the Bhāgavata Purāṇa, in his handwriting, dated L. S. 349 (A. D. 1456), still exists, so that we can know that the poet lived to a good old age. These are the only two certain dates we have in his life.

The following dates depend upon the dates mentioned in Ajodhyā Par'sād's history of Tir'hut, as those of the accessions of the various kings. Ajodhyā Par'sād's dates are as follows

King Dēva Siṁha (Dēb Siṅgh) came to the throne A. D. 1385
Çiva Siṁha (Sib Siṅgh) 1446
Two queens reigned . . . . 1449—1470
Nara Siṁha Dēva (Nar Siṅgh Dēb) 1470
Dhīra Siṁha (Dhīr Siṅgh) 1471

Now the Puruṣa Parīkṣa was according to its colophon written during the life-time of Dēb Siṅgh, i. e. before 1446. And the Durgābhakti Taraṅgiṇī was written during the reign of Nar Siṅgh Dēb, i. e. in the year 1470. We therefore can arrange the dates which we have of Bidyāpat'i Ṭhākur's life as follows, writing those which depend upon Ajodhyā Par'sād in italics.

Granted the village of Bisapī, and therefore, already a learned man.	A. D. 1400
Wrote Puruṣa Parīkṣa	before *1446*
Wrote the numerous songs dedicated to Sib Siṅgh	before *1449*
Copied the Bhāgavata Purāṇa	1456
Wrote Durgābhakti Taraṅgiṇī	*1470*

Assuming the above dates to be correct, he must have been at least 90 years old when he completed his last work.

Rājā Sib Siṅgh, Bidyāpat'i's great patron, was also named Rūp Nārāyan, which seems to have been a general title of many members of the family. He had several wives, of whom the poet has immortalized Lakhimā Ṭhakurāïn, Prānabatī, and Mōdabatī.

There is a tradition that the emperor Ak'bar[1]) summoned Sib Siṅgh to Dillī for some offence, and that Bidyāpat'i obtained his patron's release by an exhibition of clairvoyance. The emperor locked him up in a wooden box, and sent a number of the courtezans of the town to bathe in the river. When all was over, he released him, and asked him to describe what had occurred, when Bidyāpat'i immediately recited impromptu one of the most charming of his sonnets which has come down to us, describing a beautiful girl at her bath. Astonished at his power the emperor granted his petition to release king Sib Siṅgh. Another legend is that the poet feeling his end approaching, determined to die on the banks of the holy Ganges. On the way he remembered that the stream was the child of the faithful, and summoned it to himself. The obedient flood immediately divided itself into three streams, and spread its waves up to the very spot where Bidyāpat'i was sitting. Joyfully gazing on its sacred waters, he laid himself down and died. A

[1]) It is hardly necessary to point out that the real hero of this story (if it is to be believed) cannot have been Ak'bar, who did not come to the throne till 1556 A. D.

Çiva Liñga sprang up where his funeral pyre had been, and it, and the marks of the river are shown there to the present day. It is close to the town of Bāzit'pūr, in the Darbhañgā District. Such is the fitting legend of the passing away of the great old Master-singer.

Bidyāpat'i's influence on the history of the literature of Eastern Hindūstān has been immense. He was a perfect master of the art of writing the religious love sonnets which have since become, in a much degraded form, the substance of the Vaishṇava bibles. Subsequent authors have never done any thing but, *longo intervallo,* imitate him; but while the founder of the school never dealt with any subject without adorning it with some truly poetical conceit, his imitators have too often turned his quaintness into obscurity, and his passionate love songs into the literature of the brothel.

Leaving Bidyāpat'i and his successors we may now return to the extreme west, where in Mēwār Mīrā Bāī, the one great poetess of Northern India, was pouring forth her impassioned hymns to Krish'n Ran'chhōṛ. This remarkable woman who flourished in the year 1420 A. D., was the daughter of Rājā Ratiyā Rānā, the Raṭhaur, of Mer'tā, and was married in Sambat 1470 (A. D. 1413) to Rājā Kumbh'karan, son of Mōkal Dēb, of Chitaur.[1]) Her husband was killed in Sambat 1534 (A. D. 1469) by his son Ūdā Rānā. Her great work is the Rāg Gōbind, and she also wrote a much admired commentary on the Gīta Gōvinda of Jayadēva. She was devoted to that form of the God Krish'n known as Ran'chhōṛ, and the tradition is that she worshipped his image with such fervour that it came to life, and the God, descending from his shrine, embraced her, crying 'Welcome Mīrā'. On hearing these words, overcome with rapture, she died in his arms. According to Wilson,[2]) she was much persecuted by her husband's family, on account of her religious principles. She became the patroness of vagrant Vai-

[1]) According to Wilson, Udaipur.

[2]) Religious sects of the Hindūs, p. 137.

shṇavas, and visited, in pilgrimages, Brindāban and Dwārikā. Previous to leaving the latter place, she visited the temple of her tutelary deity, to take leave of him, when, on the completion of her adorations, the image opened, and, Mīrā leaping into the fissure, it closed, and she finally disappeared. Some idea of the popularity of her writings may be gained from the fact that I have collected, from the mouths of the people of Mithilā, songs purporting to be by her.[1])

Passing over a number of minor poets, including Nānak (B. 1469, D. 1539 A. D.), who was more remarkable as a religious reformer than as a literary author, we come, after the lapse of more than a century, to Malik Muhammad of Jāyas in Audh, who flourished under Shēr Shāh in the year 1540 A. D. He was the author of the Padmāwat, which is I believe the first poem, and almost the only one, written in a Gaudian vernacular, on an original subject. I do not know a work more deserving of hard study than the Padmāwat. It certainly requires it, for scarcely a line is intelligible to the ordinary scholar, it being couched in the veriest language of the people. But it is well worth any amount of trouble, both for its originality, and for its poetical beauty.

Malik Muhammad was a Musalmān *faqīr* of great sanctity. The Rājā of Amēṭhī who believed that he owed a son and his general prosperity to the saint was one of his principal devotees. When the poet died he was buried at the gate of the Rājā's fort at Amēṭhī, where his tomb is still worshipped. He was not a man of great learning, but was famed for his wisdom, and for the fact that he wrote for the people in the people's tongue.

According to the text of the Banāras edition of the Padmāvat (which is very incorrect),[2]) the poet commenced to write it in A. H. 927 (1520 A. D.); but this is probably a misreading,

[1]) Cf. Tod, I, 289; II, 760.

[2]) My friend Paṇḍit Chhōṭū Ram Tiwārī, Professor of Sanskrit at Bankipur College, has undertaken to translate and to edit a correct text of this important work for the Bibl. Ind.

for he says in the preface that Shēr Shāh of the Sūr dynasty who came to the throne in A. H. 947 (A. D. 1540) was then the ruling king. 927 is therefore probably incorrect for 947.

The outline of the story of Padmāwat is as follows, — there was a king named Ratan Sēn of Chitaur, who was informed by a parrot of the great beauty of Padminī, daughter of the king of Siṅghal Dīp (Ceylon). He journeyed to Ceylon as a mendicant, married her there, and returned with her to Chitaur. After this one Raghu, a messenger of Alāu'ddīn Khiljī informed that monarch of the great beauty of Padminī. Alāu-'ddīn in consequence attacked Chitaur, and imprisoned Ratan Sēn in order to obtain possession of her. He failed, however, in his object for she became *satī* and burnt herself with the dead body of her husband, who had, in the meantime, been killed by Rājā Dēb Pāb of Kambhal'nēr. In the final verses of his work the poet says that it is all an allegory. By Chitaur he means the body of man, by Ratan Sēn the soul, by the parrot the *guru* or spiritual preceptor, by Padminī wisdom, by Raghu Satan, by Alāu'ddīn delusion and so on.

The Story of the Padmāwat is founded on the historical facts of the siege of Chitaur, which is described by Tod (Rājāsthān, I, 262 and ff.). The substance is as follows. Lakam'sī the minor king of Chitaur came to the throne A. D. 1275. His uncle Bhīm'sī ruled during his minority. He had espoused Padminī the daughter of Hammīr Sāṅk (Chauhān) of Ceylon. Alāu-'ddīn besieged the city in order to obtain possession of her, and after a long and fruitless siege he restricted his desire to a mere sight of her extraordinary beauty, and acceded to the proposal of beholding her through the medium of mirrors. Relying on the faith of the Rāj'pūt, he entered Chitaur slightly guarded, and, having gratified his wish, returned. The Rāj'pūt, unwilling to be outdone in confidence, accompanied the king to the fort of the fortress. Here Ālā had an ambush waiting; Bhīm'sī was made prisoner, and his liberty made to depend on the surrender of Padminī. Padminī being informed of this, agreed to give herself up as a ransom for her husband, and, having provided wherewithal to secure her from dishonour, she designed with two chiefs of her own kin of Ceylon, her uncle Gōrā, and her nephew Bādal, a plan for the liberation of the prince without hazarding her life and fame. She was accompanied into Ālā's camp by a procession of litters, borne by and filled with armed men disguised as handmaids, some of whom returned taking Padminī and Bhīm'sī with them in disguise. The rest remained in the enemy's camp till the ruse was discovered, when they covered the retreat of their master and were cut down to a man in doing so. Bhīm'sī and Padminī escaped into Chitaur, and after an unsuccessful attempt at storming the citadel (in which Gōrā was killed) Alāu'ddīn raised the siege. He returned again to the siege in 1290 (Firishta says 13 years later), and one by one eleven out of twelve of Bhīm'sī's sons were slain. Then, having made arrangements for the escape of Ajaisī, his second son, to continue the family line, the Rānā himself, calling around him his devoted clans, for whom life had no longer any charms, threw open the portals, and carried death into, and met it in the crowded ranks of Ālā. 'But another awful sacrifice preceded this act of self-devotion, in that horrible rite, the *Jōhar,* where the females are immolated to preserve them from pollution or captivity. The funeral pyre was lighted within the great subterranean retreat, in chambers impervious to the light of day, and the defenders of Chitaur beheld in procession the queens, their own wives and daughters, to the number of several thousands. The fair Padminī closed the throng, which was augmented by whatever of female beauty or youth could be tainted by Tatar lust. They were conveyed to the cavern, and the opening closed upon them, leaving them to find security from dishonour in the devouring element.

'The Tatar conqueror took possession of an inanimate capital, strewed with the bodies of its brave defenders, the smoke yet issuing from the recesses where lay consumed the once fair object of his desire.'

Malik Muhammad has changed the name of the hero from Bhīm'sī to Ratan, the name of the king of Mēwār who ruled at

Chitaur about the time that the poem was written (Tod, I, 309). He has also borrowed part of his story from that of another Padmāwat, the Padmāvatī of Udayana and the Ratnāvalī. He makes his hero turn a mendicant devotee in order to gain his beloved, and the scene of the burning together of the two queens, though suggested by the terrible real tragedy, seems also to bear marks of the somewhat similar situation in the Ratnāvalī. There are also other variations from the accepted story, which it is not necessary to mention here.

From the date of the Padmāwat the literature of Hindūstān became, so to speak, crystallized into two grooves. This was due to the Vaishnava reformations of Rāmānand and Ballabhāchār'j. The first of these, who has been already mentioned, founded the modern worship of Viṣṇu in his incarnation of Rām (Rāma) and the other the worship of the same God in his incarnation of Krish'n (Kriṣṇa). From this date all the great poetical works of the country were devoted to either one or other of these two incarnations, and Malik Muhammad's work stands out as a conspicuous and almost solitary example of what the Hindū mind can do when freed from the trammels of literary and religious custom. It is true that there are examples of didactic, grammatical, and medical works in the long list of authors given in my appendix, but the fact remains that from the middle of the sixteenth century to the present day, all that was great and good in Hindūstānī[1]) literature was bound by a chain of custom or of impulse or of both to the ever-recurring themes of Rām and Krish'n. Rāmānand has already been dealt with, and his only conspicuous follower was Tul'sī Dās, concerning whom I shall hereafter deal at length. We shall now consider Ballabhāchār'j and his successors and pupils. I shall deal with this reformer at greater length than I have done with Rāmānand both because of his greater importance, and because

[1]) I use this word here, as elsewhere, as the adjective corresponding to the substantive 'Hindūstān', and not as meaning the so called Hindūstānī language.

I am able to give some particulars concerning him which have not hitherto been made available to European scholars.

Ballabhāchār'j (Vallabhāchārya) was the celebrated founder of the Rādhā-ballabhī sect.[1]) According to Harishchand'r,[2]) his father's name was Lachhman Bhaṭṭ (a Tailiṅga Brāhman of Madras), and his mother's name was Illamgārū. His father had three sons, Rām Krish'n, Ballabhāchār'j, and Rām Chand'r. Both his brothers were Vaishṇava authors of repute. Lachhman Bhaṭṭ lived at Ajodhyā, and was paying a visit to Banāras when, on the way, near the village of Chaurā in the vicinity of Betiyā in the district of Champāran in Bihār, on Sunday the 11th of the dark half of Baisākh, Sambat 1535 (A. D. 1478) Ballabhāchār'j was born.[3]) At Banāras he commenced studying under the celebrated Mādh'wāchār'j at the age of 5 years, and remained there till the death of his father, after which he led a wandering life, and visited the court of Krish'n Dēb, king of Bijainagar, apparently the same as Krish'n Rāyalū, who reigned about the year 1520 A. D. Here he overcame the Smārta Brahmans in controversy. (See Wilson, Religious sects of the Hindūs, p. 120). According to Harishchand'r, however, this took place before Sambat 1548 (A. D. 1491) when he was only thirteen years of age. In this year he made a tour to Braj where he studied the Bhāgavata Purāṇa, and subsequently returned to Banāras, preaching Vaishṇava doctrines as he went along. From Banāras he went to Gayā, Jagannāth and the Deckan, spreading his doctrines everywhere. He finished his first tour (technically called his *Digbijai* or conquest of the world) in Sambat 1554 (A. D. 1497) at the age of 19.[4]) He then made Braj his headquarters, and established an image of Shrī Nāth at Gōbardhan. From this as his head quarters he made his second mis-

---

[1]) See Wilson, Religious sects of the Hindūs, p. 120.

[2]) Prasiddh Mahātmāōn̐ kā Jīban Charit'r, II, 28.

[3]) See the 3[d] Khaṇḍ of the Ballabh Digbijai, *sambat 1535 çāke 1400 Baisākh mās krisṇa paksha rabibār madhyān.* See also a hymn by Dwārikēs quoted by Harischand'r l. c.

[4]) This is the date given by Harishchand'r.

sionary tour throughout India. He died in Banāras in Sambat 1587 (A. D. 1530), at the age of 52 years, leaving two sons, Gōpī Nāth and Biṭṭhal Nāth.

He was a voluminous author. His most admired works are a commentary on the Bhāgavata Purāṇa entitled Subōdhanī,[1] the Anubhāṣya, and the Jaiminīya Sūtra Bhāṣya. The latter two are in Sanskrit. Harishchand'r (l. c.) gives a complete list of his works. The authorship of a vernacular work of considerable authority, the Bishnu Pad or stanzas in honour of Viṣṇu, is also attributed to him. Many verses by him are included in the anthology entitled Rāg-sāgarōdbhab of Krishnānand Byās Dōb.

Ballabhāchār'j was succeeded as leader of the Rādhā-ballabhī sect by his son Biṭṭhal Nāth of Braj (fl. 1550). Biṭṭhal Nāth had seven sons, all of whom became Gosāīñs or leaders of the sect. The descendants of two of these (Gir'dhar and Jadunāth)[2] still exist in Gōkul.[3] Many of his verses are included in the Rāg-sāgarōdbhab, and he is possibly the same as a Biṭṭhal Kabi mentioned in the Sib Siñgh Sarōj as an erotic poet.

Ballabhāchār'j had four famous pupils, viz

Sūr Dās
Krish'n Dās
Par'mānand Dās
Kumbhan Dās

and Biṭṭhal Nāth had also four pupils, named

Chatur'bhuj Dās
Chhīt Swāmi
Nand Dās
Gōbind Dās.

The first four may be considered as flourishing in the year 1550, and the second four as flourishing about 1567 A. D.

[1]) According to Wilson Subōdhinī.

[2]) See Harishchand'r, II, 36.

[3]) For further information cf. Wilson, Religious sects of the Hindūs, p. 125, where he is wrongly called Vitala Nath.

These eight all lived in Braj, and wrote in Braj Bhākhā, and are named the Ashṭa Chhāp, or eight acknowledged masters of the literature of that dialect. Wilson and others speak of a work entitled the Ashṭā Chhāp, giving the lives of these poets, and I once believed in the existence of such a work myself, but I am at present of opinion that by the term Ashṭa Chhāp is simply meant this list, which, so far as I can make out, was first given and so named in some verses of Sūr Dās translated hereafter, and next in a work entitled the Tul'sī Shabdārth Prakās of Gopāl Siṅgh of Braj, whose date I have been unable to fix.

Of these eight I shall here deal with only two, Krish'n Dās Pay Ahārī, and Sūr Dās. Krish'n Dās (fl. 1550) was a graceful and sweet poet, many of whose verses will be found in the Rāg-sāgarōdbhab. There is a legend that Sūr Dās in his poetry had exhausted all that could possibly be said concerning the God Krish'n, and that, hence, when Krish'n Dās wrote anything, it was always found to be identical with something which Sūr Dās had already written. One day the latter challenged him to produce a single stanza which did not comply with this disagreeable necessity, and he failed to do so. He then promised to bring an original verse next day, and going away, spent the whole night in vain endeavouring to concoct one. In the morning he found a verse mysteriously written upon his pillow, which he took to Sūr Dās, who at once identified it as one which had been written by their master Ballabhāchār'j. In spite of this legend, which seems to point to a rivalry between the two poets, Krish'n Dās is always graceful, and as original as his subject will admit. His best known work is the Prēm-ras-rās. His most famous disciples were Agr' Dās, Kēwal Rām, Gadādhar, Dēbā, Kalyān, Haṭi Nārāyan, and Padum Nāth. Agr' Dās had Nābhā Dās, the author of the Bhakt Mālā, of whom more anon, for his disciple.

Sūr Dās deserves a more extended notice. He was, with his father Bābā Rām Dās, a singer at the court of the Emperor Ak'bar (see Āīni Akbarī, Blochmann's translation, p. 612). He and Tul'sī Dās are the two great stars in the firmament of North Indian vernacular poetry. Tul'sī was devoted to Rām *(ēkānt Rām-sēbak)*, while Sūr Dās was devoted to Krish'n *(ēkānt Krish'n-sēbak)*, and between them they are considered to have exhausted all the possibilities of poetic art.

According to tradition, preserved in the Glosses to the Bhakt Mālā and to the Chaurāsī Bārtā, he was a Sāraswat Brāhman, and his father and mother were beggars who lived at Gaū Ghāṭ or at Dillī. This fact, that books of the authority of the two above works countenance this theory, is typical of the tendency of mediæval Indian authors to trust to tradition, instead of to independent research. Subsequent writers, English and foreign have followed the Bhakt Mālā implicitly, and have all been led wrong in consequence, for we have the very best authority, that of Sūr Dās himself, that he was not a Sāraswat Brāhman, and that his father was not a beggar, and did not live at Gaū Ghāṭ.[1]) Sūr Dās wrote a collection of emblematic verses *(drishṭ kūṭ)* with the accompanying necessary commentary, and in the latter the author gives the following account of himself.[2])

'The founder of my family was Brahm Rāo[3]) of the Prath Jagāt[4]) (or first of the Jagāt) clan. From him was descended Bhās Chand.[5]) To him Prithwī Rāj (fl. 1190 A. D.) gave the country of Jwālā. He had four sons, of whom the eldest succeeded him as king *(narēs)*. The second was Gun Chand'r,

---

[1]) It must not be forgotten that Priyā Dās, the author of the gloss to the Bhakt Mālā, collected the traditions more than a hundred years after Sūr Dās' death.

[2]) The late lamented Harishchand'r of Banāras, the greatest, I had almost said the only, critic of Hindūstān was the first to draw attention to this autobiography in his 'Siddh Mahātmāoñ kā Jiban Charit'r (Bankipore, Sahib Prasad Sinha, Khadgbilas Press, 1885).

[3]) The title Rāw renders it probable that he was either a Rājā, or a Bhāt or panegyrist.

[4]) This clan is not mentioned in the list of clans of Sāraswat Brāhmans by Paṇḍit Rādhā Krish'n. Jagāt or Jagatiyā means a panegyrist.

[5]) Or simply Chand if we take *bhau* as equivalent to *huā*, 'was'.

whose son was Sīl Chand'r, whose son was Bīr Chand'r. This last used to sport with Hammīr,[1]) king of Ran'thambhōr. From him was born Hari Chand'r, who dwelt at Āg'rā. Hari Chand'r's son[2]) dwelt in Gōp'chal, and had seven sons, viz. 1) Krish'n Chand, 2) Udār Chand, 3) Jurūp Chand, 4) Buddhi Chand, 5) Dēb Chand, 6) (?) Sansrit Chand, and 7) myself Sūraj Chand. My six brothers were killed in battle with the Musalmāns; I alone, Sūraj Chand, blind[3]) and worthless, remained alive. I was fallen into a well,[4]) and though I called for help, no one saved me. On the seventh day Jadupati (Krish'n) came and pulled me out,[5]) and making himself visible to me, said 'Son, ask what thou desirest, as a boon'. I said, 'Lord, I ask for the boon of perfect devotion, for the destruction of the enemy,[6]) and that, now that I have seen the form of God, mine eyes may never see aught else'. As the Sea of Compassion heard me, he said 'So let it be. Thine enemy will be destroyed by a mighty Brāhman of the Deckan'.[7]) Then named he me Sūraj Dās, Sūr, and Sūr'syām, and disappeared, and thereafter all was darkness to me.[8]) I then went to live in Braj, where the Holy Master (Biṭṭhal Nāth) entered my name in the Ashṭa Chhāp.[9]) We thus get the following genealogy:

---

1) The famous king of Ran'thambhōr who was killed by Alā-u'ddīn, and for whom a thousand wives became satī. The date of his death was about 1300 A. D.

2) His sons name was probably Rām Chand'r, which he subsequently changed, according to Vaishnava custom to Rām Dās.

3) Either literally or figuratively. Owing to the undoubted fact of his blindness, every blind singing mendicant is now called a Sūr Dās.

4) This may either be taken literally (fallen into a dry well [*andhā kūāṅ*]) or figuratively that he was a sinner.

5) Or, taken figuratively, after seven days of internal conflict, I became converted and obtained salvation.

6) i. e. his evil passions, or perhaps the Musalmāns.

7) i. e. Ballabhāchār'j.

8) i. e. he became literally blind.—The fulfilment of his third request, '*dusarō nā dēkhō rūpa dēkhī Rādhā-Syāma*'.

9) The list of the eight great poets of Braj. See Krish'n Dās, above.

Brahm Rāo the Prath Jagāt
|
Bhāo Chand'r (fl. 1190 A. D.)
|
second son
Gun Chand'r
|
Sīl Chand'r
|
Bīr Chand'r (fl. 1300 A. D.)
|
(?) descendants unknown
|
Hari Chand'r (of Āg'rā)
|
Rām Chand'r (of Gōp'chal)
|
Sūraj Chand (fl. 1550) and six others.

It is evident that he was not of a Brāhman but of a royal stock.[1] According to tradition he was born about Sam. 1540 (1483 A. D.), and was instructed by his father, at Āg'rā in singing, in Persian, and in the vernacular. On his father's death, he took to writing hymns *(bhajan's)* and gained many disciples. At this time he signed his verses Sūr Swāmi, and under that title wrote a poem dealing with the story of Nala and Damayantī.[2] He was then in the prime of his youth, and is said to have lived at Gaū Ghāṭ, a village nine *kōs* from Āg'rā on the road to Mathurā. About this time he himself became a disciple of Ballabhāchār'j, and signed his poems with the name of Sūr Dās, Sūr, Sūraj Dās, or, as before, Sur'syam.[3] At this time he translated the Bhāgavata Purāṇa into verses in the vernacular, and he also collected his hymns into the compilation entitled the Sūr Sāgar.[4] In his old age his fame reached the ears of the emperor Ak'bar, who summoned him to his court. He died in Gōkul about Sam. 1620 (1563 A. D.).

The above tradition is certainly wrong so far as regards dates, and as regards Sūr Dās' father. For the Āīni Akbarī, which was completed in 1596—97 A. D., mentions both Sūr Dās

---

1) He calls Bhāo Chand'r's eldest son, *narēs*.
2) No copies of this are known to exist.
3) Also, possibly, Sant Dās.
4) Said to contain sixty thousand verses.

and Bābū Rām Dās as (apparently) then alive. Abu'l Fazl says that Rām Dās came from Gwāliyar, but Budāonī (II, 42) says that he came from Lakh'naū.

Another legend current throughout India concerning Sūr Dās may be mentioned. Subsequently to his becoming blind, during the absence of his amanuensis, Krish'n came himself, and wrote down for him the words which welled forth from the unsuspecting poet's mouth. At length Sūr Dās perceived that the writer was outstripping his tongue and was writing down his thoughts before he had uttered them. Recognising the Antarajāmī God by this, Sūr Dās seized him by the hand, but Krish'n thrust him away and disappeared. Sūr Dās then uttered a poem still extant, and in my opinion, by far his highest flight, the leading idea of which is that though God may thrust him away, he could not tear himself from the poet's heart.

Regarding Sūr Dās' place in literature, I can only add that he justly holds a high one. He excelled in all styles. He could, if occasion required, be more obscure than the Sphynx, and in the next verse as clear as a ray of light. Other poets may have equalled him in some particular quality, but he combined the highest qualities of all.[1]) Natives of India give him the very highest niche of fame, but I believe that the European reader will prefer the nobility of character of all that Tul'sī Dās wrote, to the often too cloying sweetness of the blind bard of Āg'rā.

We shall now anticipate the course of time a little in order to complete the history of this famous group of Braj poets. Krish'n Dās had a pupil, Agr' Dās of Gal'tā, who in turn was preceptor of Nabhā Dās alias Nārāyan Dās of the Deckan, who flourished about 1600 A. D. Under the direction of Agr' Dās he wrote the Bhakt Mālā or 'Legends of the Saints' consisting of 108 verses in Chhappai metre. It is one of the most difficult works in the Braj dialect, and, as we have it now, was avowedly edited, and perhaps rewritten by a (?) disciple of Nābhā

---

[1]) As an anonymous poet of Ak'bar's court says, 'Gang excels in sonnets, and Bīr'bal in the Kabitta metre. Kēsab's meaning is ever profound, but Sūr possess the excellencies of all three'.

Dās entitled Nārāyan Dās, who lived in the reign of Shāh Jahān. Mr. Growse, to whom I am indebted for a portion of the foregoing information, adds 'A single stanza is all that is ordinarily devoted to each personage, who is panegyrized with reference to his most salient characteristics in a style that might be described as of unparalleled obscurity, were it not that each separate portion of the text is followed by a gloss written by one Priyā Dās in the Sambat year 1765 (1712 A. D.), in which confusion is still worse confounded by a series of most disjointed and inexplicit allusions to different legendary events in the saint's life'. Priyā Dās' gloss is in the Kabitta metre. He was followed by Lāl Jī a Kayasth of Kādh'lā, who in Hij'rī 1158 (A. D. 1751), wrote a further commentary entitled Bhakt Urbasī. A few years ago Tul'sī Rām Agar'wālā of Mīrāpur translated the Bhakt Mālā into Ūrdū, calling his translation the Bhakt Māl Pradīpan.

The name Nārāyan Dās which Mr. Growse attributes to a disciple of Nābhā Dās, was, according to native writers, really the actual name of Nābhā Dās, the latter being his *nom de guerre.*

Nābhā Dās is possibly the same as a Nārāyan Dās Kabi, mentioned in the Sib Siṅgh Sarōj as born in 1558 A. D., and author of translations of the Hitōpadēça, and Rājanīti into the vernacular; and as another Nārāyan Dās, a Vaishṇava author of an undated prosody, describing fifty-two metres, entitled Chhand Sār.

Retracing now our steps, we may take a glance at the brilliant court of the emperor Ak'bar (reigned 1556—1605), and the constellation of poets which shone there. Most of the foregoing poets from Malik Muhammad downwards were contemporaries of this king, who was so celebrated a patron of learning. It may be noted that the reign of the emperor Akbar nearly coincided with that of the English queen Elizabeth, and that the reigns of both these monarchs were signalized by an extraordinary outburst of literary vigour. Nor, indeed, if Tul'sī Dās and Sūr Dās were compared with Shakespeare and Spenser, would the Indian poets be very far behind.

I have noted the following poets as having attended Akbar's court, 1) 'Abdu'r Rahīm Khān'khāna, 2) Abu'l Faiz,

3) Amrit, 4) Karan or Kar'nēs, 5) Gaṅg, 6) Jag'dīs, 7) Jagannaj, 8) Jagāmag, 9) Jōdh, 10) Jait, 11) Ṭōḍar Mal, 12) Tān Sēn, 13) Nar'hari, 14) Fahīm, 15) Bīr'bal, 16) Manōhar, 17) Mān Rāy, 18) Hōl. Of these many are historical personages. Number 1 was the celebrated son of Bairām Khān, Number 2 was the brother of Abu'l Faẓl. Ṭōḍar Mal was the great finance minister, and Bīr'bal the equally famous minister, general, and wit. Tān Sēn was a court singer and considered the greatest artist of his age.

We now approach the greatest star of Indian poetry, Tul'sī Dās. I much regret that the materials available are so scanty, and it is the more tantalizing to me that I have received information of a very full account of his life, entitled Gosāīñ Charit'r by Bēnī Mādhab Dās of Pas'kā who lived in the poet's companionship. I have never been able to obtain a copy of this work though I have long searched for it, and I have been compelled to base my account principally on the enigmatic verses of the Bhakt Mālā aided by the glosses of Priyā Dās and others. The text and literal translations of these will be found in the introduction to Mr. Growse's translation of the Rāmāyan, from which I have freely drawn.

The importance of Tul'sī Dās in the history of India cannot be overrated. Putting the literary merits of his Rāmāyan out of question, the fact of its universal acceptance by all classes from Bhagal'pūr to the Panjāb, and from the Himālaya to the Narmadā is surely worthy of note. 'The book is in every one's hands,[1]) from the court to the cottage, and is read or heard, and appreciated alike by every class of the Hindū community, whether high or low, rich or poor, young or old.' It has been interwoven into the life, character, and speech of the Hindū population for more than three hundred years, and is not only loved and admired by them for its poetic beauty, but is reverenced by them as their scriptures. It is the Bible of a hundred millions of people, and is looked upon by them as as much

[1]) Mr. Growse (from whom this quotation is taken) states that the professional Sanskrit Paṇḍits affect to despise Tul'sī Dās' work as an unworthy concession to the illiterate masses, but this has not been my experience.

inspired, as the Bible is considered inspired by the English clergyman. Paṇḍits may talk of the Vēdas and of the Upaniṣads, and a few may even study them. Others may say that they pin their faith on the Purāṇas, but to the vast majority of the people of Hindūstān, learned and unlearned alike, their sole norm of conduct is the so called Tul'sī-krit Rāmāyan. It is indeed fortunate for Hindūstān that this is so, for it has saved the country from the tantric obscenities of Shaivism. Rāmānand was the original saviour of upper India from the fate which has befallen Bengal, but Tul'sī Dās was the great apostle who carried the doctrine east and west, and made it an abiding faith.

The religion he preached was a simple and sublime one, a perfect faith in the name of God; but what is most remarkable in it, in an age of immorality, when the bonds of Hindū society were loosened, and the Mughal empire being consolidated, was its stern morality in every sense of the word. Tul'sī was the great preacher of one's duty towards one's neighbour. Vālmīki praised Bharat's sense of duty, Lachhman's brotherly affection, and Sītā's wifely devotion, but Tul'sī taught them as an example. So too, in an age of licence, no book can be purer in tone than the Rāmāyan. He himself justly exclaims, 'here are no prurient and seductive stories, like snails, frogs, and scum on the pure water of Rām's legend, and therefore the lustful crow and the greedy crane, if they do come, are disappointed'. Other Vaishnava writers, who inculcated the worship of Krish'n, too often debased their muse to harlotry to attract their hearers, but Tul'sī Dās had a nobler trust in his countrymen, and that trust has been amply rewarded.

Tul'sī Dās was a Sar'bariyā Brāhman. He was born early in the 16th century and died at a good old age in 1624 A. D. As the old rhyme says

Sambata sōraha sai asī, Asī Gaṅga kē tīra |
Sāwana sukalā sattamī, Tulasī tajeu sarīra ||

'On the seventh of the light half of Çrāvaṇa, in Sambat 1680, Tul'sī left his body on the bank of the Ganges at Asī.' According to the Bhakt Sindhu, his father's name was Ātmā Rām, and he was born at Hastināpur, but according to other authorities he was born at Hājīpur near Chitrakuṭ. The usual tradition is however, that Rājāpur in the district of Bāndā on the banks of the Jamunā has the honour of being his birthplace. As a child he lived at Sūkar'khēt (*vulgo* Sōrōñ[1]) where he was first imbued with devotion to Rām. According to Priyā Dās, his wife first persuaded him to exchange an earthly for a divine love, and incited by her remonstrances he left her and went to Banāras, where he spent the greater part of his life, visiting frequently Ajodhyā, Mathurā, Brindāban, Kuruchhēt'r, Prayāg, Purukhōttam'purī, and other holy places. The only other fact in his life about which there is any reasonable certainty (beyond the dates of some of his works) is that he was appointed arbitrator in a land-dispute between two men named Anand Rām and Kanhāy. The deed of arbitration in his handwriting is still in existence, and is dated Sambat 1669 or eleven years before his death. A photograph, transliteration and translation of it is appended to this paper.

A few legends mentioned by Priyā Dās, and given in full by Mr. Growse in the introduction to his translation of the Rāmāyan, may be briefly noted here. A grateful ghost introduced him to Hanumān, through whom he obtained a vision of Rām and Lachhman. He recognized a murderer, who piously uttered the name of Rām, as a saved man, and when challenged to prove his statement, he did so by making the guilty man's offerings accepted by Çiva. Some thieves came to rob him, but his house was guarded by a mysterious watchman, who was no other than Rām himself, and, instead of stealing, the thieves became converted, and pure of heart. He restored a Brāhman to life.[2]) His fame reached Dillī, where Shāh Jahān was emperor. The monarch called upon him to perform a miracle and to produce the person of Rām, which Tul'sī Dās refusing to do,

[1]) Rām., Ba., Dōhā, 37.

[2]) The following in nearly is Wilson's words.

the king threw him into confinement. He was, however, speedily compelled to release him, for myriads of monkeys having collected about the prison began to demolish it and the adjacent buildings. Shāh Jahān having set the poet at liberty desired him to solicit some favour as a reparation for the indignity he had suffered. Tul'sī Dās accordingly requested him to quit ancient Dillī, which was the abode of Rām; and in compliance with this request, the emperor left it, and founded the new city, thence named Shāh-Jahān-Abād. After this, Tul-sī went to Brindāban, where he had an interview with Nābhā Dās (the author of the Bhakt Mālā). There he strenuously advocated the worship of Rām in preference to that of Krish'n, though the latter god appeared in person and assured him that there was no difference between the two. Out of this tissue of childish legends it is perhaps possible to extract a few threads of fact, but till we can find a copy of the Gosāīñ Charit'r there does not appear to be much hope of our being able to do so.

His most famous work is the Rām-charit-mānas, 'the Lake of the Gestes of Rām', which he commenced to write in Ajodhyā on Tuesday, the 9th of Chaitra, Sambat 1631 (A. D. 1574—75).[1] It is often incorrectly called the Rāmāyan, or the Tul'sī-krit Rāmāyan, or (alluding to its metre) the Chaupāī Rāmāyan, but according to the 44th Chaupāī of the Bāl Kāṇḍ, the above is its full and proper name. Two copies of this work are said to have existed in the poet's own handwriting. One of them which was kept at Rājāpur, has disappeared all but the second book. The legend is that the whole copy which existed was stolen, and that the thief being pursued flung the manuscript into the river Jamunā, whence only the second book was rescued. I have photographs of ten pages of this copy, and the marks of water are evident. The other copy exists in Malihābād (so Sib Siṅgh; Growse says in the temple of Sītā Rām, at Banāras), of which only one leaf is missing.

---

1) Rām., Bā., Ch. 43.

I am in possession of an accurate literatim copy of so much of the Rājāpur MS. as exists. I have also a printed copy of the poem carefully compared with and corrected from a manuscript in the possession of the Mahārāj of Banāras, which was written in Sambat 1704 (A. D. 1647), or only about 24 years after the author's death.

Little as the Rām-charit-mānas is known to European students, still less is known of the poet's other works. Those which I have seen and read are the following:

1) The Gītābalī. This is the story of Rām told in the form of sonnets adapted for singing. There are several incorrect editions of it in print, some of which have commentaries of varying excellence.

2) The Kabittābalī or Kabitta Rāmāyan. It deals with the same subject, and is in the Kabitta metre.

3) The Dōhābalī or Dohā Rāmāyan. As its name imports, it is in the Dōhā metre. It is rather a moral work than an epic poem, and I am not sure that it is not a collection of *dōhās* from his other works by a later hand. I have at any rate been able to identify many of them.

4) The Chhappai Rāmāyan. In the Chhappai metre. I have only seen one incorrect and unintelligible manuscript of this work, from which an edition has been printed.

5) Sat Saī, a collection of emblematic *dōhās*. Written in Sambat 1642 (A. D. 1585).

6) The Panch Ratan, or five jewels, a set of five short poems usually grouped together. They are: a) the Jānakī Maṅgal, b) the Pārbatī Maṅgal, c) the Bairāgya Sandīpinī, d) Rām Lālā Kar Nah'chhū, e) the Bar'wē Rāmāyan. The first two of these are songs celebrating the marriages of Sītā and Gaurī respectively. The third is a didactic treatise. The fourth is a song in honour of the Nah'chhū or ceremonial nail-paring of Rām at his wedding, and the fifth a short history of Rām in the Bar'wai metre.

7) The Rām Agyā also called the Rām Sagunābalī is a collection of seven books of seven chapters each, of seven *dōhās* to each chapter. It is a series of omens connected with

the life of Rām. I suspect it is spurious, and partly made up of extracts from the poet's other works. I have met with one very inferior commentary to it.

8) The Saṅkaṭ Mōchan is a short didactic work. I have only seen it in one vilely printed edition.

9) The Binay Pattrikā is a collection of 279 hymns to Rām, much admired, and deservedly so. It has often been printed, and has a very fair commentary by Sib Par'kās.

10) The Hanumān Bāhuk, a collection of sonnets in honour of Hanumān, who according to tradition gave him a vision of Rām and Lachhman.

In addition to these, the Sib Siṅgh Sarōj mentions the following:

11) Rām Salākā.

12) The Kuṇḍaliyā Rāmāyan.

13) The Kaṛ'kā Rāmāyan.

14) The Rōlā Rāmāyan.

15) The Jhūl'nā Rāmāyan.

None of which I have seen. The last four are named after the metres in which they are written.

16) A Krishnābalī, in the Braj dialect is also printed and sold in the bazārs. It deals with the life of Krish'n, and I do not believe that it is by the Tul'sī Dās whom we are now considering.

Many of these have been printed, always most incorrectly, and some with commentaries. The best commentary on the Rām-charit-mānas is that of Rām Charan Dās. The best on the Gītābalī and the Kabittābalī are by Baij'nāth. Rām Charan Das' commentary has been printed by Nawal Kishōr of Lakh'naū, but is now out of print. The other commentaries can be bought in any Indian bazār. All the commentators have a great tendency to avoid difficulties, and to give to simple passages mystical meanings which Tul'sī Dās never intended. They are unfortunately utterly wanting in the critical faculty. Though there are abundant materials for obtaining an absolutely accurate text of at least the Rām-charit-mānas, the commentators have never dreamed of referring to them, but have preferred trusting to their inner consciousness. As an extreme example I may mention one who drew up a scheme of the number of Chaupāīs each section of each canto ought to have, in a numerical decreasing order, after the pattern of the steps of a landing stage, because the poem is called a lake *(mānas)*. Nothing could be prettier than this idea; and so he hacked and hewed his unfortunate text to fit this Procrustean bed, and then published it with considerable success. It never occurred to him or his readers to see if this was what Tul'sī Dās had written, and if they had done so the ludicrous nature of the theory would have been evident at the first glance.

Regarding Tul'sī Dās' style, he was a master of all varieties, from the simplest flowing narration to the most complex emblematic verses. He wrote always in the old Bais'wārī dialect, and once the peculiarities of this are mastered, his Rām-charit-mānas is delightful and easy reading. In his Gītābalī and Kabittābalī he is more involved, but still readable with pleasure, in his Dohābalī he is sententious, and in his Sat Saī as difficult and obscure as any admirer of the Nalōdaya could wish. The Sat Saī is a veritable *tour de force*, and I am glad that this, almost the oldest specimen[1]) of this kind of writing which was brought to perfection fifty years later by Bihārī Lāl (the mine of commentators), is being edited with a commentary by Professor Bihārī Lāl Chaubē in the Bibliotheka Indica. The Binay Pattrikā is again in another style. It is a book of prayers often of the most elevated description, but its difficulties are very unsatisfactorily elucidated by either of the two commentaries of it which I have seen.

Regarding his poetic power, I think it is difficult to speak too highly. His characters live and move with all the dignity of an heroic age. Das'rath, the man of noble resolves, which fate had doomed to be unfruitful; Rām of lofty and unbending rectitude, well contrasted with his loving but impetuous brother

[1]) It was written (Sat. I, 21) in Sambat 1642, i. e. A. D. 1585. Bidyāpati's emblematic verses were written about A. D. 1400.

Lachhman; Sītā the 'perfect woman nobly planned'; and Rāban like Das'rath predestined to failure, but fighting with all his demon force against his fate, almost, like Satan in Milton's epic, the protagonist of half the poem, — all these are as vividly before my mind's eye as I write, as any character in the whole range of English literature. Then what a tender devotion there is in Bharat's character, which by its sheer truth overcomes the false schemes of his mother Kaikēyī and her maid. His villains, too, are not one black picture. Each has his own character, and none is without his redeeming virtue.

For sustained and varied dramatic interest I suppose the Rām-charit-mānas is his best work, but there are fine passages in his other poems. What can be more charming than the description of Rām's babyhood and boyhood in the commencement of the Gītābalī, or than the dainty touches of colour given to the conversations of the village women as they watch Rām, Lachhman, and Sītā treading their dreary way during their exile? Again what mastery of words is there in the Sundar Kāṇḍ of the Kabittābalī, in the description of the burning of Laṅkā. We can hear the crackling of the flames and the crash of the falling houses, the turmoil and confusion amongst the men, and the cries of the helpless women as they shriek for water.

Still even Tul'sī Dās was not able to rise altogether superior to the dense cloud which fashion had imposed upon Indian poetry. I must confess that his battle descriptions are often repulsive, and sometimes overstep the border which separates the tragic from the ludicrous. To native minds these are the finest passages which he has written, but I do not think that the cultivated European can ever find much pleasure in them. He was hampered too by the necessity of representing Rām as an incarnation of Viṣṇu, which leads him into what, although only meet adoration to the pious believer, sounds to us *mlēchchhas* as too gross hyperbole.

The reasons for the excellence of this great poet's work are not far to seek. The most important of all was the great modesty of the man. The preface to the Rām-charit-mānas is one of the most remarkable portions of the book. Kālidāsa may begin his Raghuvaṁça with a comparison of himself to a dwarf, and of his powers over language to a skiff on the boundless ocean, but from under this modest statement there gleams a consciousness of his own superiority. His modesty is evidently a mock one, and the poet is really saying to himself all the time, 'I shall soon show my readers how learned I am, and what a command I have over all the nine *rasas*'. But (and this is another reason for his superiority), Tul'sī never wrote a line in which he did not believe heart and soul. He was full of his theme, the glory and love of his master, and so immeasurably above him did that glory and that love seem, that he was full of humility with regard to himself. As he expresses it; 'My intellect is beggarly, while my ambition is imperial. May good people all pardon my presumption, and listen to my childish babbling, as a father and mother delight to hear the lisping prattle of their little one.' Kālidāsa took Rām as a peg on which to hang his graceful verses, but Tul'sī Dās wove wreathes of imperishable fragrance, and humbly laid them at the feet of the God whom he adored. One other point I would urge, which has I believe escaped the notice of even native students of our author. He is, perhaps, the only great Indian poet who took his similes direct from the book of nature, and not from his predecessors. He was so close an observer of concrete things, that many of his truest and simplest passages, are unintelligible to his commentators, who were nothing but learned men, and who went through the beautiful world around them with eyes blinded by their books. Shakespeare, we know, spoke of the white reflection of the willow leaves in the water, and thus puzzled all his editors, who said in their wisdom that willow leaves were green. It was, I think, Charles Lamb who thought of going to the river and seeing if Shakespeare was right, and who thereby swept away a cloud of proposed emendations.[1]) So too it has been

[1]) The under surface, and therefore the reflection, of the willow leaf is white.

reserved to Mr. Growse to point out that Tul'sī Dās knew far more about nature than his commentators do.

It remains now to point out the necessity there is of printing a correct text of this poet's works. At present, the printed *bazār* editions available are very deficient. The best of them is that by Paṇḍit Rām Jasan, but he, like all the other editors has printed only a modernized copy of the *textus receptus*. I have carefully compared the latter with the original text, and am in a position to state that anything more misleading can hardly be imagined. Tul'sī Dās wrote phonetically the words as they were pronounced at his time, and in an archaic dialect. In the printed books the dialect is altered to the standard of modern Hindī, and the spelling improved (?) according to the rules of Pāṇini. Examples of the modernization of the dialect are the following. Tul'sī Dās uses the short *u* as the termination of the nominative singular, leaving the crude base in *a* for its legitimate purposes in composition, thus following the rules of Apabhraṁça Prākṛit. Thus he wrote *kapi-kaṭaku,* an army of monkeys, *prabala-mōha-dalu,* a band of powerful delusions, and so on, but all the modern editions give *°kaṭaka,* and *°dala,* according to the modern pronunciation. So also modern editors write *prasāda,* favour, for the original *pasāu, bhujaṅginī,* snake, for original *bhuaṅginī, yajñavalkya* for *jagabaliku, bandauñ,* I revere, for *bandaũ, bhakti,* faith, for *bhagati,* and so on. Examples can be gathered in almost every line. Instances of alteration of spelling are equally numerous. One example must suffice. Tul'sī Dās evidently pronounced the name of Rām's father as *Dasarathu,* for that is the way he wrote it, but modern editors write the Sanskrit *Daçaratha,* which is not even the way in which it is pronounced now-adays. But there are other and even greater errors than this in the *textus receptus.* It abounds in *lacunoe.* Whole pages are sometimes omitted and minor changes occur in every page. In short, opening the printed edition at random, I count no fewer than 35 variations from the original, some most important ones, in one page of 23 lines.

In conclusion, I here give samples of the true text of the Rām-charit-mānas, founded on the Banāras and Rājāpur MSS. already alluded to, together with photographs of the originals. The footnotes show the readings of the *textus receptus.* I also exhibit my copies of these manuscripts. I hope that these will serve to show the absolute necessity of the publication of an accurate text.

Appendix.

I) Specimens from the Rāmāyaṇa.

1) From the Bāl Kāṇḍ (Banāras MS.). [Pl. II. B.]

Chaupāī.

Kō Shiwa[1]) *sama Rāmahi*[2]) *priya bhāī* ||

Dōhā.

Prathamahi mai kahi Shiwa charita
Būjhā maramu tumhāra |[3])
Suchi sēwaka tumha[4]) *Rāma kē*
Rahita samasta bikāra || *104* ||[5])

Chaupāī.

Mai[6]) *jānā tumhāra guna sīlā* |
Kahauṅ sunahu[7]) *aba Raghu-pati-līlā* ||
Sunu muni āju samāgama tōrē |[8])
Kahi na jai[9]) *jasa sukhu*[10]) *mana mōrē* ||[11])
Rāma-charita ati amita munīsā |
Kahi na sakahi[12]) *sata kōṭi ahīsā* ||
Tadapi jathā shruta[13]) *kahauṅ bakhānī* |
Sumiri Girā-pati Prabhu dhanu-pānī ||

---

[1]) *Siwa.* — [2]) *Rāmahī.* — [3]) *Prathama kahē maiṅ Siwa charita būjhā marama tumhāra* | — [4]) *tuma.* — [5]) *112.* — [6]) *maiṅ.* — [7]) *sunahū.* — [8]) *tōrē.* — [9]) *jāya.* — [10]) *sukha.* — [11]) *mōrē.* — [12]) *sakahī.* — [13]) *sruta.*

Sārada dāru-nāri-sama, Swāmī |
Rāmu[1]) *sūtra-dhara antara-jāmī* ||
Jehi para kṛipā karahi janu[2]) *jānī* |
Kabi-ura ajira nachāwahi[3]) *Bānī* ||

TRANSLATION.

(Yajñavalkya says to Bharadvāja) 'who, brother, is as dear to Rāma as Çiva is'.

Dōhā 104.

I began by telling thee Çiva's deeds, for well understand I thy secret, that thou art a pure servant of Rāma, free from all variableness.

Chaupāī.

I understood thy character and disposition, listen therefore while I tell thee Raghu-pati's incarnation. Hear, O saint; I cannot tell how happy is my heart at my meeting with thee to-day. Though Rāma's deeds are, Holy saint, beyond measure, and though a hundred times ten million serpent kings could not tell them, still I tell thee the tale as it hath been revealed, after meditating on the Master, bow in hand, the lord of the goddess of eloquence. For Saraswatī is as it were but a puppet, and the Master Rāma, the knower of the heart, the manager who pulleth the strings. When he findeth a true believer, he graciously maketh her to dance in the court-yard of the poet's heart.

2) Conclusion of the Kis'kindhā Kāṇḍ[4]) (Banāras MS.). [Pl. II B.]

(The two following extracts are given for the sake of the Colophons.)

Chhand.[5])

(Jō sunata gāwata kahata sa)mujhata parama pada nara pāwaī |
Raghu-bīra-pada-pāthōja madhu-kara Dāsa Tulasī gāwaī ||

---

[1]) *Rāma.* — [2]) *karahī jana.* — [3]) *nachāwahī.* One edition of *text. rec.* gives *ānī* for *bānī.* — [4]) These are the names of the *kaṇḍs* as given in the printed edition. Tul'sī Dās, it will be seen, gave other names. — [5]) Passages in the Chhand metres are always in highly Sanskritized style, and hence are seldom altered in the printed texts.

Dōhā.

Bhawa-bhēkha-ja-Raghu-nātha-jasu [1])
Sunahi jē nara aru nāri |
Tinha kara sakala manōratha
Siddha karahī Trisirā-'ri ‖[2])

Sōraṭhā.

Nīlōtpala tana [3]) *syāma*
Kāma kōṭi sōbhā adhika |
Sunia [4]) *tāsu guna-grāma*
Jāsu nāma agha-khaga-badhika ‖ *30* ‖[5])

Iti Çrī [6])-*Rāma-charita-mānasē sakala-kali-kaluṣa-vidhvaṁsanē, Visuddha*[sic]-*santōṣa-sampādinī* [7])-*nāma chaturthas sōpānaḥ samāptaḥ* ‖ *Çubham astu* [8]) ‖ *Sambat 1704 samaē, Paukha-shūdi-dwārasi* [9]) *likhitaṁ Raghu Tīvāri Kāsyāṁ* ‖

TRANSLATION.

Chhand.

That man who heareth, singeth, reciteth, or understandeth this lay, gaineth the highest place in heaven. And therefore doth Tul'sī Dās, like the honey-bee, ever sing the (glory of the) lotus feet of Raghu Vīra.

Dōhā.

That man or woman who heareth the glory of Raghu Nātha,—that panacea for the ills of existence, all the desires of his heart will Rāma,—the slayer of Triçiras,[10]) fulfil.

---

[1]) *jasa.* — [2]) *Tripurā-'ri.* — [3]) *tanu.* — [4]) *Suniya.* — [5]) System of numbering different from that of the printed text which here has 2. — [6]) In Sanskrit passages, I transliterate श by ç, in Gaudian passages by *sh.* — [7]) *vimala-vairāgya-sampādanō.* — [8]) *Çubham astu* | *Siddhir astu.* — [9]) A very interesting form. This date is of course omitted in the printed editions. — [10]) The reading of the *textus receptus, Tripurāri,* i. e. Çiva, makes nonsense here.

Sōraṭhā.

List ye then to the tale of his virtues, whose name is the fowler to the (unclean) birds of sin, with his body dark-hued as the blue-lotus, and his beauty greater than that of a myriad loves.

Here endeth the fourth descent (entitled the Bestower of Purity and Continence) into the Lake of the Gestes of Rām, which destroyeth all the defilement of this Kali age. Written on the 12th of the light half of Paukh, Sambat 1704 (at Banāras by Raghu Tiwārī.

3) Conclusion of the Laṅkā Kāṇḍ (Banāras MS.). [Pl. II. B.]

Chhand.

(Mati-manda Tulasī) Dāsa sō Prabhu mōha-basa bisarāïyō ‖
Yaha Rāwanā-'ri-charitra pāwana Rāma-pada-rati-prada sadā |
Kāmā-''di-hara bigyāna-kara sura-siddha-muni gāwahī mudā ‖

Dōhā.

Samara-bijaya Raghu-mani-charita [1])
Sunahī je sadā sujāna | [2])
Bijaya bibēka bibhūti nita
Tinhahī[3]) *dēhī Bhagawāna* ‖
Yaha Kali-kāla malā-''yatana
Mana kari dēkhu bichāra |
Shrī Raghu-nāyaka-nāmu[4]) *taji*
Nahi kachhu āna adhāra[5]) ‖ *120* ‖[6])

Iti Çrī-Rāma-charita-mānasē sakala-kali-kaluṣa-vidhvaṁsanē, Vimala-vijñāna-sampādinī[7])*-nama ṣaṣṭhas sōpānaḥ samāptaḥ*[8]) | *Çubham astu* ‖ *Sambat 1704 samaē* ‖ *Māgha-sūdi pratipad likhītaṁ Raghutīvārī Kāsyāṁ (?) Tōlā-kasmīrē* ‖ *Çrī-Rāmō jayati* | *Çrī-Viçva-nāthāya namaḥ* ‖ *Çrī-Vindumādhavaē* (? sic) *namaḥ* ‖

---

[1]) *Samara-bijaya Raghubīra kē.* — [2]) *Charita je sunahī sujāna.* — [3]) *Tinahī.* — [4]) *-natha-nāma.* — [5]) *Nāhina āna.* — [6]) *118.* — [7]) *vimala-jñāna-sampādanō.* — [8]) Printed editions omit all after this.

Translation.

Chhand.

Dull of soul, O Tul'sī Dās, is he who in his delusion forgetteth such a Lord. Gods, saints, and sages joyfully sing these gestes of the foe of Rāvaṇa. For they are purifying, and ever fill one with devotion to Rāma's feet, the destroyers of fleshly lusts, and causers of true wisdom.

Dōhā.

The wise man who ever listeth to Raghu Mani's deeds and to his victories in the battle, to him doth God give victory, discrimination, and fame for ever. This sinful Kali age is the very abode of impurity, therefore consider thou and understand. If thou desert the name of the holy Raghu Nāyaka, none other refuge wilt thou have.

Here endeth the sixth descent (entitled the Bestower of a Pure Understanding) into the Lake of the Gestes of Rām, which destroyeth all the defilement of this Kali age. Written on the first day of the light half of Māgh, Sambat 1704, at Banāras, Kāshmīrī Ṭōlā (?), by Raghu Tiwārī.

4) From the Ajodhyā Kāṇḍ (Rājāpur MS.). [Pl. I.]

Chaupāī.

(Dēhī ku)chālihi kōṭi ka[1]) *gārī* ‖
Jarahī bikhama jara[2]) *lēhi usāsā* |
Kawani[3]) *Rāma binu jīwana-āsā* ‖
Bipula[4]) *biyōga prajā akulānī* |
Janu[5]) *jala-chara-gana sūkhata pānī* ‖
Ati bikhāda-basa lōga logāī |[6])
Gayē mātu pahī[7]) *Rāmu*[8]) *gosāī* ‖[9])
Mukhu[10]) *prasanna chita chau-guna chāū* |
Miṭā sōchu[11]) *jani rākhaï*[12]) *rāū* ‖

---

1) *hu.* — 2) *jwara.* — 3) *kawana.* — 4) *Bikula.* — 5) *Jimi.* — 6) *lugāī.* — 7) *pahā̃.* — 8) *Rāma.* — 9) *gusā̃ī.* — 10) *Mukha.* — 11) *Ihai sōcha.* — 12) *rākhahī.*

Dōhā.

Nawa gayandu Raghu-bīra-manu[1]
Rāju[2] *alāna samāna* |
Chhūṭa jāni bana-gawanu[3] *suni*
Ura-anandu[4] *adhikāna* ‖ *51* ‖[5]

Chaupāī.

Raghu-kula-tilaka jōri doū[6] *hāthā* |
Mudita mātu-pada nāyeu[7] *māthā* ‖
Dīnhi[8] *asīsa lāī ura līnhē* |
Bhūkhana basana nichhāwari kīnhē ‖
Bāra bāra mukha chumbati[9] *mātā* |
Nayana nēha-jalu[10] *pulakita gātā* |
Gōda rākhi puni hṛidaya lagāē |[11]
Shrawata[12] *prēma-rasa payada suhāē* ‖[13]
Prēmu pramōdu[14] *na kachhu kahi jāī* |
Raṅka Dhanada-padawī janu pāī ‖
Sādara sundara badanu[15] *nihārī* |
Bōlī madhura bachana mahatārī ‖
'*Kahahu, Tāta, jananī bali-hārī* |
Kabahī lagana muda-maṅgala kārī ‖
Sukṛita-sīla-sukha-sīwa[16] *suhāī* |
Janama-lābha kaï awadhi[17] *aghāī* ‖

Dōhā.

Jehi chāhata nara-nāri saba
Ati ārata ehi[18] *bhāti* |
Jimi chātaka-chātaki trikhita[19]
Briṣṭi sarada-ritu[20] *swāti* ‖ *52* ‖[21]

---

1) *gayanda Raghu-bansa-mani.* — 2) *Rāja.* — 3) *gawana.* — 4) *ānâda.* — 5) *50.* — 6) *dwau.* — 7) *nāyaū.* — 8) *Dīnha.* — 9) *chūmati.* — 10) *jala.* — 11) *lagāī.* — 12) *Srawata.* — 13) *suhāī.* — 14) *Prēma-pramōda.* — 15) *badana.* — 16) *sīwa.* — 17) *Janma-lābha kahi* (or *lahi*) *awadha.* — 18) *ihi.* — 19) *chātaki-chātaka triṣita.* — 20) *ritu.* — 21) *51.*

Chaupāī.

Tāta, jāū̃ bali, bēgi nahāhū |[1])
Jō mana bhāwa madhura kachhu khāhū ||
Pitu samīpa taba jāyehu bhaiā |
Bhaï baḍi[2]) *bāra jāi bali maiā'* ||
Mātu-bachana suni[3]) *ati anukūlā* |
Janu sanēha-sura-taru kē phūlā ||
Sukha-makaranda-bharē Shriya[4])*-mūlā* |
Nirakhi Rāma-manu bhawaru[5]) *na bhūlā* ||
Dharama[6])*-dhurīna dharama*[7])*-gati jānī* |
Kaheu mātu sana ati mṛidu bānī ||
'Pitā dīnha mohi kānana-rājū |
Jahā̃ saba bhā̃ti mōra baḍa[8]) *kājū* ||
Āyesu dēhi[9]) *mudita mana mātā* |
Jēhi[10]) *muda-maṅgala kānana jātā* ||
Jani sanēha-basa ḍarapasi bhōrē̃ |[11])
Ānādu amba[12]) *anugraha tōrē̃* ||[13])

Dōhā.

Barakha[14]) *chāri-dasa bipina basi*
Kari pitu-bachana-pramāna |
Āï[15]) *pāya puni dēkhihau*
Manu[16]) *jani karasi malāna'* || *53* ||[17])

Chaupāī.

Bachana binīta madhura Raghubara kē |
Sara sama lagē mātu-ura kara kē ||
Sahami sūkhi suni sītali[18]) *bānī* |
Jimi jawāsa pare[19]) *pāwasa pānī* ||
Kahi na jāï kachhu hṛidaya-bikhādū |
Manahū̃ mṛigī suni[20]) *kēhari-nādū* ||

---

1) *anhāhū.* — 2) *baṛi.* — 3) Here ends leaf 28 of the MS. — 4) *Shrī.* — 5) *Rāma-mana bhā̃wara.* — 6) *Dharma.* — 7) *dharma.* — 8) *baṛa.* — 9) *Āyasu dēhu.* — 10) *Jehi.* — 11) *bhōrē.* — 12) *Ānāda mātu.* — 13) *tōrē.* — 14) *Barkha.* — 15) *Āya.* — 16) *Mana.* — 17) 52. — 18) *sītala.* — 19) *para.* — 20) *janu sahamē kari.*

Nayana sajala,[1] *tana*[2] *thara thara kāpī* |[3]
Mājahi khāi mīna janu māpī ‖[4]
Dhari dhīraju[5] *suta-badanu*[6] *nihārī* |
Gadagada[7]*-bachana kahati mahatārī* ‖
'*Tāta pitahi tumha*[8] *prāna-piārē* |
Dēkhi mudita nita charita tumhārē ‖
Rāju[9] *dēna kahū̃*[10] *subha dina sādhā* |
Kaheu jāna bana kehi aparādhā ‖
Tāta sunāwahu mōhi nidānū |
Kō dina-kara-kula bhayeu[11] *kṛisānū*' ‖

Dōhā.

Nirakhi Rāma-rukha sachiwa-suta.
Kāranu[12] *kaheu bujhāī* |
Suni prasaṅgu[13] *rahi mūka jimi*[14]
Dasā barani nahi[15] *jāī* ‖ *54* ‖[16]

Chaupāī.

Rākhi na sakaī[17] *na kahi saka jāhū* |
Duhū̃ bhā̃ti ura dāruna dāhū ‖
Likhata sudhā-kara'gā[18] *likhi Rāhū* |
Bidhi-gati bāma sadā saba kāhū ‖
Dharama[19]*-sanēha ubhaya mati ghērī* |
Bhaī gati sā̃pa chhuchhundari kērī ‖
Rākhau̐ sutahi karau̐[20] *anurōdhū* |
Dharamu[21] *jāī aru bandhu-birōdhū* ‖
Kahau̐ jāna bana tau baḍi[22] *hānī.* |
Saṅkaṭa sōcha bibasa[23] *bhaī rānī* ‖
Bahuri sumujhi tiya-dharamu[24] *sayānī* |
Rāmu Bharatu doū[25] *sutasama jānī* ‖

---

[1] *Salila.* — [2] *tanu.* — [3] *kā̃pī.* — [4] *Mā̃jā manahū̃ mīna kahā̃ byāpī.* — [5] *dhīraja.* — [6] *badana.* — [7] *Gadgada.* — [8] *tuma.* — [9] *Rāja.* — [10] *kahā̃.* — [11] *bhayau.* — [12] *kāraṇa.* — [13] *prasaṅga.* — [14] *mūka-gati.* — [15] *nahī̃.* — [16] *53.* — [17] *sakahī̃.* Here ends leaf 29 of MS. — [18] *likhi gā.* — [19] *Dharma.* — [20] *hōī.* — [21] *Dharma.* — [22] *baṛi.* — [23] *bikala.* — [24] *dharma.* — [25] *Rāma Bharata dwau.*

Sarala subhāü[1]) *Rāma-mahatārī* |
Bōlī bachana dhīra dhari bhārī ‖
'*Tāta, jāū̃ bali, kīnhehu*[2]) *nīkā* |
Pitu-āyesu[3]) *saba dharama ka*[4]) *ṭīkā* ‖

Dōhā.

Rāju[5]) *dēna kahi,*[6]) *dīnha banu*[7])
Mōhi na sō[8]) *dukha-lēsa* |
Tumha[9]) *binu Bharatahi bhu-patihi*
Prajahi prachaṇḍa kalēsa ‖ 55 ‖[10])

Chaupāī.

Jaun̐[11]) *kēwala pitu-āyesu*[12]) *tātā* |
Tau jani jāhu jāni baḍi mātā ‖[13])
Jaun̐[14]) *pitu-mātu kaheu*[15]) *bana jānā* |
Tau kānana sata Awadha samānā ‖
Pitu bana dēwa, mātu bana-dēwī |
Khaga mṛiga charana-sarōruha-sēwī ‖
Antahu uchita nṛipahi bana-bāsū |
Baya bilōki hiya hōï[16]) *harāsū* ‖
Baḍa[17]) *bhāgī banu,*[18]) *Awadha abhāgī* |
Jō[19]) *Raghu-bansa-tilaka tumha*[20]) *tyāgī* ‖
Jaun̐[21]) *suta kahaun̐ saṅga mohi lēhū* |
Tumharē hṛidaya hōï sandēhū ‖
Pūta[22]) *parama priya tumha*[23]) *saba-hī kē* |
Prāna prāna kē jīwana jī ke ‖
Tē tumha[24]) *kahahu mātu bana jāū̃* |
Mai[25]) *suni bachana baithi pachhitāū̃* ‖

Dōhā.

Ehi[26]) *bichāri nahi*[27]) *karaū̃ haṭha.*
Jhūṭha sanēhu baḍhāï |[28])

---

1) *subhāwa.* — 2) *kīnheü.* — 3) *āyasu.* — 4) *dharma ke.* — 5) *Rāja.* — 6) *kahā̃.* — 7) *bana.* — 8) *muhi na sōcha.* — 9) *Tuma.* — 10) *54.* — 11) *Jau.* — 12) *āyasu.* — 13) *jāï bali mātā.* — 14) *Jau.* — 15) *kahain̐.* — 16) *hōta.* — 17) *Baṛa.* — 18) *bana.* — 19) *Jau.* — 20) *tuma.* — 21) *Jau.* — 22) *Putra.* — 23) *tuma.* — 24) *Tuma.* — 25) *Main̐.* — 26) *Yaha.* — 27) *nahī̃.* Here ends leaf 30 of the MS. — 28) *sanēha baṛhāï.*

Māni mātu kara[1]) *nāta bali*
Surati bisari jani jāï ‖ 56 ‖[2])

Chaupāī.

Dēwa pitara saba tumhahi gosāī̃ |[3])
Rākhahū[4]) *palaka nayana kī nāī̃* ‖
Awadhi ambu, priya parijana mīnā |
Tumha[5]) *karunā-"kara dharama*[6])*-dhurīnā* ‖
Asa bichāri soï karahu upāī |
Saba-hi jiata jēhi[7]) *bhē̃ṭahu āī* ‖
Jāhu sukhēna banahī bali jāū̃ |
Kari anātha jana parijana gāū̃ ‖
Saba kara āju sukṛita phala bītā |
Bhayeu karālu kālu[8]) *biparītā* ‖
Bahu-bidhi bilapi charana lapaṭānī |
Parama abhāgini āpuhi jānī ‖
Dāruna dusaha dāhu[9]) *ura byāpā* |
Barani na jāhī[10]) *bilāpa-kalāpā* ‖
Rāma uṭhāï mātu ura lāī |[11])
Kahi mṛidu bachana bahuri samujhāī ‖[12])

Dōhā.

Samāchāra tehi samaya suni
Siya uṭhī akulāï |
Jāi sāsu-pada-kamala-juga[13])
Bandi baiṭhi siru[14]) *nāï* ‖ 57 ‖[15])

Chaupāī.

Dinhi[16]) *asīsa sāsu mṛidu bānī* |
Ati sukumāri dēkhi akulānī ‖
Baiṭhi namita mukha sōchati Sītā |
Rūpa-rāsi pati-prēma-punītā |

---

1) *kē.* — 2) *55.* — 3) *tumahi gusāī̃.* — 4) *Rākhahu.* — 5) *Tuma.* — 6) *dharma.* — 7) *jiyata jehi.* — 8) *Bhayē karāla kāla.* — 9) *dāha.* — 10) *jāī.* — 11) *lāwā.* — 12) *bahuta samujhāwā.* — 13) *paga-kamala-yuga.* — 14) *sira.* — 15) *56.* — 16) *Dīnha.*

'*Chalana chahata bana jīwana-nāthū* |[1])
Kehi sukṛitī[2]) *sana hoïhi sāthū* ‖[3])
Kī tanu-prāna, ki kēwala prānā |
Bidhi karatabu[4]) *kachhu jāï*[5]) *na jānā*' ‖
Chāru charana-nakha lēkhati dharanī |
Nūpura mukhara madhura kabi baranī ‖
Manahū̃ prēma-basa binatī karahī̃ |
'*Hamahī Sīya-pada jani pariharahī̃*' ‖
Mañju bilōchana mōchati bārī |
Bōlī dēkhi[6]) *Rāma-mahatārī* ‖
'*Tāta sunahu Siya ati sukumārī* |
Sāsu sasura parijanahi piārī ‖[7])

Dōhā.

Pitā Janaka bhūpāla-mani
Sasura bhānu-kula-bhānu |
Pati rawi-kula-kairawa-bipina-
Bidhu guna-rūpa-nidhānu ‖ *58* ‖[8])

Chaupāī.

Maĩ puni putra-badhū priya pāī |
Rūpa-rāsi guna-sīla suhāī ‖
Nayana-putari kari[9]) *prīti baḍhāī* |[10])
Rākheũ prāna Jānakihi lāī ‖
Kalapa-bēli[11]) *jimi bahu bidhi lālī* |
Sī̃chi sanēha-salila pratipālī ‖
Phūlata phalata bhayeu[12]) *bidhi bāmu* |
Jāni na jāi kāha parināmā ‖
Palãga pīṭha taji gōda hĩḍōrā |
Siya na dīnha[13]) *pagu awani kaṭhōra* ‖
Jiana-mūri[14]) *jimi jogawata*[15]) *rahaū̃* |[16])
Dīpa-bāti nahi[17]) *ṭārana kahaū̃* ‖[18])

---

1) *nāthā.* — 2) *Kawana sukṛita.* — 3) *sātha.* — 4) *karataba.* — 5) *jāta.* — 6) Here ends leaf 31 of MS. — 7) *parijanahi piyari.* — 8) 57. — 9) *iwa.* — 10) *baṛhāī.* — 11) *Kalpa-bēli.* — 12) *bhayē.* — 13) *dīna.* — 14) *Jīwana-mūri.* — 15) *jugawati.* — 16) *raheũ.* — 17) *nahī̃.* — 18) *kaheũ.*

Soī[1]) *Siya chalana chahati bana sāthā* |
Āyesu[2]) *kāha*[3]) *hōi Raghu-nāthā* ‖
Chanda[4])*-kirana-rasa-rasika chakōrī* |
Rawi-rukha nayana sakai kimi jōrī ‖

Dōhā.

Kari kēhari nisi-chara charahī
Dusṭa jantu bana bhūri |
Bikha-bāṭikā ki sōha suta
Subhaga sãjīwani[5]) *mūri* ‖ *59* ‖[6])

Chaupāī.

Bana hita kōla kirāta-kisōrī |
Rachi Birañchi bikhaya-sukha[7])*-bhōrī* ‖
Pāhana-kṛimi jimi kaṭhina subhāū |
Tinahi kalēsu[8]) *na kānana kāū* ‖
Kai tāpasa-tiya kānana jōgū |[9])
Jinha[10]) *tapa-hētu tajā saba bhōgū* ‖
Siya bana basihi tāta kehi bhātī |[11])
Chitra-likhita kapi dēkhi ḍerātī ‖
Sura-sara-subhaga-banaja-bana-chārī |
Ḍābara-jōgu[12]) *ki hansa-kumārī* ‖

TRANSLATION.

(The town folk heaped upon) the wicked (Kaikēyī) countless abuse. They burn with a fierce fever, and sob, crying, 'without Rāma, what hope of our life is left'? Distraught at the long banishment were the people like creatures of the deep when the water drieth up. Men and women were overpowered by grief; but the holy Master Rāma went to his mother, with his face suffused with happiness, and fourfold joy in his heart, for he had overcome sorrow, (only now fearing) lest the king should detain him.[13])

[1]) *Sō.* — [2]) *Āyasu.* — [3]) *kahā.* — [4]) *Chandra.* — [5]) *sajīwana.* — [6]) *58.* — [7]) *rasa.* — [8]) *Tinahī kalēsa.* — [9]) *yōgū.* — [10]) *Jina.* — [11]) *bhāti.* — [12]) *yōga.* — [13]) The passage is difficult. The *textus receptus* is quite easy, 'fearing only that the king might detain him'. Ram Charan Dās, in his comm., reads *hṛidaya sōcha.*

Dōhā 51.

The soul of the hero of Raghu's race was like a young elephant, with a kingdom for its chain. The sentence of banishment was as it were its loosening, and as he heard of it, great became the joy of his heart.

Chaupāī.

The crown of Raghu's race clasped his hands, and joyfully bowed his head at his mother's feet. She gave him her blessing and then clasped him to her bosom, as she scattered over him gifts of jewels and raiment. Again and again with thrilling limbs doth she kiss his face, as the water of love rushed to her eyes. Then taking him in her lap, she pressed him to her heart, while drops of affection oozed from her comely breasts. None can describe her rapture and her love,— she who seemed like a beggar made rich as Kuvēra. Adoringly gazing on his fair countenance, his mother uttered words full of sweetness. 'Tell me, my darling[1]) (and may the blessing of thy mother be upon thee), what hour hath been fixed for the happy and propitious ceremony (of thy coronation), the delightful horizon of piety, amiability and happiness, and the extreme bound of the fruition of my birth,

Dōhā 52.

'For which the people, men and women, all long for anxiously, as a thirsty *chātaka* and his mate long, in the autumn season, for the rainfall of Arcturus.

Chaupāī.

'My darling, haste, with my blessing, and bathe. Then eat thou something sweet in which thy soul delighteth. Afterwards approach thou thy father; I, thy mother, protest that there is too much delay.' Rāma heard his mother's most loving words,

[1]) Rām's mother has not yet heard of the sentence of banishment, and is asking what date is fixed for Rām's installation as heir to the throne.

which seemed like flowers of the Paradise-tree of love, brimming over with the honey of happiness, and rooted in prosperity; but, as he gazed upon her, his bee-like soul forgot not its duty. Perfect in virtue, he followed virtue's path, and thus, in tender language did he address his mother. 'The realm which my father hath given me is the forest, where I shall in every way have much work to do. Give thy command, my mother, with a joyful heart, so that I may joyfully and auspiciously depart thereto. Under the influence of thy love, fear thou not causelessly; for my happiness, mother mine, dependeth on thy consent.

Dōhā 53.

'When I shall have dwelt for fourteen years in the woods, and thus made good my father's word, then will I return and again behold thy feet. Let not thy heart be sad.'

Chaupāī.

The dutiful sweet words of Raghu Vara pierced like arrows through his mother's breast. As she heard his chilling speech, she withered in her terror, as the *jawāsa* plant droopeth under a shower in the rainy season. Aught of the anguish of her soul I cannot tell. 'Twas e'en as when an elephant shrinketh at the roar of a tiger. Her eyes were filled with tears, and her whole form shivered, as a fish drunk with the scour of a flooded river.[1]) Summoning up her courage, Rāma's mother gazed upon her son's face, and thus spake she words broken by her sobs. 'My darling, thou art the beloved of thy father's life-breath, and it ever is his joy to gaze upon thy doings. He hath fixed a lucky day for giving thee his kingdom; for what crime hath he sentenced thee to the forest? My darling let me hear the end. Who hath become the destroying fire of the solar race?'

---

[1]) This is one of the passages which has puzzled commentators who were not observers of nature. It was Mr. Growse who first pointed out that the literal meaning is quite correct. See Translation, II, 30, 80.

Dōhā 54.

After a glance at Rāma's countenance the minister's son explained to her the cause. Like one struck dumb she heard the tale; words cannot tell her state.

Chaupāī.

She cannot hold him back, nor can she tell him 'Go'. In either way was her bosom filled with a fire of agony. 'Twas e'en as if one who would write the word 'Moon', had found that he had written 'Eclipse'. The way of fate seemed ever hostile to all. Two (foes) Duty and Affection had laid siege against her soul. Her fate was like that of the snake and the muskrat.[1] 'If I make my son to stay, and disobey (the king),—my virtuous deeds will be obliterated, and my relations will hate me. If I tell him to depart to the forest, great will be my loss.' In these conflicting thoughts became the queen distraught. And then again discreetly recalled she her wifely duty, and remembered that Rāma and Bharata were both equally her sons. Then in her simple nature did Rāma's mother summon up her courage and slowly speak these words. 'Darling, receive my last blessing,—thou hast done aright. (Obedience to) a father's command is the crown of every duty.

Dōhā 55.

'He said that he would give to thee the kingdom,—he hath given thee the forest;—and that he hath done so is not a cause of a trace of the sorrow in my heart. But without thee, terrible will be the distress of Bharata, of the king and of the people.

Chaupāī.

'Yet, darling, if it be only thy father that biddeth thee to go, then go thou not, but hold thy mother still greater. But if

[1]) 'If it swallows the rat, it dies; if it disgorges it, it goes blind; such is the popular belief.' Growse, Trans., ad l.

both father and mother[1]) banish thee to the forest, then to thee will the wood be as an hundred Awadhas. The sylvan God will be to thee a father, and the sylvan Goddess a mother. The birds and deer will serve thy lotus feet. In declining years retirement to the forest is meet for a king, but when I think upon thy (tender) age fear fills my heart. Blessed will be the forest, and unblessed will be Awadha, when thou, the crown of Raghu's line, dost leave it. If, son, I say unto thee, "take thou me with thee", and if there be doubt thereat within thy heart,—O, my child, thou art dearest of all to all, breath of our breath, life of our life—and if thou say unto me, "mother, I depart into banishment alone",—when I hear thy words, will I sit at home and lament?'

Dōhā 56.

'Thinking thus, I will not be perverse (and insist upon my going with thee) with a feigned affection. But remember thou the relation that I bear to thee, and forget me not.[2])

Chaupāī.

'Be thou guarded, noble boy, by the Gods and all the spirits of thy ancestors, as closely as the eyeball is guarded by its lids. The period of thy banishment is like the sea, and thy beloved ones are its fish. Thou alone art, as it were, the All-Merciful, the Perfect in Justice. Remember this, and so arrange thou thy plans, that when thou returnest, thou mayest find all alive. Go thou in peace to thy banishment, with thy mother's blessing, leaving, the while, the people, thy friends, the whole city bereft of its lord. To-day hath passed away for ever all the fruit of their good deeds, for dreadful Death himself is opposed

[1]) Kaikēyī, Rām's step-mother, is considered as his mother; just as Kausalyā considered Bharat (Kaikēyī's child) as her own son.

[2]) According to the commentators, Kausalyā is purposely made incoherent here. She wants to go with Rām, and tries to explain to him that this is not because, she is afraid of his forgetting her, which is the doubt in his mind to which she refers a few lines further back. At the same time the fear of his forgetting her is present in her mind, and she discloses it here.

to them'. Thus many times lamenting, and clinging to his feet, did she count herself to be the most hapless of women. A cruel unbearable fire pervaded her breast, nor can the tale of her lamentations be told in full. But Rāma arose and took his mother to his bosom, and again and again consoled her with his gentle words.

Dōhā 57.

Just then heard Sītā the tale of what had happened, and rising in agitation, came she and reverenced with bowed head the lotus feet of Rāma's mother.

Chaupāī.

Her mother blessed her with gentle words, and as she saw her tender frame became yet more distressed. With bended face Sītā, the perfection of the beautiful, pure in her wifely devotion, sitteth in thought. 'The Lord of my life is about to go into banishment, by what good deed can (I earn the claim) to be his companion in his wanderings? Shall I go with him in soul and body, or only in soul?[1] I know not, for the appointments of God are inscrutable'. She writeth on the dust with her dainty toe-nails, her anklets, the while, giving forth sweet music, like a poet's song. They ring out, as it were, the loving prayer 'May we never leave the feet of Sītā'. Rāma's mother saw the tears flowing from her tender eyes and cried, 'My darling, hearken! Sītā is delicate of form, and dear is she to her husband's parents and his kindred.

Dōhā 58.

'Her father is Janaka, a jewel among kings, and her father-in-law the sun of the Solar race. Her lord is the moon of the lily forest of the sun's offspring, full of virtue and of beauty.

Chaupāī.

'I too have obtained in her a beloved bride for my son, beautiful, virtuous, and charming. My love for her, the apple

[1]) i. e. alive or dead.

of mine eye, increaseth ever. And I but remain [1]) alive for Sītā's sake. [2]) In many varied ways is she charming as the jasmine of paradise, and as I tended her did I water her from the spring of love. But as she beareth blossom and fruit, hath fate become averse, nor doth one know what the end will be. If e'er she left her couch or seat, became my lap her cradle; never hath Sītā put her foot upon the hard earth. Like the root of my life did I nurture her, nor did I e'er e'en ask her but to move aside the wick of a lamp. Yet it is she who wisheth to go to the forest with thee. What is thy command, O Raghu Nātha? Can the hen *chakōr* who delighteth in the nectar of the moon-ray, bear to turn her eyes towards the sun?

Dōhā 59.

'Elephants and lions, demons, and evil beasts wander manifold throughout the forest. O son, can the sweet tree of life bloom in such a poison-garden?

Chaupāī.

'God hath created the forest to be dear to Kōles and to the women of the Kirātas, who scorn a life of ease. Their nature is tough as the stone-worm, nor, to them, is there any hardship in the woods. Or a hermit's wife, who for penance hath abandoned every joy, is fit for the woods. But, darling, how can Sītā dwell in the forest;—she who is terrified if she see but a pictured ape. Is the hen-cygnet, who hath wandered through the sweet lotus forests of the Ganges, fit for dwelling in a swamp? . . . . . .'

---

[1]) i. e. After thy departure.

[2]) A pun here in the original, on *Prān*, or *Jān*, the first syllable of Jānakī.

II. Deed of arbitration in the handwriting of Tul'sī Dās, dated Sam. 1669 (A. D. 1612), with photograph of original,[1]) transliteration, and translation.

I take this opportunity of thanking J. A. Reid Esq. Secretary to Govt. N. W. P. and Audh, and Rājā Shiva Prasād C. S. I., to whom I am indebted for the photographs of the deed and manuscripts accompanying this paper, and for the copies of the Banāras MS., and of the Rājāpur fragment.

I have also to express my acknowledgment to my old friend and teacher Mīr Aulād 'Alī, Professor of Arabic, Persian, and Hindūstānī, at Trinity College, Dublin, for much assistance rendered in transliterating and translating the Persian and Arabic portions of the deed.

(Transcription.)

Çrī-Jānakī-vallabhō vijayatē.

Dviç çaraṁ nābhisaṁdhattē dvis sthāpayati nāçritān | Dvir dadāti na 1
chārthibhyō Rāmō dvir naiva bhāṣatē ‖ 1 ‖. Tulasī jānyō Daçarathahī dha- 2
ramu na satya samāna ‖ Rāmu tajō jehi lāgi binu Rāma pariharē prāna ‖ 3
Dharmō jayati nādharmas satyaṁ jayati nānṛtaṁ | Kshamā jayati na krōdhō 4
Viṣṇur jayati nāsurāḥ ‖ 1 ‖ 5

Allāhu Akbar.

Chū̃ Anad Rām bin Tōdar bin Dēō Rāy wa Kanhāē bin Rām Bhadar bin Tōdar mazkūr 6
dar ḥuẓūr āmada qarār dādand ki dar mawāẓi'i matrūka ki tafṣīli ā̃ dar Hindwī mazkūr ast 7
bilmunāṣafa batarāẓī i jānibain qarār dādēm. Wa yak ṣad o pinjāh (?) bīghā zamīn ziyāda (?) qismati munāṣafa khūd[2]) 8
dar mauẓa'i Bhadainī Anand Rām mazkūr ba Kanhāē bin Rām Bhadar mazbūr tajwīz namūda 9

---

[1]) See Plate II, A. — [2]) Or *(?) az ḥiṣṣa qismati munāṣafa.*

10 *barī̃ ma'anī rāẓī gashta i'tirāf ṣaḥīḥ shar'ī namūdand banābari ā̃*
11 *muhr karda shud*

(Seal) ? *Ṣādullāh bin . . . . . .*

12 *Qismati Anad Rām.*	*Qismati Kanhāē.*
13 *qariyā Bhadainī, do ḥiṣṣa. qariyā Lahartārā, darōbast.*	*qariyā Bhadainī, sih ḥiṣṣa. qariyā Shiūpūr darōbast.*
14 *qariyā Naipūra, ḥiṣṣa i Tōdar tamām.*	*qariyā Nadēsar ḥiṣṣa i Tōdar tamām.*
qariyā Chhitūpūra khūrd ḥiṣṣa i Tōdar tamām.	*(?) Iṭṭala'a'alaih* (illegible)

Srī Paramēswar.

15 *Sambat 1669 samae, Kuār sudi tērasī, bār sub dīnē likhītaṁ patra Anand*
16 *Rām tathā Kanhaï su(bha)ṁ, ans bībhāg purbamu āgē̃ mai āgya dunahu janē bhāg*
17 *jē āgya bhai sē pramān mānā. Dunahu janē bīdīt ta asīlu ans Ṭōḍar Malu*
18 *me bhaï jeṣṭ bhāg padu hōt. Rā . . . .*

19 *Ans Ānand Rām. Maujē Bhadainī maï an-*	*Ans Kanhaï. Maujē Bhadainī maï ans pā̃ch, tehī*
20 *-s pā̃ch, tehī maï ans duï Ānand Rāmu.*	*maï tīnī ans Kanhaï. Tathā maujē Sīpurā.*
21 *Tathā Lahar'tārā sagarē u. Tathā Chhītu-*	*Tathā Nades'rī ans Ṭōḍar Malu ka. Hīl(ā)*
22 *-purā ans Ṭōḍar Malu ka. Tathā Naipurā An-*	*hujatī nāstī*
23 *-s Ṭōḍar Malu ka. Hīl(ā) hujatī nāstī.*	*Līkhītaṁ Kanhaï, jē upar līkhā, sē sahī.*
24 *Līkhītaṁ Anand Rām, jē upar līkhā, sē sahī.*	

Here follow the witnesses signatures, ending.

25 *Shahada*	*Shahada*
26 *bimāfīhi Jalāl Makbūlī*	*bimāfīhi Ṭāhir ibni Khwāja*
27 *bikhaṭṭihi*	*Daulatī Qānūngōī.*

VII. Orient.-Congress, Ar. Sect.

Lichtdruck von Jaffé & Albert, Wien.

Plate I.

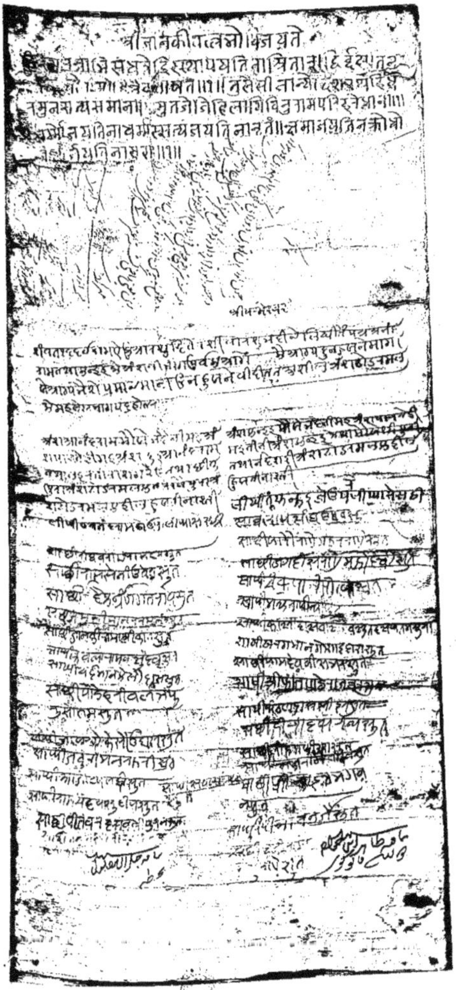

A

B

Plate II.

Lichtdruck von Jaffé & Albert, Wien.

(TRANSLATION.)

(Sanskrit.) Victory to the husband of Çrī Jānakī.

Two arrows cannot be shot at one time, Two supports cannot be given to one refugee. Twice over benefits are not given to applicants. Rāma does not speak in two ways.

(Old Bais'wārī.) O Tul'sī, Das'rath knew no virtue equal to the truth. He left Rām for it, and without Rām he gave up his life.

(Sanskrit). Virtue conquers and not vice, truth and not falsehood. Mercy conquers and not anger. Viṣṇu conquers and not the Asuras.

(Persian.) God is great.

As Anand Rām son of Tōdar son of Dēō Rāy, and Kanhāē son of Rām Bhadar son of Tōdar aforesaid appeared before me, and acknowledged that with their mutual consent the inheritance,—villages as detailed in Hindwī, have been equally divided, and the said Anand Rām has given to the said Kanhāē son of Rām Bhadar 150 bīghās of land in village Bhadainī more than his own half share; they are satisfied, and have lawfully made correct acknowledgment. Their seal has been affixed heretò.

Share of Anand Rām.	Share of Kanhāē.
Village Bhadāīnī, 2 shares.	Village of Bhadāīnī, 3 shares.
Village Lahar'tārā, whole.	Village of Shiūpūr, the whole.
Village Naipūra, the whole of Tōdar's share.	Village of Nadēsar, the whole of Tōdar's share.
Village Chhitūpūra the lesser, the whole of Tōdar's share.	(?) I am informed of this (?) (illegible).

(Old Bais'wārī.) To the most high God.

In the Sambat year 1669, on the 13th of the bright half of Kuār, on the auspicious day of the week, was this deed written by Anand Rām and Kanhaï. We both know the order with regard to the division of property.[1]) The order which has been passed that we recognize as authoritative. Both parties recognize the division of Tōdar Mal's share, with due allowance for the elder brother.

Share of Anand Rām. In village Bhadainī, out of five shares, two to Anand Rām. Also the whole of Lahar'tārā. Also Tōdar Mal's share in Chhitupūrā, and in Naipurā. There is no evasion or reservation. Signed, Anand Rām. What is written above is correct.

Share of Kanhaï. In village Bhadainī, out of five shares, three to Kanhaï. Also the village of Sīpurā. Also Tōdar Mal's share in Nades'rī. There is no evasion or reservation. Signed, Kanhaï. What is written above is correct.

Witnesses. Rāghab Rām son of Rām Dat. Rām Sēnī son of Udhab. (U)dai Karn son of Jagat Rāy. Jamunī Bhān son of Paramānand. Jānakī Rām son of Srī Kānt. Kāwalā Rām son of Bāsudēb. Chand Bhān son of Kēsau Dās. Pāṇḍē Harībal-labh son of Purusōtam. Bhāwarī son of Kēsauu Dās. Jadu Rām son of Nar'barī. Ājodhya son of Lachhī. Sabal son of Bhīkham. Rām Chand son of Bāsudīw (sic). Pitāmbar Das'wadhī son of Puran. Rām Rāï Garīb Rāï (?) sons of Makuṭirī Karn (?). (Arabic.) Witness to whatever is in this Jalāl Maq'būlī, with his own hand.

Witnesses. Rām Sīgh son of Uddhab. Jādau Rāē son of Gahar Rāē. Jagadīs Rāē son of Mahōdadhī. Chakrapānī son of Siwā. Mathurā son of Pīthā. Kāsī Dās son of Bāsudēwa (by the hand of Mathurā). Kharag Bhān son of Gosāi Dās. Rām Dēw son of Bīsa(m)bhar. Srī Kānt Pāṇḍē son of Rājbaktra (?). Bīṭhāl Dās son of Harihar. Hīrā son of Das'rath. Lōhag son of Kīshnā. Man(ī) Rām son of Sītal. Krīshn Dat son of Bhag'-wan. Bīnrāban son of Jai. Dhanī Rām son of Madhu Rāē.

(Arabic.) Witness to whatever is in this Ṭāhir son of Khwājah Daulatī the Qānūngōī.

[1]) The meaning of this passage is not clear.

Two new grants of the Chalukya dynasty.

By

Paṇḍit Bhagvânlâl Indrâjî, Ph. D., Hon. M. R. A. S.

The two grants which form the subject of this paper, possess a considerable interest. They are important for fixing the beginning of the Traikûṭaka era which was commonly used on the western coast of India and in the Dekhan up to the eighth century A. D. Moreover, they furnish interesting information regarding the minor kingdoms, which existed during the last mentioned period in Western India as well as regarding an expedition of the Arabs, undertaken shortly before 740 A. D. which reached the district of Nausâri in southern Gujarât.

The plates, on which grant nro 1 is written, come from Surat. I owe them to the kindness of Râo Bahâdur Bhîmbhâi Kirpârâm, Ass[t] Director of Agriculture, who obtained them from Mr. Lalubhâi, a merchant of Surat. They are two in number and measure 10½ inches by 7½. The outer sides are left blank; on the inner sides the lines run breadthwise as on the Valabhi plates. Two rings a plain one and one with a seal attached, held the plates together, passing through the holes in the bottom of the first and in the top of the second. The former has been lost, while the latter remains in its proper position. The seal has the shape of an inverted cone with a round top, 1½ inches in diameter, and closely resembles that of grant A.[1]) It bears the inscription *Śrî-Dharâśraya,* the name of the donor's father. Below this is the representation of a flower, resembling a blown lotus. The characters of the grant are very similar to those of Professor Dowson's Gurjara plates from Kaira. The engraver has done his work exceedingly well and the state of preservation is good. The language is pure and correct Sanskrit.

Grant nro II comes from Nausâri. The plates, also two in number, were kindly made over to me for publication by Mr. Sheriarjî Dâdâbhâi Bhârûchâ, Asst master in the Sir Cavasji Jahângir Mudressa at Nausâri. They measure each $11\frac{1}{2}$ inches by $9\frac{1}{2}$. In the arrangement of the letters and of the rings they resemble grant nro I. The seal shows two human figures, probably, I think, intended to be likenesses of the donor's parents. When I received the plates, they were covered with a thick coating of verdigris and mud, and not a letter could be made out. After a careful cleaning nearly the whole inscription has become readable. Some letters, which have been cut very shallow, are much worn but still recognisable from the traces which remain. A few remain doubtful. The letters resemble in the body of the grant those of the Valabhî grants, which have been derived from Dekhan originals. The royal signature at the end, *Svayam âjñâ* shows the northern Nâgarî alphabet of the eighth century. The language is good and pure Sanskrit. The few mistakes, which occur, are probably due to the engraver.

Both grants begin with the *maṅgala,* addressed to Vishṇu in his boar-incarnation, which is found in nearly all Chalukya inscriptions. Nro II has also a remarkable verse in honour of Vinayâditya-Satyâśraya-Vallabha, the reigning king of the main or Dekhan line of the family. Then follows in both documents the usual description of the Chalukyas, who are stated to belong to the Mânavya *gotra,* to be sons of Hârîtî etc. Next comes the genealogy, which comprises both some kings

[1]) The grant, which in this paper I call grant A, is that issued by Śryâśraya-Śîlâditya, the donor of grant nro I, in Saṁvat 421. I have published it in the Jour. Bo. Br. Roy. As. Soc. vol. XVI. pp. 1—7.

of the Dekhan or main line and some princes of the Gujarât branch. Grant nro I gives the following names:

Pulakeśi-Vallabha-Satyâśraya

A. Dekhan line | B. Gujarât Branch

Vikramâditya-Satyâśraya-Vallabha — Jayasiṁhavarman-Dharâśraya

Vinayâditya-Satyâśraya-Pṛithivîvallabha — Śîlâditya-Śryâśraya

Grant nro II somewhat differs, and names the following rulers:

Kirtivarman-Satyâśraya-Pṛithivîvallabha

Pulakeśi-Vallabha-Satyâśraya

A. Dekhan line | B. Gujarât Branch

Vikramâditya-Satyâśraya — Jayasiṁhavarman-Dharâśraya

Maṅgalarasarâja — Pulakeśi-Vallabha

As regards the details of the historical statements, Kirtivarman receives the usual attributes "performer of a horse-sacrifice" etc. and is called *mahârâjâdhirâja* and *parameśvara*. Of his son Pulakeśi grant nro I says that his head was purified by the final both at a Bahusuvarṇaka and a horse-sacrifice, as well as, that he defeated Harshavardhana, the lord of the north. The latter point is noticed also in grant nro II. Pulakeśi's son Vikramâditya (670—680 1, A. D.) is described in grant nro I as the destroyer of the Pallava dynasty, which ruled over Kâñchî and as the conqueror of the Trairâjya kingdom, while according to grant nro II he conquered the hereditary (*kramâgata*[1]) kingdoms of the Chera, Chola and Pâṇḍya.[2]) Grant nro II says further that he obtained his kingdom by the help of his excellent and unique horse Chitrakaṇṭha. This statement is rather curious, as in the inscriptions of the Chalukyas of Badâmi, the possession of the steed Chitra-

---

[1]) Possibly *kramâgata* may mean 'situated in a row, one behind the other'.

[2]) Whether these three kingdoms are the Trairâjya, mentioned in grant nro I, or whether there some other kingdom is meant cannot be made out. For in another grant Vikramâditya is described as 'taking to himself his father's glory, which had been obscured by three kings' and also as conquering the Chola, Chera and Kirâta kingdoms.

kaṇṭha is ascribed to Pulakeśi II. Vikramâditya's son, Vinayâditya (680/1—696 A. D.), receives in the genealogical portion of grant I the high titles *mahârâjâdhirâja, parameśvara* and *bhaṭṭâraka*. For this reason as well as on account of the fact that the second verse in the beginning of the grant (l. 2—3) is addressed to him, there can be no doubt that he was the paramount souvreign to whom the donor owed allegiance. The latter, the *yuvarâja* Śryâśraya-Śîlâditya, is described as the son of Vinayâditya's paternal uncle, the illustrious Dharâśraya-Jayasiṁhavarman and as intent on worshipping his father's lotus-feet. This description of Śîlâditya agrees in the main with that, given in grant *A*, where his title is the same and his father is described in the same manner. Grant *A* adds, however, that "Jayasiṁhavarman's prosperity had been augmented by his elder brother, the illustrious Vikramâditya-Satyâśraya-Prithivîvallabha and omits Vinayâditya's name. The latter circumstance may be accounted for by the supposition that Vinayâditya was not yet on the throne and that his father Vikramâditya was still reigning as head of the Chalukyas at Badâmi, while Śîlâditya governed Gujarát, subordinate to him, as heir-apparent of Jayasiṁhavarman. For grant nro 1 is dated twenty two years later than grant *A*. The fact that Śîlâditya is called *yuvarâja* in both shows that his father was alive during this whole period.

Grant nro II mentions after Vikramâditya, Jayasiṁhavarman as his younger brother and calls him *paramamâheśvara, paramabhaṭṭâraka*, Dharâśraya. The second epithet seems to have been given to him, because he was the founder of the Gujarât branch of the Chalukyas.

This grant says nothing of Śîlâditya, but mentions Maṅgalarasarâja as the son of Jayasiṁhavarman and with royal attributes. One of his attributes "who had obtained his own piece of territory by the prowess of his own arms", shows that in his reign the Gujarât Chalukyas were high in power. His other epithets are the same as those of his father, save that his own *biruda* was Jayâśraya.

The reason why Śîlâditya Yuvarâja is omitted in the genealogy of this plate, probably is that he died as heir-apparent without becoming king. Maṅgalarasarâja, the other son of Jayasiṁhavarman, who is mentioned in his stead, is, I have no doubt, the same as Maṅgalarâja, the donor of Dr Bhâû Dâji's Balsâr grant, as the latter, too, is called a son of Jayasiṁhavarman.[1])

His successor was his younger brother Pulakeśi, the donor of this grant, who has got the same royal attributes as his predecessors. He is mentioned as having defeated the army of Tâjiga. In the description of this army it is said that it had destroyed with its swords the great kings of Saindhava, Kachchhella, Saurâshṭra, Châvoṭaka, Maurya, Gurjara and others. After defeating these kings it advanced so far south as Nauasâri, on its way to the conquest of the Dekhan. There Pulakeśi met and vanquished it in a great battle. This victory is said to have earned for him four titles from a king named Vallabhanarendra.

Grant nro I is made by Śîlâditya from his camp at Kusumeśvara near Kârmaṇeya, probably the Kamaṇijja of another plate and the modern Kâmlej about ten miles from Surat. The object of the grant is a field on the eastern boundary of Osumbhalâ, a village within the limits of the Kârmaṇeya *Âhâra*. The boundaries of the field are, on the east, the limits of the village of Âlluraka, on the south a *śamî* tree, an ant-hill and the bank of a pond, on the west a tamarind-tree and on the north two ponds, called Mallâvi and Madhuka, and a field of the village-goddess *(gramâdevî)*. The donee is a Bra-

---

[1]) Journ. Bo. Br. Roy. As. Soc. vol. XVI, p. 5. The pedigree in the Balsâr grant is:

Kîrtivarman
|
Pulakeśi-Vallabha
|
Satyâśraya-Vikramâditya — Jayasiṁhavarman
|
Vinayâditya-Yuddhamalla-Jayâśraya-Maṅgalarâja, (donor, Śakasaṁvat 653).

hman of Kârmaṇeya, Dîkshita Mâtṛiśvara, son of Nannasvâmin, of the Śâṇḍilya *gotra*, belonging to the community of the hall of the *Chaturvedins (châturvidyaśâlâśâmânya)* and specially studying the Kâṇva *śâkhâ*. The *Dûtaka* of the grant is a military officer Ammagopa and the writer another military officer Chella.

The village granted in grant nro II is Padraka in the Kârmaṇeya district, apparently also Kâmlej. The donee is a Brahman, a native of Banavâsi in North Kânarâ. His name may rather doubtfully be read as Kâñchaḷi and his father's name Govindaḷi. The writer of the grant is the minister for peace and war, a noble named Bappabhaṭṭa, son of the great military officer Haragaṇa. The inscription concludes with the royal signature "our command".

The place of issue is not mentioned in grant nro II, while that of grant nro I is, as already mentioned, a royal camp at Kusumeśvara near Kârmaṇeya. With respect to grant A we learn that the order was given by Śîlâditya, "who was living at Navasârikâ" *(navasârikâm adhivasatâ)*. The latter expression makes it probable that Nausâri was the capital of the Chalukyas of the Gujarât branch. To this conclusion points also the fact that Pulakeśi according to grant nro II gave battle to the invading army of Tâjika near Nausâri, as well as the circumstance that most of the plates have been found there.

The era, used in these grants of the Gujarât Chalukyas which are dated 1) Grant *A*. *Saṁvatsara* 421, *Mâgha śuddha* 13, 2) Grant nro I *Saṁvatsara* 443, *Śrâvaṇa śuddha* 15 and 3) Grant nro II *Saṁvatsara* 490, *Kârttika śuddha* 15, appears to be the same as that employed by the Gurjaras. I have discussed the subject at length in a paper "on a new Gurjara copper-plate grant",[1]) in which I have tried to show that this era begins about *Śaka* 167, or, 245 A. D., or a little later about 250 A. D. Professor Bhâṇḍârkar does not accept this date, but says:—

[1]) Indian Antiquary, vol. XIII, p. 70—81.

"Paṇḍit Bhagvânlâl has recently published a facsimile, transcript, and translation of a grant by Śryâśraya Śîlâditya, son of Jayasiṁhavarman the founder of the Gujarât branch of the early Châlukya dynasty. The date occurring in it is 421. The Paṇḍit also mentions a grant by Vinayâditya Yuddhamalla,[1]) the brother of Śryâśraya the date of which is Śaka 653. What era the first date refers to is not stated, but it certainly cannot be the Śaka or the Vikrama. It must therefore be the Gupta which was one of those in ordinary use in Gujarât and which the Valabhî princes themselves are said to have used." . . . .

"Paṇḍit Bhagvânlâl, however, in a paper recently published refers Śryâśraya's date to an unknown era with 250 A. D. as its initial date. But even thus the interval between the two brothers becomes sixty years, which unquestionably is too long. For Śryâśraya's 421 corresponds under the supposition to 671 A. D. and Vinayâditya's 653 Śaka to 731 A. D. The grounds adduced for the supposition of a new era appear to me to be very questionable. Dadda II of the Gûrjara dynasty, whose date is 380, is spoken of in a grant to have protected a prince of Valabhî who had been hard pressed by Harshadeva. This Harshadeva is supposed by the Paṇḍit to be Harshavardhana of Kanoj, the contemporary of Hwan Thsang and Pulakeśi II of the Dekkan. But the Chinese traveller represents the king of Valabhî as the son-in-law of Harshavardhana's son and consequently a friend of the monarch rather than an enemy." . . . .

"The second ground on which the supposition of the existence of a new era is based is that in the opening passage of another grant of Śryâśraya, Vinayâditya Satyâśraya Vallabha is praised. This Vinayâditya the Paṇḍit identifies with the sovereign of the Dekkan of that name. But I should think it to be more natural to understand him as the brother of Śryâśraya, the donor of the grant dated 653 Śaka. For this last is not called Yuvarâja while Śryâśraya is, and from this it appears that the latter was his brother's associate in the administration

[1]) Professor Bhâṇḍârkar has left out the real name, which is Maṅgalarâja.

and governed a prince as his Viceroy. It is on this account that the brother's name is mentioned at the beginning of the grant. The title Satyâśraya Vallabha was promiscuously applied to all Chalukya rulers. The date Śaka 653 of Vinayâditya Yuddhamalla of Gujarât also does not harmonize with the supposition that his brother was the contemporary of Vinayâditya of the Dekkan."[1])

These objections do not appear to me very formidable, nor can I agree with Professor Bhâṇḍârkar's own combinations. I have shown in the Gurjara paper that Śryâśraya's latest date has been found to be 443, i. e. 443 + 250 = 693 A. D. This reduces the interval between the two brothers to thirty-eight years. Grant nro II shows that the date of the Balsâr grant, Śaka 653, i. e. 731 A. D., must fall near the end of Maṅgalarasarâja's reign as his younger brother's grant (II) is dated 490 or 490 + 250 = 740 A. D. Hence the long interval of 47 years between Saṁvat 443—490 must be assumed to be filled by Maṅgalarasarâja's reign. As to Professor Bhâṇḍârkar's contention that the Vinayâditya with whose praise grant nro I begins, may be Yuddhamalla Maṅgalarâja of the Balsâr grant, whose second name is Vinayâditya, that is refuted by facts. The Dekhan Vinayâditya is distinctly mentioned in the genealogy of grant nro I, l. 12, and it is clearly stated that Śryâśraya was his cousin and contemporary. The Vinayâditya of the Balsâr grant, whom Professor Bhâṇḍârkar takes to be the elder brother and overlord of Śryâśraya, is not even mentioned in the genealogy, though, if he were the overlord, a mention of his name might be expected. But the fact is, I have no doubt, that he was a younger brother of Śryâśraya and hence could not possibly find a place in the genealogy of his elder brother's grant. The circumstances which make this conclusion inevitable, are the following. We have 1) two grants (A. and I) of Śryâśraya, the son of Jayasiṁhavarman, who in both is called *yuvarâja* or heir-apparent, 2) one grant (Balsâr) of Vinayâdi-

[1]) Early History of the Dekkan, p. 102.

tya-Yuddhamalla-Maṅgalarâja-Jayâśraya, another son of the same Jayasiṁhavarman, who bears the title "king", 3) one grant (II) of Pulakeśi, a third son of Jayasiṁhavarman, who is likewise "a king" and who mentions his elder brother Maṅgalarasarâja-Jayâśraya as his predecessor (Grant nro II, l. 21). The identity of Maṅgalarasarâja-Jayâśraya with the donor of the Balsâr grant cannot be doubted in spite of the slight difference in one of the two names [1]) and the omission of two *birudas*. Hence the relation in which the donor of the Balsâr grant stood to that of grant nro II is perfectly clear. That Śryâśraya was older than both of them, follows from his being Jayasiṁhavarman's *yuvarâja* for twenty-two years. The title *yuvarâja* is usually given to the eldest son. For this reason alone we should be justified in concluding that Śryâśraya was Jayasiṁhavarman's eldest son. The fact that he bore this title for a long time, and the circumstance that we find in other inscriptions two other sons of Jayasiṁhavarman, who are called 'kings' and who omit to mention him, make this conclusion still more probable. They clearly indicate that he died during his father's life-time and never ascended the throne, which was occupied after Jayasiṁhavarman's death, first by Maṅgala or Maṅgalarasarâja and afterwards by Pulakeśi. If these combinations are correct, Professor Bhâṇḍârkar's supposition that Śryâśraya's dates, Saṁvat 421 and 443, refer to the Valabhî era, becomes untenable. The Valabhî or Gupta era begins in *Śaka* 242 and *Saṁ* 421 and 443 would correspond to *Śaka* 663 and 685. Thus Śryâśraya would have reigned as *yuvarâja* from ten to thirty-two years later than his younger brother, Maṅgalarâja, who was a 'king'. This is clearly impossible. Śryâśraya's dates must refer to an era, the beginning of which lies before that of the Valabhî or Gupta *Saṁvat*. This condition is satisfied by the era of 249—250 A. D., which, as I have shown, occurs also in the Gurjara grants. General

[1]) Compare also the name of the western Chalukya king Maṅgalîśa, for which the forms Maṅgalîśvara and Maṅgalarâja occur.

Sir A. Cunningham and Mr. Fleet[1]) declare this to be the *Chedisaṁvat,* the era of the Kulachuris or Haihayas of Tripura. The latter begins, indeed, about the same time. But it remains to be explained, how the era of a dynasty, whose possessions lay far away in Central India, came to be used in Gujarât. The inscriptions of the Kulachuris furnish no assistance for this purpose. They show only late centuries of the *Chedisaṁvat* and give no information regarding the early history of the family. Some recent discoveries, made in Western India, help us, it seems to me, to a solution of the problem.

If we consider by themselves the facts which the grants from Gujarât reveal, we find that the dates of the era of 249—250 A. D. range between the years 380 and 490. The Gurjara plates show *Saṁ* 380, 385, 436 and 486,[2]) those of the Chalukyas *Saṁ* 421, 443 and 490. The era cannot have been founded by the latter, because the western Chalukyas of the main line of the family, use the *Śaka* era. It is also improbable that the Gurjaras established it. As far as we know, their kingdom was a small one and they were vassals of greater monarchs. Hence it may be reasonably doubted, that among their earlier rulers, there were men powerful enough to found an era. The probability is, that both the Gurjaras and the Chalukyas adopted the era, because they found it prevalent in Gujarât. If we now look out for the source from which they could have derived it, it would seem that the grant of the Traikûṭaka king Dahrasena, which I have recently published,[3]) furnishes us with an indication. This grant comes from the same part of Gujarât, where those of the Chalukyas and some of the Gurjara plates were found. It is dated in exactly the same manner with the simple notation *Saṁ* and shows an earlier date the year 207. Hence it is not at all improbable, that the era is the same as that used by the Gurjaras and

---

[1]) Note on my paper 'On a new Gurjara inscription' in the Indian Antiquary, vol. XIII, p. 80.

[2]) Found on the Kaira, Navsâri and Kâvi plates.

[3]) Journ. Bo. Br. Roy. As. Soc., vol. XVI, p. 346.

Chalukyas. If that is the case, this era probably owes its origin to the Traikûṭakas. Dahrasena tells us that he offered a horse-sacrifice, and thereby clearly indicates that he was an independent sovereign. The era which he uses, may, therefore, be supposed to be that of his own family. Moreover, we have in Dr Bird's grant from Kanheri clear proof that the Traikûṭakas had an era of their own. That document[1]) begins with the words, *Traikûṭakânâm pravardhamânavijayarâjyasaṁvatsaraśatadvaye pañchachatvâriṁsaduttare* "in the year 245 of the prosperous and victorious rule of the Traikûṭakas". The question which we have now to consider, is who these Traikûṭakas really were. Their name is evidently derived from Trikûṭa which in the Raghuvaṁsa and the Râmâyaṇa is mentioned as a considerable town in Aparânta, i. e. the Konkan. The beginning of their era, 249—250 A. D. or about *Śakasaṁvat* 170, falls in the time when Gujarât and the adjacent provinces were in the hands of the Western Kshatrapas. By the evidence of the coins it appears that the rule of this dynasty was once interrupted by an invader who assumed the titles *râja* and *kshatrapa* and founded an era, distinct from that of the descendants of Chashṭana. This was king Îśvaradatta who probably fought with the Kshatrapas and for a short time deprived them of their power. For his coins which are struck according to the model of those of the Kshatrapas, are dated in the first and second years of his reign. Other kings, bearing names which end in *datta,* have left their records in the caves of Nasik,[2]) and state that they are Âbhîras by caste. This circumstance permits us to infer that they belong to the Âbhîra dynasty which, probably coming by sea from Sindh, conquered the western coast and made Trikûṭa its capital. Îśvaradatta whom I consider to belong to it, probably attacked and obtained a victory over the Kshatrapas. After he had consolidated his power, he issued his own coins,

---

[1]) Archaeological Survey of W. I., nro 10, p. 57.

[2]) Archaeological Reports of W. I., vol. IV, p. 103.

coins, copying the Kshatrapa currency of the district. His coins particularly resemble those of the Kshatrapa Vîradâman and of his brother Vijayasena. The end of the reign of the latter falls, as the coins show, in the year 170 of the Kshatrapa era. If we take this to be the *Śaka* era, the time of Îśvaradatta's conquest will fall just about the same time as the foundation of the Traikûṭaka or Kulachuri era. This agreement induces me to consider Îśvaradatta its founder. It seems, further, that the reign of the Traikûṭakas did not last long, as Vîradâman's son, Rudrasena appears to have regained power and to have driven his foe out of the country. The Traikûṭakas then probably retired to the Central Provinces and there assumed the names Haihaya and Kulachuri. Afterwards the kings of this dynasty appear to have again taken possession of their former capital Trikûṭa at the time of the final destruction of the Kshatrapa power. Dahrasena must have ascended the throne just about this time which was the year 207 + 170 or 377 of the *Śaka* era. This was the year of the end of the reign of Svâmin Rudrasena, son of Svâmin Rudradâman.

A new coin of another Traikûṭaka king, belonging to the period after the final destruction of the Kshatrapa power, has been obtained by me from Daman. It resembles in all respects the coins of the last Kshatrapa king. On the obverse, it bears the king's bust, like the Kshatrapa coins, and on the reverse the symbol consisting of three semi-circular arches, and the following inscription:

Mahârâjendravarmma [1]*-putra-paramavaishṇavaśrî-Mahârâja-Rudragaṇa.*

I belive this must be the first king after the revival of the Traikûṭaka power. No other later coin of this dynasty

[1]) This may also be read °*jendradanna* or °*datta*.

has been discovered. So it is probable that they again were defeated by either the Mauryas, or the Chalukyas, or the Gurjara kings. They however seem to have retained in their inscriptions the same era that was prevalent in the time of their reign.

A matter of great historical interest in grant nro II is the mention of Pulakeśi's fight with Tâjika's army. The real proper name of the leader of the army is not mentioned. The word Tâjika, the first part of the compound *tâjikânîka,* the Tâjika-army, is commonly used by Indian writers to denote the Arabs, and a number of astronomical works, made according to Arab originals, is still known as Tâjaka or Tâjika.

The date of Pulakeśi's fight cannot be far distant from that of this grant, *Saṁ* 490 or about 740 A. D. If we take the year of its occurrence to be 730 A. D., it falls in the time, when Mahommed, son of Kâsim, conquered Sindh and went very far into the interior of India.[1])

With respect to the kings which the Tâjika-army is said to have conquered (grant II, l. 24), it may be noted that Saindhava is, doubtlessly, the king of Sindh, probably one of the Sumrâs of that place.

Kachchhella may be the Kachchva Rajputs or the Kachchha kings known by this name at this time. The Saurâshṭra must be a king of Soraṭh or Kâṭhiâvâḍ. It is not certain what king of Kâṭhiâvâḍ may be meant. But the time is that both of those of Valabhî and of the Jeṭhvas.

The Châvoṭakas appear to be the Châpoṭakas or Châvaḍâs, and the date approximates closely to the defeat or death of Jayaśekharin of Pañchâsar. Jayaśekharin's son, Vanarâja, is known to have established his kingdom of Aṇahilavâḍ in *Vikramasaṁvat* 802 or 746 A. D. The traditional Jain stories about the Châvaḍâs say that their king of Pañchâsar, Jayaśekhari, was defeated by the Chalukya king

[1]) Vide Elliot's history, vol. I, pp. 432—439, also Sindh Gazetteer, pp. 24—25.

Bhûvaḍ who, as they allege, reigned in Kalyâṇa in *Vikramasaṁvat* 750 or 696 A. D. But it is still doubtful whether Kalyâṇa was a Chalukya capital at that time. Moreover there is no king of the name of Bhûvaḍ among the hitherto known Chalukya kings, and the history, written by the Jains, is chiefly in praise of the Solaṅkî kings who were the descendants of the Chalukyas, ruling at Kalyâṇa. It is possible that the latter, having themselves obtained the Châvaḍâ kingdom, tried to show that it had been formerly conquered by their ancestors. One account shows that the Châvaḍâs were destroyed by the Arabs about 735 A. D., eleven years before Vanarâja's foundation of the Aṇahilavâḍ kingdom in 746 A. D. The story about Vanarâja that his mother was with child at the time of his father's decease, appears to have been fabricated to explain his name,—witness the parallel instance of the Jain story of the birth at Nâsik of Dvidhaprahâra, the founder of the Châvaḍâ Yâdavas. It is more probable that the Arabs destroyed the Châvaḍâ kingdom and killed the king, and that Vanarâja, as the invasion was a passing raid, immediately afterwards repaired the loss and, after they left, established himself on the throne about 740 A. D.

The Mauryas, we know from the Vâḍû inscription, were ruling in the Konkan about the fifth century, [1]) and the Aiholi inscription shows that they continued to rule till at least 610, when their defeat by Pulakeśi II is recorded. But the mention of the Mauryas in our grant shows that they had possessions north of Nausâri in the eighth century. Hence it may be inferred that there was another Maurya state in upper Gujarât. The Gurjaras are probably the Gurjaras of Broach, the latest known of whom Jayabhaṭa, we know, was ruling at least as late as *Saṁvat* 486 or 736 A. D. or just about the time of this raid. [2])

---

[1]) Bombay Gazetteer, XIV, p. 373.

[2]) Indian Antiquary, vol. XIII, p. 76.

Grant nro I.

Transcript.

Plate I.

1. Oṁ jayatyâvishkṛitaṁ Vishṇor-vvârâhaṅ-kshobhitârṇṇavam | dakshiṇonnatadaṁshṭrâgraviśrântabhuvanaṁ vapuḥ ‖ [1]
2. Narasiṅhavikkramastutavimalayaśâ jagati vijayate vîraḥ [|] sthirabala-Vinayâdityaḥ Satyâśraya-Va-
3. llabhaḥ śrîmân ‖ [2] svasti Kârmmaṇey'-opakaṇṭha-Kusumeśvar'-âvâsitavijayaskandhâvârâchchhrîmatâṁ sa-
4. kalabhuvanasaṁstûyamâna-Mânavya-sagotrâṇâṁ Hârîtîputrâṇâṁ saptalokamâtṛibhis saptamâ-
5. tṛibhir aharahar abhivarddhitânâṅ-Kârttikeyaparirakshaṇaprâptakalyâṇaparamparâṇâm bhagavan-Nârâya-
6. ṇa-prasâdasamâsâditavarâhalâñchhaneekshaṇakshaṇavaśîkṛitâśepamahîbhṛitâñ[1])-Chalukyânâṅ-ku-
7. lam alaṅkarishṇur-bbahusuvarṇṇakâśvamedhayâgâvabhṛithasnânapavitrîkṛitaśirâ Nṛiga-Nahusha-Yayâti-
8. Dhundhumârâ[-ra-A]mbarîshapratimas sakalottarâpatheśvara-Śrîharshavarddhana-labdhayuddhapatâkas Satyâśraya-
9. Śrî-Pulakeśivallabha-mahârâjas tasya sutas tatpâdânuddhyâtonivâritavîryyavilaṅghitânyâ-
10. laṅghyâribhûpâlabalakh Kâñchîpurîśa-Pallavânvayapramâthî parigṛihîtatrairâjyarâjyaḥ śrî-
11. Vikkramâditya-Satyâśraya-Vallabhamahârâjas tasya putras tachcharaṇânuddhyâtovinayâdyasâdhâraṇarâ-
12. jaguṇâlaṅkṛito Vinayâditya Satyâśraya-Śrîprithivîvallabha[2])-mahârâjâdhirâjaparameśvarabhaṭṭâ-
13. rakas tasya pitṛivyasyânekasamaravijayasamudbhûtaviśuddhakîrtteph paramamâheśvarasya Dharâśra-
14. ya-śrî-Jayasiṅhavarmmaṇaph putras tachcharaṇamalârâdhanaparo nayapratâpavijṛimbhitânyamahîpâ-

[1]) Read °śesha°.

[2]) Read pṛithivî°.

15. lachakkras sakalakalâpravîṇo ratichaturavilâsinîjanamanohârirûpalâvaṇyasaubhâgyasa-

16. meto vidhyâdharachakkravarttîva | Śryâśraya-śrî-Śîlâditya-yuvarâjas sarvvân eva râjasâmantavisha-

17. yapatigrâmabhogikamahattarâdîn yathâsambaddhyamânakân samâjñâpaya-

18. ty astu vas saṁviditam ‖ mayâ mâtâpitror âtmanaś cha puṇyayaśobhivṛiddhaye

PLATE II.

19. Kârmmaṇeyachâturvvidyaśâlâsâmânya-Śâṇḍilya-sagotrâddhvaryyu-Kâṇva-sa-

20. brahmachâriṇe brâhmaṇa-Naṇṇasvâmi-putra-Dîkshita-Mâtṛîśvarâya[1]) bhûmichchhidra-

21. nyâyena Kârmmaṇey-ahâravishayântarggata[2]) Osumbhalâ-grâme pûrvvasyâṁ sîmni kshetraṁ yasya pûrvvataḥ A-

22. llûraka-grâmasîmâ | dakshiṇataḥ śamîvṛikshavalmîkataḍâkikâpâliḥ paśchimatombilakâvṛikshau | utta-

23. rato Mallâvi-taḍâkapâli-Madhukaṁ-taḍâkikâ grâmadevîkshetrasîmâ | evam etachchatuḥsîmâbhya-

24. ntarapratishṭhitam pañchamahâyajñâdikriyotsarppaṇâya putrapautrânvayabhogyam âchandrârkkârṇavakshiti-

25. sthitisamakâlînaṁ sarvvadityavishṭiprâtibhedikâdiparihînaṁ puṇye tithau śrâvaṇapaurṇṇamâsyâ-

26. m udakâtisarggeṇa pratipâditam | yatosmadvaṁśyair anyair-vvâgâmibhadranṛipatibhi<u>kh</u> kadalîgarbbhasâraṁ

27. saṁsâraṁ jalabudbudopañ[3])-cha jîvitam avadhâryya śirîshakusumasadṛiśâpâyañ-cha yauvanaṁ girinadîsa-

28. lilagatvarâṇi chaiśvaryyâṇi | prabalapavanâhatâśvatthapatrachañchalâ cha râjalakshmîr iti śaśikararu-

29. chiraṁ sthâsnu yaśaśchichîshubhir ayam asmaddâyonumantavyap<u>h</u> pâlayitavyaś-cha yo vâjñânatimirapaṭalâ-

---

1) Read Mâtrîśvarâya.

2) Read °yâhâra°.

3) Read °dopamañ-cha.

30. vṛitamatir âchchhindyâd âchchhidyamânaṁ vânumodeta | sa pañchabhir-mmahâpâtakais sopapâtakaiś cha saṁyuktaḥ
31. syâd api choktam ṛishipravekena vikachakuvalayanikaratarasubhagavapushâ[1]) Satyavatînandanena bhaga-
32. vatâ vedavyâsena Vyâsena | shashṭiṁ varshasahasrâṇi svargge modati bhûmidaḥ âchchhettâ chânumantâ cha
33. tâny eva narake vaset || Vindhyâṭavîshv atoyâsu śushkâkoṭaravâsinaḥ[2]) krishṇâhayo hi jâyante bhûmidâ-
34. yaṁ haranti ye || bahubhir-vvasudhâ bhuktâ râjabhiḥ Sagarâdibhir-yyasya yasya yadâ bhûmis tasya tasya tadâ pha-
35. laṁ || pûrvvadattâṁ dvijâtibhyo yatnâd raksha Yudhishṭhira | mahîm mahîmatâṁ śreshṭha dânâch-chhreyonupâlanaṁ ||
36. saṁvatsaraśatachatushṭaye trichatvâriṁśadadhike śrâvaṇaśuddhapaurṇṇamâsyâṁ | saṁvatsara 443 śrâvaṇa
37. śudi 15 dûtako balâdhikṛitâ[ta-A]mmagopaḥ likhitañcha balâdhikṛita-Chellene'-ti ||

Translation.

Om. Victorious is the boar-manifestation of Vishṇu which agitated the ocean and on the tip of the right raised tusk of which rested the universe. Triumphant in the universe is the illustrious Vinayâditya Satyâśrayavallabha of steady power, a hero of renowned unsullied fame, and like Narasiṁha in heroism.

Hail! From the victorious camp stationed at Kusumeśvara near Kârmaṇeya.

(There was) the illustrious great king Satyâśraya Pulakeśivallabha adorning the family of the illustrious Chalukyas who belong to the Mânavya *gotra* praised in the whole world, and are the descendants of Hâritî, who were nourished by the seven Mothers, the mothers of the seven worlds, who enjoy a continued succession of prosperity acquired under the protection of Kârttikeya, and by whom all princes were subdued (at the)

[1]) Read °*nikarasubhagatara*°.
[2]) Read śushkako°.

very moment that they saw the boar-emblem obtained by the favour of divine Nârâyana,—he (Pulakeśi) whose head has been purified by the final bath at the Bahusuvarṇaka and Aśvamedha sacrifics,—who is equal to Nṛiga, Nahusha, Yayâti, Dhundhumâra and Ambarîsha, who has obtained in battle the banner of the illustrious Harshavarddhana, the lord of the whole northern country. His son who meditated on his (father's) feet, (was) the illustrious great king Vikramâditya Satyâśraya Vallabha who by his irresistible valour conquered hostile kings unconquerable by others, (who was) the destroyer of the Pallava dynasty ruling over Kâñchî, who took the Trairâjya-kingdom. His son who meditated on his (father's) feet, was the supreme lord and *Bhattâraka*, the great king of kings, the illustrious Vinayâditya Satyâśraya Pṛithvîvallabha adorned by humility and other unusual royal qualities. The son of his paternal uncle, the illustrious Dharâśraya Jayasiṁhavarman, a great Śaiva who obtained unsullied fame by victories in numerous battles, (is) the illustrious heir apparent Śryâśraya-Śîlâditya intent on worshipping his (father's) lotus feet, who has pleased the multitude of other kings by his policy and majesty, (who is) proficient in all the arts, who possesses beauty, loveliness and handsomeness attracting the minds of courtezans clever in amorous sports, and who resembles the emperor of the Vidyâdharas (Jîmûtavâhana); (he) addresses (this) order to all royal nobles, *vishayapatis, grâmabhogikas, mahattaras* and others wherever posted; 'Be it known to you that, for the increase of my own and my parents' merit and glory I have given, on a holy day, the fifteenth of Śrâvaṇa, with a libation of water, to Dîkshita Mâtrîśvara, the son of the Brâhmaṇa Nannasvâmi, a member of the Śâṇḍilya *gotra*, an *adhvaryu*-priest, a *Kâṇva brahmachârin*, a member of the community of the *châturvidyâśâlâ* of Kârmaṇeya according to the familiar reasoning of the ground and the sky [1]) a field on the eastern boundary of the village of Osumbhalâ which is situated in the territory of the Kârmaṇeya district. To the east

[1]) See Indian Antiquary, XIII, 80, note 45.

of this (lies) the boundary of the village of Allûraka; to the south the bank of the Valmîka pond[1]) and a Śamî(-tree); to the west two tamarind trees; to the north the bank of the Mallâvi pond and the small Madhuka pond and the boundary of the field granted to the village goddess. This (field) which thus lies within the (above-mentioned) four boundaries (has been granted) for the performance of the five great sacrifices and other ceremonies, is to be enjoyed by sons, grandsons and other heirs, is to remain (with the donee and his family) as long as the moon, the sun, the ocean and the earth last, (and is) exempted from the *ditya,* forced labour, *prâtibhedika* and other rights. Therefore future good kings of our own dynasty or others, believing the world to be as fragile as the inner part of a plantain, life to be comparable a waterbubble, youth as fading as the Śirîsha-flower, dominion as little lasting as the water of a mountain torrent, and royal fortune as tremulous as an Aśvattha leaf that is struck by a powerful gust of wind,—and being eager to collect an undying fame as beautiful as the moon's rays, should approve of and maintain this our grant. But he who, his mind being obscured by the veil of ignorance will cancel this or permit it to be cancelled, will be guilty of the five great sins and of the minor sins. And it has been said by the venerable Vyâsa, the arranger of the Vedas, the son of Satyavatî, the chief of sages, whose body is as fine and beautiful as a group of the petals of a blown lotus: 'The giver of land dwells for sixty thousand years in heaven; (but) the confiscator (of a grant), and he who assents (to such confiscation) shall dwell for the same member of years in hell.' 'Those who confiscate a grant of land, are born as black snakes dwelling in the dried up hollows of trees, in the forests of the waterless Vindhya (mountains).' 'The earth has been enjoyed by many kings, commencing with Sagara; to him who for the time being possesses the earth, belongs at that time the reward (of this grant that is now made).' 'O Yudhisthira, best of kings, carefully preserve

---

[1]) (Or an anthill and the bank of a small pond.)

land formerly granted to Brâhmaṇas, the preservation (of a grant) is better than (making) a grant.' On the fifteenth of the bright (fortnight) of Śrâvaṇa in the year four hundred, exceeded by forty three. Samvatsara 443 Śrâvaṇa Śudi 15. The Dûtaka (of this grant) is the military officer Ammagopa. (This has been) written by the military officer Chella.

Grant nro II.

Transcript.

Plate I.

1. Oṁ Jayaty âvishkṛitaṁ vishṇor-vvârâhaṁ kshobhitârṇṇavaṁ | dakshiṇonnatadaṁshṭrâgraviśrântabhuvanaṁ vapuḥ ||

2. śrîmatâṁ sakalabhuvanasaṁstûyamâna-Mânavya-sagotrâṇâṁ [1]) saptalokamâtṛibhis sapta[mâtṛibhi]r abhiva-

3. rddhitâ[nâṁ] Kârttikeyaparirakshaṇaprâptakalyâṇaparaṁparâṇâṁ bhagavan-Nârâyaṇa-prasâdasamâsâdi-

4. tavarâhalâṁchhanekshaṇakshaṇavaśîkṛitâśeshabhûbhṛitâṁ Chalukyânâṁ kulam alaṁkarishṇu[r aśvamedhâ]vabhṛita- [2])

5. snânapavitrîkṛitagâtronekanarapatimakuṭa [3]) taṭaghaṭitamaṇigaṇakiraṇasamulla[sita]dyotitachara-

6. ṇakamalayugalas Satyâśraya-Prithivîvallabha [4])mahârâjâdhirâjaparameśvaraśrî-Kîrttivarmmarâjas tasya

7. sutas tatpâdânudhyâtaḥ paramadevatâviśeshavad vaṁdanîyatamas sakalaśâstrârtthatatvajñakh karika-

8. ranishṭhuraprakoshṭhakarakalitaniśitanistṛiṁśa [5])prahâradalitapramukhâgatavairivâraṇakuṁbhasthalochchhala-

9. tpratyagradhavalanirmmalamuktâphalaprakarakuṁbhastabakasamabhyarchchitasamaradharitrîtalaḥ śrîmaduttarâpa-

10. thâdhipati-Śrîharshavarddhana-parâjayopalabdhograpratâpaph paramamâheśvaroparanâmâ Satyâśra-

---

[1]) The word *Hârîtîputrâṇâṁ* has been omitted.

[2]) Read °*vabhṛitha*°.

[3]) Read °*mukuṭa*°.

[4]) Read *Pṛithivî*°.

[5]) Read °*nistriṁśa*°.

11. yaḥ¹) śrî-Pulakeśivallabhas tasya sutas tatpâdânu-dhyâtonekanarapatisâmantamakuṭa²)koṭighṛishṭachara-

12. ṇâravindayugalo Meru-Malaya-Mandara-Viṁdhyasamâ-nadhairyyoharahar-abhivarddhamânavarakarituragaratha-

13. padâtibalo manojavaika-Chitrakaṁthâkhyapravaratu-raṁgamenopârjjitasvarâjya[ḥ] vijita-Chera-Chola-Pâṁ-

14. ḍya-kramâgatarâjyatrayaph paramamâheśvaraph para-mabhaṭṭârakas Satyâśrayaḥ śrî-Vikramâditya-râjas tasyâ-

15. nujo vijitasakalârâtipakshaś chaturudadhiparyyantamâ-lâmekhalâyâḥ kshiter-mmaṇḍanabhûto matte-

16. bhakuṁbhamaṇḍalavidâraṇaḥ kesarikiśorair³)iva vikramaikarasas samastadiṅmaṁḍalaprakhyâtakîrttiḥ pa-

17. ramamâheśvaraph paramabhaṭṭâraka-Dharâśrayaḥ śrî-Jayasiṅghavarmma-râjas tasya sutas tatpâdânu-

18. dhyâtas sakalajanamanânaṁda⁴)bhûtonekasamarasaṁ-kaṭapramukhâgatanihataśatrusâmantakulavadhû-

19. prabhâtasamayaruditachchhalodgîyamânavimalanistriṁ-śapratâpo nijabhujaprabhâvopârjjitasva-

20. kîyabhûbhâgamaṇḍalaph paramamâheśvaraph parama-bhaṭṭâraka-Jayâśraya-śrî-Maṅgalarasa-râjas tasyânu-

21. jas tatpâdapaṁkajârâdhanânudhyâta⁵)pratidinam upa-chîyamânodayaḥ śaiśavâd eva samastaguṇagaṇâ-

22. dhishṭhânabhûtaḥ svayaṁvarayaiva⁶) râjalakshmyâ samâsâditavakshasthalo dhavalayaśovitânavimalikṛitasa-

23. kalajaganmaṇḍalaḥ paramamâheśvaraḥ paramabhaṭṭâ-rakaḥ Śarajhaḥ sîramudgarodgâriṇi taralataratâraravâridâ-

24. ritoditasaindhava-Kachchhella-Saurâshṭra-Châ-voṭaka-Mauryya-Gûrjjarâdirâje niḥśeshadâkshiṇâtyakshi-tipatiji-

---

¹) Read Satyâśrayâparanâmâ.
²) Read ºmukuṭaº.
³) Read ºkiśora.
⁴) Read ºmana ânandaº.
⁵) Read ºnudhyâtaḥ.
⁶) Read svayaṁvarayeva.

25. [gî]shayâ Dakshiṇâpathapraveś[âbhilâshama]nâḥ [1]) prathamam eva Navasârikâ-vishayaprasâdhanâyâgate [tvarita]-

Plate II.

26. turagakharamukharakhurotkhâtadharaṇidhûlidhûsaritadigantare kuntaprântanitântavimardyamânarabhasâbhidhâvito-

27. dbhaṭasthûlodaravivaravinirggatâṁtrapṛithutara [2]) rudhiradhârâraṁjitaka[vacha]bhîshaṇavapushi svâmimahâ-

28. sanmânadânagrahaṇanikhkrayîkṛita [3])svaśirobhir abhimukham âpatitair adayadaśanâgradashṭaushṭhapuṭair ane-

29. kasamarâjiravivaravari- [4])karikaṭitaṭabadha-(?)vighaṭanaviśâlitaghanarudhirapaṭalapâṭalitapaṭukṛipâṇapaṭṭair api mahâ

30. yodhair alabdhaparabhâgaiḥ vipakshakshapaṇâkshepakshiprakshiptatîkshṇakshuraprapraharâvilûnavairiśirakhkamalagalanâlair â-

31. havarasarabhasaromâṁchakaṁchukâchchhâditatanubhir anekair api narendravṛiṁdavṛiṁdârakair ajitapûrvvaiḥ vyapagatam asmâka-

32. m-ṛiṇam anena svâminaḥ svaśiraḥpradânenâdya tâvad ekajanmîyam ity eva mishopajâtaparitoshânantaraprahatapaṭupa-

33. ṭaharavapranṛittakabandhabaddharâsamaṁḍalîke | samaraśirasi vijite Tâjikânîke śauryyânurâgiṇâ Śrîvallabhanareṁ-

34. dreṇa prasâdikṛitâparanâmachatushṭayas tad yathâ Dakshiṇâpathasâdhâra- [5])Chaluki[ka]kulâlaṁkâra-Prithivîvallabhâ [6])[a-A]nivarttakaniva-

35. rttayitr-Avanijanâśraya-Śrî-Pulakeśirâjas sarvvân evâtmîyân asmadvaṁśajân anyâṁś cha yathâsaṁbadhyamânakân visha-

---

[1]) The letters, placed between brackets, are very doubtful. [I believe the correct reading is *abhilâshiṇi*. G. B.]

[2]) Read °*pṛithutara*°.

[3]) Read °*nishkrayîkṛita*°.

[4]) Read °*vara*°.

[5]) Read °*sâdhaka*°.

[6]) Read *Pṛithivî*°.

36. yapatigrâmabhogikavâsâvakâyuktaviniyuktakâdîn samanudarśayaty astu vaḥ saṁviditaṁ | yathâsmâbhir-mmâtâpi-

37. tror âtmanaś cha puṇyayaśobhivṛiddhaye balicharuvaiśvadevâgnihotrâdikriyotsarppaṇârtthaṁ Vanavâsi-vinirggata-Vatsa-

38. sagotra-Taittirika-sabrahmachâriṇe dvivedabrâhmaṇa-Kâñchaḷe (?) brâhmaṇa-Govindaḷi-sûnune[1]) Kârmmaṇey'-âhâravishayâṁtarggata-

39. Padraka-grâmas sodraṁgas saparikaras sadânapradânakaḥ achâṭabhaṭaprâveśyo bhûmichhidranyâyenodakâtisarggeṇa Mahâ-

40. kârttikyâṁ putrapautrânvayabhogyaḥ pûrvvapradattadevabrahmadâyavarjjo dharmmadâyatvena pratipâdito yatosyâ-

41. grahârasthityâ bhuṁjataḥ krishataḥ[2]) karshayato vâ na kaiśchid vighâte sthâtavyam âgâmibhadranṛipatibhir asmadvaṁśyair anyair-vvâ

42. vidyullolâny anityâny aiśvaryyâṇi tṛiṇâgralagnajalabinduchaṁchalam âyur avekshyâsmaddâyonumaṁtavyonupâlayitavya-

43. ś-cha yâś-châjñânatimirapaṭalâvṛitamatir âchchhiṁdyâd âchchhiṁdyamânaṁ[3]) vânumodeta sa pañchabhir-mmahâpâtakais sopapâtakai-

44. s-saṁyuktaḥ[4]) syâd ity uktaṁ cha bhagavatâ vedavyâsena Vyâsena | shashṭir-vvarshasahasrâṇi svargge[5]) tishṭhati bhûmidaḥ âchchhettâ châ-

45. numaṁtâ cha tâny eva narake vaset ‖ Viṁdhy'-âṭavîshv atoyâsu śushkakoṭaravâsinaḥ kṛishṇâhayo hi jâyaṁte bhûmidâyaṁ

46. haraṁti ye ‖ bahubhir-vvasudhâ bhuktâ râjabhis Sagarâdibhiḥ yasya yasya yadâ bhûmis tasya tasya tadâ phalaṁ ‖ svadattâṁ

---

1) Read *sûnave.*
2) Read *kṛishataḥ.*
3) Read *âchchhidya°.*
4) Read *°saṁyuktaḥ.*
5) Read *shashṭiṁ varsha°.*

47. paradattâṁ vâ yatnâd rakshya[1]) Yudhishṭhira | mahîn[2]) mahîmatâṁ śreshṭha dânâchchhreyonupâlanaṁ || yânîha bhuktâni[3]) purâ na-

48. reṁdrair-ddânâni dharmmârtthayaśaskarâṇi nirbhuktamâlyapratimâni tâni ko nâma sâdhuḥ punar âdadîta || samvatsaraśa-

49. ta[4]) 490 kârttikaśuddha 15 likhitañ chaitan mahâsândhiviggrahikaprâptapañchamahâśabdasâmantaśrî-Bappa[bha]-

50. [ṭi]nâ [mahâ]balâdhikṛita-Haragaṇa-sûnunâ | nyûnâksharam adhikâksharaṁ vâ sarvvaṁ pramâṇaṁ || || ||

51. svayam âjñâ

Translation.

Victorious in the boar-manifestation of Vishṇu which agitated the ocean and on the raised tip of whose right tusk rested the earth. Adorning the family of the illustrious Chalukyas who belong to the Mânavya *gotra* praised in all the worlds, who have been nourished by the seven mothers, the mothers of the seven worlds, who have obtained an uninterrupted succession of prosperity through the protection of Kârttikeya, by whom all kings have been subdued at the moment they saw the boar-emblem obtained by the favour of the divine Nârâyaṇa, (ruled) the supreme lord and overlord of great kings, the illustrious Kîrtivarmarâja Satyâśraya Pṛithivîvallabha, whose body was purified by the final bath at a horse-sacrifice,—whose pair of lotus feet shone and glittered with the rays proceeding from the multitude of jewels set in the surfaces of the crowns of numerous kings. His son who meditated on his (father's) feet,—who was most worthy of being worshipped like some great divinity,—who knew the principles of the meaning of all Śâstras,—who worshipped the surface of the battle-field with flower-bunches, (poured out) from pots, in the shape of multitudes of fresh, white and spotless pearls, issuing from the attacking hostile

---

[1]) Read *raksha.*

[2]) Read *mahîṁ.*

[3]) Read *dattâni.*

[4]) The writer has omitted *chatushṭaye navatyadhike saṁvat.*

elephants' temples, that were torn by the blows of his sharp word, swung by an arm the forepart of which was as hard as the trunk of an elephant,—who gained dread glory by defeating the illustrious Harshavardhana, the lord of the north,—(was) the great Śaiva, the illustrious Pulakeśivallabha whose other name was Satyâśraya.

His son who meditated on his (father's) feet,—the pair of whose lotus feet was rubbed by the edges of the crowns of numerous kings and vassals,—who was equal in firmness to (the mountains) Meru, Malaya, Mandara and Vindhya,—whose army consisting of excellent elephants, horses, chariots and fortsoldiers was daily increasing,—who obtained his kingdom through his excellent and unique horse, named Chitrakaṇṭha, fleet as the wind,—who conquered the three hereditary kingdoms[1]) of Chera, Chola and Pândya,—(was) the great Śaiva, the great Bhaṭṭâraka, the illustrious king Satyâśraya Vikramâditya.

His younger brother who conquered all the partisans of the enemy,—who was the ornament of the earth that is girt by the belt of the four oceans,—who, like a lion-cub, tore open the rounded temples of rutting elephants,—whose only pleasure was heroism,—whose fame was spread in all directions,—(was) the great Śaiva, the great Bhaṭṭâraka, the illustrious king Dharâśraya-Jayasiṁhavarman.

His son who meditated on his (father's) feet,—who was the delight of the hearts of all men,—the glory of whose bright sword was proclaimed by songs that assumed the guise of the morning-wail of the noble wives of feudatories and enemies killed, as they came face to face (with him), in the thick of numerous battles,—who gained his own piece of territory by the prowess of his own arms—(was) the great Śaiva, the great Bhaṭṭâraka, the illustrious Jayâśraya-Maṅgalarasarâja.

His younger brother who meditated with respect[2]) on his (brother's) lotus feet,—whose good fortune is growing every day,

---

[1]) *Kramâgata* may also mean situated one after the other.

[2]) The word *ârâdhanâ* is unnecessary here. The usual phrase is *tatpâdânudhyâtaḥ*, for which perhaps the writer of this plate meant to put *tatpâ-*

—who is from his very chilhood the abode of all good qualities, —whose chest was taken possession by the Goddess of Fortune, as if she were a bride left free in her choice of a husband,—who illumines the whole universe by the country of his brilliant glory —(is) the great Śaiva, the great Bhaṭṭâraka, Śarajha,[1]) the illustrious king Pulakeśi, whom the illustrious Vallabhanarendra, taking delight in valour, favoured with the following four other names, 'the ornament of the Chalukika family, the conquerors of Dakshiṇâpatha *(Dakshiṇâpathasâdhaka-Chaluki[ka]kulâlaṁkâra)*', 'the husband of the earth *(Prithvîvallabha)*', 'the repulser of the non-retiring *(Anivarttakanivarttayitṛi)*', and 'the refuge of men on earth *(Avanijanâśraya)*', when the army of the Tâjika,—which vomited forth arrows and *mudgaras*,[2])—which destroyed by its brightly glittering very sharp swords the prosperous Saindhava, Kachchhella, Saurâshtra, Châvoṭaka, Maurya and Gurjjara kings and others—which, wishing (?) to enter the Dakshiṇâpatha with the desire of conquering all the southern kings, came in the first instance to reduce the Navasârikâ-country—which darkened the regions of the sky with dust from the ground, that was dug up by the hard and noisy hoofs of its quick horses,—whose (warriors') bodies were frightful, their coats of mail being coloured by large streams of blood (flowing) from the intestines that issued out of the cavities of the fat bellies of great warriors who rushed furiously to the attack and were completely pierced by the heads of spears,—had been conquered in a battle, in which quadrilles were formed by head-less trunks, dancing to the loud noise of the drums, beaten (by them) after (they felt) the satisfaction produced by the thought 'to day we have paid for one birth our debt to our lord by sacrificing our heads for him', by even countless chiefs of hosts of kings, unconquered before,—who had paid with their heads for the acceptance of

---

dârâdhâkaḥ. But again thinking it advisable to use the ordinary form ending in *anudhyâtaḥ*, wrote *arâdhanâ* and joined the whole incongruously.

[1]) Śarajha would appear to be one of the names of the donor.

[2]) *Mudgara* is a common Sassanian weapon, consisting of a thick iron head with an wooden handle.

great honour and presents (bestowed) by their lord,—who had rushed to the attack,—who had fiercely bitten their lips with their teeth,—whose excellence was not equalled by great warriors, though sharp blades (of the latter) had been reddened by quantities of thick blood that profusely poured forth in consequence of their splitting the—and the haunches of excellent elephants in the van of various battles,—who had cut off the stalk-like necks of the lotus-like heads of their enemies with the blows of sharp daggers that were quickly and disdainfully thrust forward in order to destroy the adversaries,—whose bodies were covered by a coat of mail, as it were, in consequence of the sudden erection of the hair that was produced by the excitement of the fight—

He (king Pulakeśi) addresses the following order to all his *vishayapatis, grâmabhojikas, vâsâvakas, âyuktas, viniyuktakas* and others wherever posted, whether of our own lineage or others: 'Be it known to you that for the increase of our own and our parents' merit and fame we have given as a religious gift, with a libation of water on the great Kârttikî (the full moon day of Kârttika), the village of Padraka, included in the country of the Kârmaṇeya district, to the Brâhmaṇa Kâñchaḷi (?), son of the Brâhmaṇa Govindaḷi, who knows two Vedas, is a student of (the) Taittirîka *(śâkhâ)*, belongs to Vatsa *gotra*, (and originally) came from Vanavâsi, for the performance of the *bali, charu, vaiśvadeva, agnihotra* and other rites. (The village has been granted) according to the reasoning from the familiar instance of the earth and the sky, *sodranga, soparikara, sadânapradânaka*, with the exception of former gifts to gods and Brahmans; is not to be entered by irregular or regular soldiers, is to be enjoyed by (the donee's) sons and grandsons. Therefore while (the donee) enjoys it, cultivates it or causes it to be cultivated in the way (suitable) for an *agrahâra*, no one should come in the way. Future kings of our own lineage and others should sanction this our grant and maintain it, considering that wealth is as little enduring and as transient and as a flash of lightning, and life as evanescent as a drop of water adhering to the end of a blade of grass. And he who, his mind being obscured by the veil of the darkness of ignorance, will revoke this or abet its revocation, will be guilty of the five great sins and of the minor sins. And it has been said . . . . . .[1]) Samvatsara [four] hundred (plus ninety) 490 Kârttika bright half 15. This has been written by the illustrious, noble Bappabhaṭi, the great minister of peace and war, who has obtained the five great *śabdas,* son of the great military officer Haragaṇa. All is authoritative, whether letters be wanting or in excess.

Our own Command.

---

[1]) The portion left untranslated contains five of the usual imprecatory verses against the resumption of gifts of land.

Inhalt.

Ueber gewisse Kürzungen des Wortendes im Veda, von R. v. Roth . 1
Der Ursprung des Rumänischen, von P. Hunfalvy 11
I Návagvāḥ e i Dáṣagvāḥ del Ṛigveda, di G. Lignana 59
Die Geschichte der classisch-armenischen Schriftsprache, von Johann Thumajan 69
Ueber die Entwickelung der philosophischen Ideen bei den Indern und Chinesen, von M. Straszewski 79
Ueber Jasna XXIX, 1—2, von Friedrich Müller 95
The Râmânujîya and the Bhâgavata or Pâñcharâtra, by R. G. Bhâṇḍârkar 101
On a newly discovered form of Indian character (with one plate), by Cecil Bendall 111
On the Bakhshālī Manuscript (with three plates), by R. Hoernle . . 127
The original Gypsies and their language, by Charles Godfrey Leland 149
The Mediæval vernacular Literature of Hindūstān, with special reference to Tul'sī Dās (with two plates), by G. A. Grierson 157
Two new grants of the Chalukya dynasty (with four plates), by Bhagvânlâl Indrâjî 211

Verlag von Alfred Hölder, k. k. Hof- und Universitäts-Buchhändler,

Wien, I., Rothenthurmstrasse 15.

A grant of the Chalukya Yuvarâja Śilâditya of saṁvat 443.

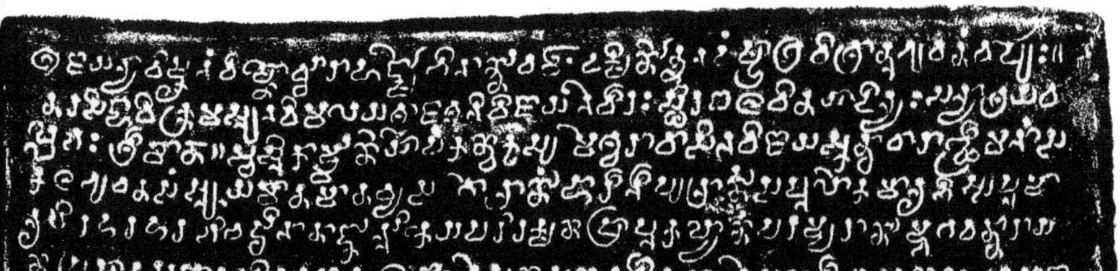

Lichtdruck von Jaffé & Albert, Wien.

Plate I.

A grant of the Chalukya Yuvarâja Śilâditya of saṁvat 443.

VII. Orient.-Congress, Ar. Sect.

Lichtdruck von Jaffé & Albert, Wien.

Plate II.

A grant of the Chalukya king Pulakeśi of saṁvat 490.

VII. Orient.-Congress, Ar. Sect.

Lichtdruck von Jaffé & Albert, Wien.

Plate I.

A grant of the Chalukya king Pulakeśi of saṁvat 490.

VII. Orient.-Congress, Ar. Sect.

Lichtdruck von Jaffé & Albert, Wien.

Plate II.

www.ingramcontent.com/pod-product-compliance
Lightning Source LLC
Chambersburg PA
CBHW050336170426
43200CB00009BA/1614
9782019597825